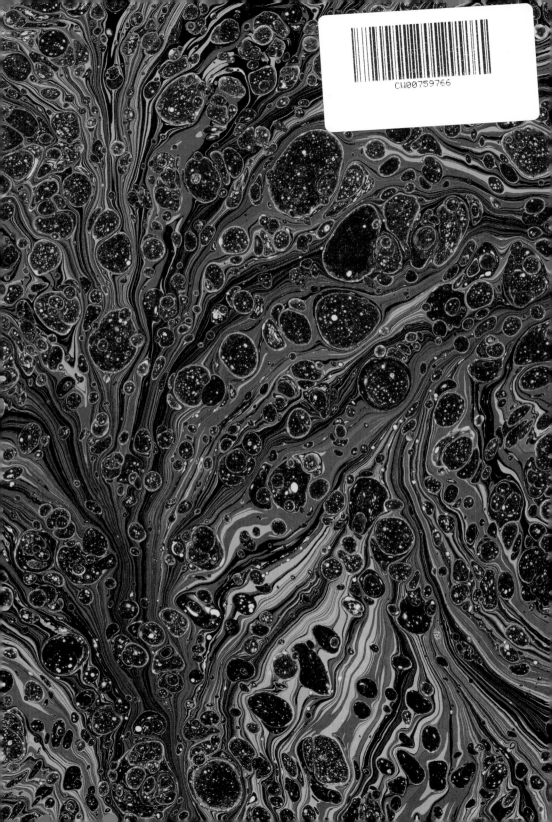

BAYERLEIN:

The Denazification Trial of Rommel's Chief-of-Staff,
and Panzer Lehr Division Commander,
Generalleutnant Fritz Bayerlein

BAYERLEIN:

The Denazification Trial of Rommel's Chief-of-Staff, and Panzer Lehr Division Commander, Generalleutnant Fritz Bayerlein

P.A. Spayd & Nicole Insanally

Schiffer Military History
Atglen, PA

Dedication

Frau Helga Morstien Woods is my steadfast and beloved friend through our eleven years of research, travel, and writing of *General* Bayerlein's saga. We never had an idea that four books documenting the history of this man were possible. Without Helga's help and friendship, I couldn't have succeeded in finding the people that brought Bayerlein's story to fruition. Research in archives is one facet of writing, however, the part that lives in our hearts is the friendship and love we find along our journey.

With Herr Fritz Dittmar-Bayerlein, Frau Anna Schwarz, and Frau Woods aiding in every step, this journey has now come to its completion. Frau Woods had no idea her innocuous phone call to my small notice in the Würzburg newspaper, "Main Post" would lead us to four books on her father's landlord.

I will always hold you dear in my heart, Dear Friend, Helga.

With Love,
Pat

Book design by Robert Biondi.

Copyright © 2011 by P.A. Spayd and Nicole Insanally.
Library of Congress Catalog Number: 2011934253.

Printed in China.
ISBN: 978-0-7643-3954-7

We are always looking for people to write books on new and related subjects. If you have an idea for a book, please contact us at the address below.

Published by Schiffer Publishing Ltd.
4880 Lower Valley Road
Atglen, PA 19310
Phone: (610) 593-1777
FAX: (610) 593-2002
E-mail: Info@schifferbooks.com.
Visit our web site at: www.schifferbooks.com
Please write for a free catalog.
This book may be purchased from the publisher.
Please include $5.00 postage.
Try your bookstore first.

In Europe, Schiffer books are distributed by:
Bushwood Books
6 Marksbury Ave.
Kew Gardens, Surrey TW9 4JF
England
Phone: 44 (0)20 8392-8585
FAX: 44 (0)20 8392-9876
E-mail: info@bushwoodbooks.co.uk
www.bushwoodbooks.co.uk

CONTENTS

INTRODUCTION

In the years following the liberation of Europe from the tyranny of Adolf Hitler and the Third Reich, the Allies sought to bring to justice those responsible for the millions of deaths of innocent men, women and children. Against this backdrop of change and prosecution *Generalleutnant* Fritz Bayerlein, Chief of Staff to Field Marshal Erwin Rommel and Commander of the Panzer Lehr Division, attempted to comply with the multitude of rules and laws that would ultimately judge his battlefield conduct and his pre-war private life as well. Bayerlein knew the ultimate consequence of being held accountable for war crimes – death by hanging – and the potential for heavy fines and imprisonment for lesser offenses. Lives and fortunes were at stake. Bayerlein, and his former *Wehrmacht* colleagues, as well as thousands of his countrymen, were subjected to screening and judgment of their actions dating back to Hitler's Munich *Putsch* in 1923. Bayerlein answered detailed questions about his war record, his conduct in the field, all aspects of his career, the uniform he wore each day, the occupied areas under his custody, civilians, his personal finances and his personal beliefs. Even his family's principles came under scrutiny.

The post-war denazification program was complex and underwent constant change; its requirements were misunderstood by many. The program was either a bane of condemnation or a boon for exoneration to the people involved. The Allies had an enormous task in processing the cases of over twelve million people in the U.S. zone of occupation alone. The Allies sought to ensure justice was done and to ensure a day of reckoning for those who profited from Nazism, those who committed criminal acts and the fanatics who still supported the principles of the Third Reich. A balance of fairness, equal justice and punishments befitting the crimes was weighed to convince the German populace of the benefits of a democracy. The program had its weaknesses, the ones that slipped through with help from comrades and political ties. This file is provided here in its entirety translated into English, so readers can make up their own minds if it was effective in this instance.

General Bayerlein's *Spruchkammerakte,* Denazification Tribunal folder, lay in the Hesse regional office since 1947 along with thousands of others, unread and forgotten in history's wake. His file was unusually large as Bayerlein submitted overwhelming evidence of his innocence and testimony from witnesses substantiating the positive actions he took during the war to protect people he did not know – at risk to himself and the endangerment of his friends and his beloved family – his sister Ellen and his nephew Friedrich. Even the woman who loved him all of her life, Hanna, would answer for his actions, her fate cast with his under the terrible scrutiny of Himmler's political secret police – the dreaded Gestapo.

Had Bayerlein profited from National Socialism? Who could testify as an independent third party to his behavior? Who could he rely on to help him? Who would come forward to be his witness? What is your judgment?

General Bayerlein's Gestapo file and the Denazification Tribunal file are presented in this fourth book on his life and military career. The documents from the German archives have been translated by my new, dynamic and young co-author, Nicole Insanally, in great detail. My co-author with our prior book, Mr. Gary Wilkins, applied his translation skills in the detailed Gestapo chapter file, other forms and narratives, identification of uniforms and armor. He is an invaluable friend who had dropped what he was doing to help. Three of us were dedicated to bring these rare and valuable documents that lend insight into the time periods – the terror of the Gestapo under Himmler – the war – and difficult post war years, the retribution as well as the more humane goals sought by the Allies. We examined how they affected Bayerlein and his senior contemporaries. Bayerlein found himself trapped between "fire and hell" – coping with the political policies of his own oppressive Third Reich dictatorship under the control of a madman, his sense of honor and obligations as a military officer to his country and his troops, his sense of morality and human decency and the United States military government's moves for retribution against its defeated foes. The U.S. goals were to instill a democratic government free of national socialism and hatred – noble goals that we seek today – whether understood by the populace at the time is yet another arguable point.

The *General*'s nephew, Mr. Fritz Dittmar-Bayerlein, has again generously opened his collection of family and wartime photographs for this book – included are pre-war family activities and vacations, girlfriends, army field exercises, and rare behind-the-scenes photographs from the Polish and Russian fronts.

Also brought to light are details from previously unpublished post-war interrogations of Bayerlein's superiors who awaited war crimes investigations, trials, or were witnesses – *General* Guderian, Field Marshals von Weichs and Kesselring – and insight from other generals on Hitler's views of his commanders and the General Staff Officers. Compared to the post-war Allied treatment of German commanders in Europe is a rare glimpse of what happened to the generals who were captured or surrendered in Africa and were transferred to camps in the United States.

The authors wish to emphasize the use of the term *Führer Befehl* i.e. "Hitler's Order" to commanders and the degree of obligation to obey, that it imposed upon the military, as well as potential consequences to one's family of not obeying. There was no logic, argument, explanation accepted. Hitler expected his commanders to blindly obey his orders, under penalty of death following a short court-martial for treason. Not only was the commander held responsible for his actions in the field, his entire family served as hostages for his exact following of Hitler's orders.

What would you do?

ACKNOWLEDGEMENTS

Never before in history have occupational powers sought to ferret out the opposition in the beliefs of its enemy and push them to accept the enlightenment of freedom and democracy. The files of the denazification tribunals, the benefits, the pitfalls, are all there for the understanding that it gives us about a time in our past. Whether one agrees or disagrees with the process, its effect, the goal to bring about stability in the population and government were daunting efforts by the Allies. While the methodology used was imperfect, it does give one pause in thought for the intentions.

We can say, perhaps, the goals were achieved by the end result – a democratic society of free people – we hope and pray to achieve in many areas of unrest in our world today.

Bayerlein loved and protected his small group of family and friends. His sister, Ellen, adored her older brother and ensured through preservation that parts of his life and career could be brought back to life for another generation to study and to understand survival under the tyranny of Hitler's government. It is due to her foresight and the cooperation and generosity of Bayerlein's nephew, Herr Fritz Dittmar-Bayerlein, that the legacy of *Generalleutnant a.D.* Fritz Bayerlein survives.

The tireless diligence, telephone calls, research and the close friendship of Frau Helga Woods immeasurably aided the completion of the forth and final in our series of the career and private life of Fritz Bayerlein. He was a neighbor and landlord to her family, and she was *Herr* Morstein's pretty daughter. *Frau* Christine Singer and her husband, *Herr* Dieter Singer, cherished neighbors, shared insight into "*Herr General*" and his home life postwar. With the help and perseverance of *Herr* Frank Lippold this book was made possible through his discovery of these valuable files in Hesse and Würzburg.

Ms. Nicole Insanally persevered and translated *General* Bayerlein's daunting original *Spruchkammerakte*. Without her dedication, care, attention to detail and hard work, this book would not be possible. Friend Mr. Gary Wilkins translated the *Gestapo* files, no easy feat. I owe both a debt of gratitude throughout this monumental endeavor of bringing to light part of history long forgotten in the Hesse German archives.

Germany:
From *Würzburg* Germany: *Frau* Helga Woods, *Herr* and *Frau* Dieter Singer, *Herr* Peter Hulaski, *Herr* Eugen Grätz for his POW photograph collection, *Herr* Willi Dürrnagel for offering valuable additions from his enormous collection, and *Herr* Helmuth Henke.

Herr Manfred Rommel and his lovely wife Lisl from Stuttgart provided great insight into Bayerlein and *Feldmarschall* Rommel's thoughts and beliefs.

Organizations: The dedicated friends from the *Kameraden – Kreiskameradschaft Verband*, Stuttgart, *Redaktion: Herr* Claus Bittner, *Herr* Götz Eberbach, and *Herr & Frau* Friedbert Limmerroth; the *Verband Deutsches Afrika-Korps* Würzburg and its president Georg Richter; *Bundesarchiv Koblenz – Frau* Brigitt Kuhl; *Bundesarchiv – Militärarchiv Freiburg – Herr* Günther Montfort; *Hessisches Hauptstaadtarchiv, Wiesbaden; Herr* Mile Penava of the Associated Press of Frankfurt.

A silent partner of mine was *Herr Oberst a.d.* Helmut Ritgen, whose photos he loaned me in the first book – on the sly – because of his dislike for Bayerlein. "I don't want my old comrades to think I'm a big liar to help this *Amerikanerin biographin* on Bayerlein!" He wished to remain anonymous for so many years, but behind the scenes, he told me great stories, shared his photos, dined with me many times in his home village, phoned his comrades to speak with me, putting me in touch with many, to include *Herr* Hellmuth Henke (of the Nuts surrender ultimatum fame), and *Herr* Bernd Wernecke, Panzer Lehr Division Logistics officer. The ultimate aide was a tour of the Panzer Museum in Muenster, Germany, conducted by a retired German *Bundeswehr* General and his staff. Everyone loved *Herr Oberst*, and I must say the same.

Sweden:
Mr. Tore Erickson, former AK Engineer.

Portugal:
Mr. Paulo Henriques – dedicated *Afrikakorps* webmaster – for his aid in obtaining information and photographs.

USA:
Our thanks go to our dedicated and supportive senior military editor at Schiffer Publishing, Mr. Bob Biondi, who placed his confidence in the authors' desire to present this unusual view into history. Mr. and Mrs. Peter Schiffer of Schiffer Publishing – Peter told me to keep busy – 'give me more books' after the death of my husband. Peter, also, has joined with Jack. Mr. Danny Parker, military author, great friend and advisor. Ms. Andrea Harris, my "old Army buddy," whose friendship, confidence, support and advice span the ocean from Fort Belvoir, Virginia to Eltville am Rhein, Germany. Mr. Robert W. Hasbrouck, Jr., and his lovely wife, Astrid, for their friendship, and Bob's interest and dedication in editing all the draft manuscripts. Friends Mr. Niels Cordes and his wonderful wife, Ms. Virginia Labar for their kindness, patience and support. Niels aided me immeasurably in guiding me through German archive culture. Many thanks to Commander Randy Heller, USN, and his lovely wife, Pam, for their encouragement and support in advertising and promoting our work. My long suffering friend and 'old Army buddy,' Mrs. Susan Kowalewski, who stayed with me the dark days after my husband, Jack, died – with me in my writing and always encouraging. And, longtime friend Mrs. Sandra Stewart.

Organizations: Library of Congress, Washington, D.C.; National Archives and Records Administration II, College Park Maryland – Mr. David Giordano, Mr. Robin Cookson, Mr. John Taylor; the Photo Archives Staff, U.S. Army Military History Institute, Mr. Jay Graybeal and Mr. Clifton Hyatt.

1
Erasing National Socialism

"To live as free men in a society of free men requires courage and determination."
— *General Lucius D. Clay, Deputy Military Governor U.S. Zone of Occupation*

At the end of the Second World War in Europe on May 8, 1945 the overwhelming task of the Allied powers was rebuilding the European continent and bringing those responsible for war crimes to justice. Adolf Hitler and his National Socialist Democratic Workers Party (NSDAP)[1] leaders were the originators of the terror wrought by the Third Reich. Measures for their identification, capture and war crimes trials were among the Allies' first priorities. This task along with problems providing the necessities of life, health, food, housing, clothing, education, transportation, and medical care combined into an overwhelming mission for the Allies. The problems needed to be addressed and solved quickly to avoid unrest and rebellion and to provide support for the building of a democratic society from the ruins. Hungry, cold, homeless and destitute people needed the basic requirements of life attended to before accepting the benefits of democracy. Before the D-Day invasion on June 6, 1944, the U.S. Army Military Government officers and staff members were trained and in place to take over from the Army field troops once an area had been secured.

Field Marshal Erwin Rommel's *Afrikakorps* chief of staff, and commander of the elite Panzer Lehr Division, former German *Generalleutnant* Fritz Bayerlein experienced the rapidly changing political policies and turbulence of the rebuilding of his war-torn country. Bayerlein was interred as a prisoner-of-war after surrendering his LIII *Armee Korps* in the Ruhr Pocket to General Robert W. Hasbrouck's "Lucky 7th" Armored Division on April 16, 1945. Two years later he was released from captivity on April 2, 1947.[2] As a general officer in the *Wehrmacht*, Bayerlein was held accountable for his actions during the war, and faced automatic arrest and the potential of filing of war crime charges against him. Many of his peers and superiors would be tried and some convicted of war crimes while others would testify as witnesses against SS and SD[3] atrocities on the battlefields. *General* Bayerlein was no exception; he would have his turn with the *Spruchkammer* (Denazification Tribunal). After two years confinement in a U.S. Army prisoner-of-war camp, Bayerlein faced possible imprisonment in a civil internment camp while awaiting his Denazification hearing. The verdict of his countrymen would decide his fate and fortune. But Bayerlein was a thorough and resourceful man – with a good attorney and a lot of support from friends, subordinates and colleagues.

Field Marshal Erwin Rommel, his Chief of Staff, Oberst Fritz Bayerlein, and another officer have a discussion over their maps. Photograph was taken shortly after Rommel's return to Africa in late October 1942. (Photo courtesy of Dittmar-Bayerlein Family Collection.)

Oberstleutnant Fritz Bayerlein modeling the Ritterkreuz awarded to him for fighting off an attack of British tanks on his supply column on the Via Balbia in November 1941. Photo taken on February 13th, 1942. (National Archives)

Since D-Day in Normandy, Allies had collected and imprisoned over four million prisoners of war in Europe. With the surrender of the Third Reich in May 1945 three million more prisoners were added to the tally – an overwhelming seven million German prisoners or – as some were later classified by the Allies – disarmed enemy soldiers. The U.S. Army alone was responsible for five million of these prisoners. The task fell on the U.S. Army to sort from a long list those who were war criminals, National Socialists, automatic arrest candidates, and fanatics.[4] From April until November 1945 most of the prisoners were sieved into a final manageable number, roughly about 200,000 in the United States zone of authority, that the Army wanted to examine more closely. The Allied Control Council[5] required the return of all prisoners of war, with the exceptions of those under arrest, to the zone where their official residence was located. The massive shifting of displaced persons, prisoners of war, and disarmed enemy soldiers kept the U.S. Army's deuce and a half's – the dependable 2 1/2 ton cargo trucks – moving all throughout the summer, fall and winter of 1945.

The war crimes trials at Dachau and international war crimes trials in Nuremberg began in mid-November 1945.[6] The indictments and trials would wind their way from the top down – from the top Nazi leaders and senior military staff closest to Hitler. Within two years justice would weave its way to reach the field commanders.

A staff car conference: Rommel, Bayerlein and Italian Marshal Ugo Cavellero. Marshal Cavellero, an admirer of Rommel and German efficiency, was removed by Mussolini in January 1943 after the fall of Tripoli. (Photographer: Eberhard Dohm, Propaganda Kompanie, North Africa. Photo courtesy of Mr. Bernd Peitz)

Rommel and his Chief of Staff, Bayerlein, in their staff car – photo taken during attack on Tobruk. (Robert Hunt Library)

General Robert W. Hasbrouck, CG of the 7th Armored Division, returns the salute of the defeated enemy, General Bayerlein, Commander of the LIII Armee Korps, on April 16, 1945. Colonel Jack Ryan, 7th AD Chief of Staff (back to camera), stands ready while Lt. Schwarz salutes with Bayerlein. The surrender of Bayerlein in the Ruhr Pocket caused the collapse of all resistance and surrender of over 300,000 German troops. During his captivity as a prisoner of war, Bayerlein was viewed with disdain and contempt by many of his senior contemporaries for his defeatism and disloyalty. Bayerlein was a realist who saw no point to continued fighting. (U.S. Army Signal Corps)

The massive surrender in the Ruhr Pocket: Generalleutnant Bayerlein, LIII Armee Korps commander, with two of his division commanders, Oberst Zollenkopf, CG of the 9th Panzer Division, and Generalmajor Hammer. The middle-aged German officers listen attentively to instructions from young Lieutenant John Schwarz, Officer in Charge of POW Team 73, 7th Armored Division. (U.S. Army Signal Corps)

Colonel Ryan and Lt. Schwarz speak with Bayerlein before sending him to the Headquarters, First U.S. Army, G-2 (Intelligence) later the same day. General Ernst Hammer listens to his Corps commander. According to Lieutenant Schwarz, Bayerlein showed respect and courtesy to members of the 7th AD, especially General Hasbrouck. As a result General Hasbrouck transported him and General von Waldenburg to First Army Headquarters via a staff car. The more arrogant and unrepentant generals were herded into trucks and then left standing with their troops in POW enclosures made up of muddy cattle fields. (U.S. Army Signal Corps)

The 7th Armored Division POW Interrogation Team gathers weapons and documents from Bayerlein's officers. Surrender was near Menden and collection points near Iserlohn in open farm fields. The cease-fire was scheduled for 0300, and at 0700 on April 16th, 1945 Colonel Ryan and Lt. Schwarz, an Austrian-American who translated the surrender terms to Bayerlein, gave the LIII Armee Korps commander orders for troop collection points. (U.S. Army Signal Corps)

The end of the Ruhr resistance (which resulted in the collapse of the Western front) has been blamed on General Bayerlein. Surrendering in the Ruhr would end, as Bayerlein phrased it, "further useless bloodshed" in spite of orders to fight to the last man. (U.S. Army Signal Corps)

Nazi general, Bayerlein, Rommel's former chief of staff, whose elite, quadruple-strength tank division, organized to repel the D-Day invasion, was cut to pieces before it reached the front.

Oberleutnant Bayerlein attending a pre-war military parade (front row, center). Sitting directly behind him in the second row is his brother-in-law, Mäthias Dittmar, a reservist and successful Würzburg businessman. Sister Ellen is sitting next to her husband. Hanna Huber, Bayerlein's long-time girlfriend, can be seen in part on the second row; sitting with her is young nephew, Friedrich (nicknamed Fritz, after his Uncle Fritz.) (Photo courtesy of Dittmar-Bayerlein Family Collection.)

The first prisoner-of-war photograph taken of General Bayerlein shows his resigned expression as he awaits his fate at the hands of the Americans. His hometown of Würzburg, Germany, and the POW camp at Oberursel were in the U.S. Zone – a fortunate break for him and his family. From the time of his surrender he cooperated fully with the Americans. (Library of Congress photo, by U.S. Army Signal Corps.)

Only surviving photograph taken by Bayerlein at the 1938 Olympics shows the crowd saluting Hitler. Note the international flags in the background. (Photo courtesy of Dittmar-Bayerlein Family Collection.)

Pre-war military parade in Frankfurt am Main, Germany, about 1938. Ellen captures a photo of her brother Fritz (center on roadway, foreground) as he walks by a line of officers. (Photo courtesy of Dittmar-Bayerlein Family Collection.)

Officers review the soldiers in field packs, Frankfurt, 1938. (Photo courtesy of Dittmar-Bayerlein Family Collection.)

Sister Ellen catches the beginnings of the parade from her seat. More soldiers arrive, lining both sides of the street. (Photo courtesy of Dittmar-Bayerlein Family Collection.)

ELIMINATION OF WAR POTENTIAL

Goals of the Allies European Advisory Council were "to ensure the destruction of nazism and militarism and that Germany would never again disturb the peace of the world ... to remove and destroy war equipment, to control industry having war potential, punish war criminals." Internal U.S. Zone posters were used to educate troops on post-war goals. (NARA, Records of the Office of Military Government, U.S. Zone, (OMGUS), RG 260/390/50/2/3)

After the Surrender

The National Socialist doctrine permeated local German governments, national civil service, education, the legal system and the economy; all areas of German life under the Third Reich were closely governed.[7] Sorting out these elements in order to establish a free and democratic process would take active oversight on the part of the Allies and years of occupation. Using the German government structure and organization as a model, the Civil Affairs Committee (CAC) under Supreme Headquarters of the Allied Expeditionary Force (SHAEF) went to work on an occupational plan in 1944. Plans were necessary to control regional and local German governments as the Allies defeated the German Army and advanced through German territory since the Allies forecasted a complete breakdown of German governmental services. The basic assumption by SHAEF was that the occupation ultimately would be a joint Allied effort.[8] The occupational plan contained a controversial booklet entitled, *Handbook for Military Government for Germany.* Although a handbook is usually a small part of an overall plan, Secretary of the Treasury, Henry Morgenthau, intervened at SHAEF and brought it to the attention of President Franklin D. Roosevelt. Even after three revisions with Morgenthau influencing his viewpoint the President wasn't satisfied with the Handbook's provisions and didn't concur with its policies.[9] Secretary Morgenthau believed the denazification proposals were too "easy" on the Germans. He believed they, as a nation, should atone for their treatment of the Jews, for the destruction and aggression in Europe and should, "forfeit any claim to ordinary humanity as defeated people." Morgenthau's proposals were vindictive and based upon revenge.[10] The President later drew away from the extreme proposals of Secretary Morgenthau shortly after the Allied Quebec Conference during September 1944. After the President's death the Morgenthau Plan was totally scrapped. With President Harry S. Truman taking office as the President, Morgenthau resigned and withdrew back into civilian life.

The most significant organization to influence the occupation of Germany was the European Advisory Commission (EAC) established in London in 1944.[11] Made up of the ambassadors of the U.S., Britain, Russia and France, it included political advisors and staff furnished by the State Department or Foreign Office. The EAC developed three basic agreements. The most familiar is the *Declaration Regarding the Defeat of Germany,* which provided for Germany to be divided into four zones rather than the previous recommendations for a joint Allied administration. There was much bantering about amongst the Allies, as France had originally been left out of the tripartite plan. The French asked for inclusion in post-war occupational plans and wanted control of a zone. The Soviets refused to allow "their" German territory to be reduced to accommodate the French request.[12] As a result, the French zone of occupation was carved from the U.S. occupational territory. The second agreement provided for national zone commanders (military governors), who would confer on matters affecting Germany as a whole. The third agreement established joint administration and control of Berlin by all four of the Allied powers.[13]

During the Yalta Conference held from February 3-11 in 1945 each member of the Allies concurred with the zone of occupation concept proposed by the European Advisory Council. The Allies decided on their goals in regard to post-war Germany. An immediate concern related to the liquidation of the National Socialist party and imprisonment of Nazi leaders. They wanted to ensure the destruction of, "Nazism and militarism and that Germany would never again disturb the peace of the world, to disband and disarm

Germany's armed forces, break up the General Staff; to remove and destroy war equipment, to control industry having war potential, punish war criminals, eliminate the Nazi party, its institutions, laws and remove Nazi and militarist influences from public offices, cultural and economic life."[14]

The U.S. Forces European Theater (USFET) command changed from General Dwight D. Eisenhower to General Joseph T. McNarey on November 26, 1945.[15] As Theater Commander, General McNarey also had dual responsibility as Military Governor of the U.S. Zone of Occupation. To run the occupation zones, the choice of a good deputy military governor was needed. The name of General Lucius D. Clay arose, and he was appointed as the Deputy Military Governor, basically as a "title without a job."[16] He was placed in command of the U.S. Control Council and also served on the joint Allied Control Council with the Russian, British and American governments. General Clay noted that the Yalta Conference was not, "devoted entirely to punitive and security measures ... it was not the Allied purpose to destroy the German people and that they could hope for a decent life and a return to the family of nations when Nazism and militarism were extirpated."[17]

The control of the U.S. occupation zone required development of a large and complex bureaucracy. By autumn of 1945 this organization (now named Office of the Military Government of the United States for Germany OMGUS) contained 12,000 officers, men and civilians. Since American civilians had a high salary and expensive transfer cost from the continental U.S. to Europe, the OMGUS opted to employ a large German staff.[18] Regional offices were set up in Bavaria, Baden-Württemberg, Greater Hesse and Bremen. Employment with the American Military Government, although highly prized at the time by the German nationals, had an unfortunate downside in the following months and years. As the old axiom goes "revenge is a dish best served cold" their fellow countrymen judged by the *Spruchkammer* grumbled that the Americans "had to leave sometime" and planned their future revenge on these "so-called" German traitors.

"Painfully Negative" – Joint Chiefs of Staff Directive 1067

The U.S. directive for the American Commander on Military Government was known as Joint Chief of Staff (JCS) 1067, and was a bitter pill for the Germans to swallow; however, the White-Morgenthau program was much worse.[19] Secretary Morgenthau's plan for Germany was to de-industrialize the entire country and thus eliminate its war potential. He envisioned an agrarian society and country defined as a "cabbage patch." However, Morgenthau's primary supporter was FDR; and with his death Morgenthau's radical and unrealistically vindictive plans were cast aside as more humane, viable and realistic solutions were sought. The primary purpose of the JCS 1067 directive was to address denazification, proclaim the dissolving of the National Socialist party and all of its organizational elements whether associated, affiliated and supervised and prohibit their reconstitution. Party property was to be confiscated and Nazi records seized. The Directives additional requirements were:

> All members of the Nazi party who have been more than nominal participants in its activities, all active supporters of Nazism or militarism and all other persons hostile to Allied purposes will be removed and excluded from public office and from positions of importance in quasi-public and private enterprises such as (1) civic,

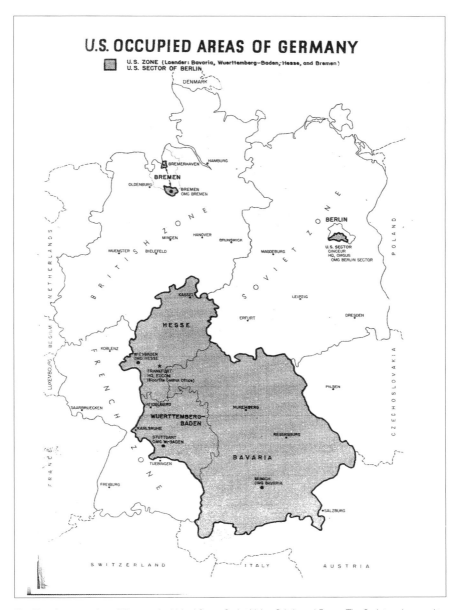

U.S. OCCUPIED AREAS OF GERMANY

U.S. ZONE (Laender: Bavaria, Wuerttemberg–Baden, Hesse, and Bremen)
U.S. SECTOR OF BERLIN

Quadripartite occupation of Germany by United States, Soviet Union, Britain and France. The Soviets only agreed to allow France their own zone if the territory was taken from the British and French. (NARA, Records of the Office of Military Government, U.S. Zone, (OMGUS), Records of the Denazification Branch; Monthly Report of the Military Governor, U.S. Zone, 20 November 1945, RG 260/390/50/2/3, Box 297)

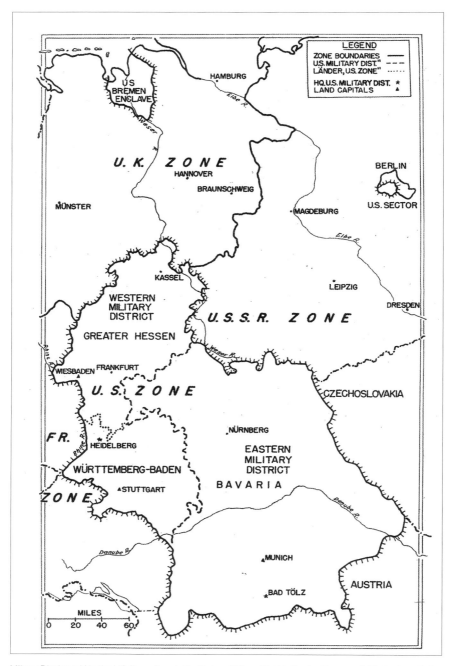

Military Districts within the U.S. Zone: Bavaria, the Eastern Military District; Greater Hesse and Württemberg-Baden, comprised the Western Military District. (NARA, Records of the Office of Military Government, U.S. Zone, (OMGUS), Records of the Denazification Branch; Monthly Report of the Military Governor, U.S. Zone, 20 November 1945, RG 260/390/50/2/3, Box 297)

economic, and labor organizations, (2) corporations and other organizations in which the German government or subdivisions have a major financial interest, (3) industry, commerce, agriculture and finance, (4) education, and (5) the press, publishing houses, and other agencies disseminating news and propaganda. Persons are to be treated as more than nominal participants in Party activities and as active supporters of Nazism or militarism when they have (1) held office or otherwise been active at any level from local to national in the party and its doctrines, (2) authorized or participated affirmatively in any Nazi crimes, racial persecutions or discriminations, (3) been avowed believers in Nazism or racial and militaristic creeds, or (4) voluntarily given substantial moral or material support or political assistance of any kind to the Nazi Party or categories of employment listed above because of administrative necessity, convenience or expediency.[20]

General Clay's opinion was that the original JCS 1067's mandatory removal provisions did, "initially result in handicapping to some extent the operations of railroads, communication systems and other essential facilities. However, in spite of these handicaps, we believe that our prompt action in removal of Nazis has speeded up the application of democratic processes in Germany and will result in stronger organizations at an earlier date than would have been obtained by a more gradual release of Nazis."[21]

With respect to the civil and economic rehabilitation, the American Military Government also held oversight over heavy industry such mining, chemical, lumber, and coal production.[22] Early planning under the supervision of the Combined Chiefs of Staff (CCS) was outlined in a directive, CCS 551, titled, *Directive for Military Government in Germany Prior to Defeat or Surrender.*[23]

The American Denazification Policy

The goal of the United States and Allied denazification program was to eliminate Nazi and militaristic influences from German life. Two extremes defined the denazification policy efforts of the U.S. One was an overzealous effort to transform the population described as, "a band of international outlaws, murderers, looters, and the like through prison sentences, confiscation of property, and fines to decent representatives of the human race and responsible citizens of the world."[24] After all, it was the Germans who had started the war, according to those whose opinions favored retribution and revenge on the German people. No doubt the goal was a purge of the National Socialist beliefs from German society. The opposite perspective was that the American denazification program in Germany was "one of the worst travesties on justice in all history."[25] The early confusion in policy among officials in Washington, D.C. did not lead to an easy implementation of the program. As the pendulum would swing from one extreme to the other and all points in between, claims that the U.S. was "easy" in their attitude or "hard" in the treatment of the Germans fanned the flames of American public opinion.

In March 1946 the denazification program was transferred to the control of the German Minister Presidents for Bavaria, Baden-Württemberg and Greater Hesse. This action gave the Germans active participation in the law the Ministers approved in order to weed out National Socialists and militaristic elements in their government and society. Whether they wanted it or not was often the subject of debate. General Clay issued general

Military Governor General Lucius D. Clay (2nd from right) and General Tedford Taylor (3rd from right) listen to war crime proceedings. (NARA Still Photo Branch)

Original Caption reads: Munich Stockade Inspection – General Lucius D. Clay, EUCOM Commander, on tour of Munich; Brigadier General Dalbey, Commander of Munich Military Post; Major General Milburn. Dated 7 May 1947. (NARA, U.S. Army Signal Corps Photo SC 284941)

Prisoners of war German Generals write battle histories for the U.S. Army Historical Division. Seated from right to left: Generallt Fritz Bayerlein, General der Panzertruppen von Lüttwitz, SS General Paul von Hausser, Generalmajor Freiherr von Gersdorff (left), Generallt. Mahlman, Geyr von Schweppenburg (right), pose with U.S. Army historian, Lieutenant J.F. Scroggin. A series of posed photographs of the original group of general officers was taken in February 1946. The men were issued fabric for prison tailors to make them new clothing. Bayerlein elected to have a civilian suit made in lieu of a uniform – another factor that alienated him from his contemporaries. (NARA, U.S. Army Photos, RG 319, Records of the Army Staff, Records of the Officer of the Chief of Military History)

Bomb damage in Bayerlein's hometown of Würzburg showing the horrendous destruction of the fire-bombing on March 15th, 1945. British Air Force General "Bomber Harris" ordered the ferocious attacks on the German populace to demoralize the civilians and strike at rumored military targets or factories – Würzburg had neither. Bayerlein took the photo on one of his furloughs from prison camp, about Christmas 1946. (Photo courtesy of Dittmar-Bayerlein Family Collection.)

instructions to the Ministers citing that, "you will be held strictly accountable for effective and just enforcement of the law ... You will take all steps necessary to assure the selection of persons well qualified to administer the law. The Ministers of Denazification, and all other officials entrusted with the enforcement of the law, must be anti-Nazis of long-standing, pro-democratic, anti-militaristic, and in complete agreement with the policies of denazification. You will maintain constant check upon the work of such officials in order to assure that they are carrying out both the letter and the spirit of the law."[26] Clay's letter also required that forfeited property be held pending instructions from the Military Government. He also required the submission of periodic reports on the denazification program's progress.

General George Patton's personal interpretation of the denazification program caused his removal as military governor of Bavaria and Commanding General of the Third Army. In a letter to Eisenhower on 11 August, 1945 in reference to Nazism, Patton wrote, "It is no more possible for a man to be a civil servant in Germany and not have paid lip service to Nazism that it is for a man to be a postmaster in America and not have paid lip service to the Democratic Party or the Republican Party when it is in power."[27] Concerned with Patton's opinion, Eisenhower reminded him of the goals of the war, which stressed obliterating Nazism; the defeat of Nazism was a "major U.S. war aim."[28] In an interview with newspaper reports, Patton expounded on his personal views of denazification, ignoring his superior's advice and stating to reporters that: "The Nazi thing is just like a Democratic-Republican election fight."[29] This statement created a shock wave of great consternation across the Atlantic. Patton's removal by Theater Commander Eisenhower was quick. General Lucian K. Truscott was appointed commander of Third Army and the Eastern Military District. General Truscott's position was vastly different from Patton's live-and-let-live implementation of the denazification. Truscott stated later for reporters: "I have left too many white crosses across North Africa, Italy, and France and I have seen too many young men wounded and maimed not to be in complete sympathy with any policy that designs to eradicate, root and branch, the evil force, Nazism, that loosed this holocaust on the world."[30]

General Clay noted later that obviously a universal interpretation of the denazification programs goals had to be agreed upon. Clay believed that political stability couldn't be fully realized until the denazification program had been fully completed.[31]

In part, the Patton incident along with another controversial issue the appointment of 'rumored Nazi supporter' Friedrich Schaeffer[32] as Bavarian Minister President created a backlash of anti-nazism which resulted in Military Government Law No.8. This law prohibited Nazi party members in business in any capacity other than common labor. It included "executives, managers, as well as private owner-operators such as grocers, barbers, bakers, and butchers."[33] Military government also further tightened control and applied the law to public employment. What would be the next step, the Germans could only guess. However, the sheer number of questionnaires the Denazification Program required the Germans to prepare proved impractical in the reality of dismissing from employment and placing on trial every person who owned a small business or was a clerk in a government office. Further changes were in store for the Program.

As the tally and the effects of the Denazification Program dawned upon the Military Government in December 1945, General Clay recommended terminating the automatic

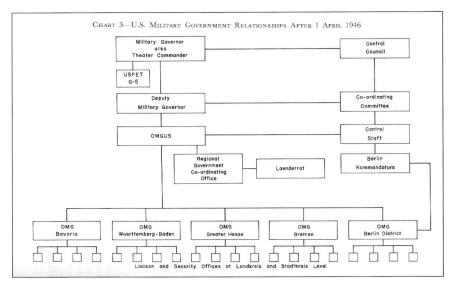

Organization Chart of the Military Governor and Deputy Military Governor. General Eisenhower was Theater Commander with dual responsibility as Military Governor until command transferred to General McNarey on November 26, 1946. General Lucius D. Clay was appointed Deputy Military Governor. (Army Historical Series, The U.S. Army in the Occupation of Germany 1944-1946, Earl F. Ziemke, U.S. Government Printing Office, Washington, D.C.)

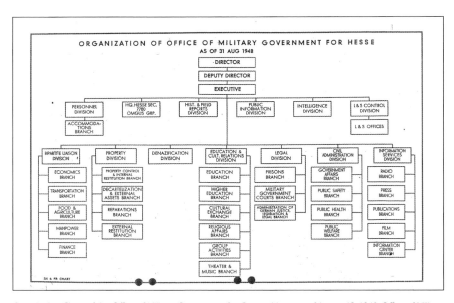

Organization Chart of the Office of Military Government for Greater Hesse, as of August 13, 1948. Office of Military Government, U.S. Zone of occupation was identical for Bavaria, Baden-Württemburg, Greater Hesse, Bremen and the Berlin District. (NARA, OMGUS, Records of the Denazification Branch, RG 260/390/49/27/5-7, Box 1127, OMGUS Monthly Reports)

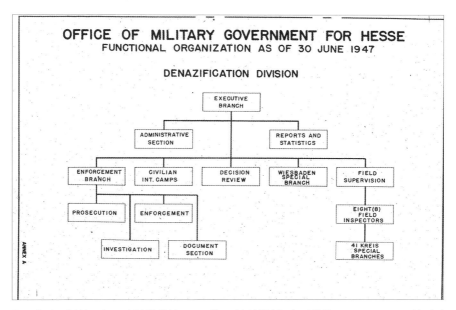

Denazification Division chart of OMGUS Hesse as of June 30, 1947. All other U.S. Zone governments are identical. (NARA, OMGUS, Records of the Denazification Branch, RG 260/390/49/27/5-7, Box 1127, OMGUS Monthly Reports)

arrest of all categories (classes) that were not under indictment by the International Tribunal at Nuremberg. Clay stated, "Our total arrestees in mandatory categories now exceed 90,000 exclusive of approximately 25,000 members of military and paramilitary organizations in prisoner-of-war enclosures. Arrestees are continuing at substantial rate under mandatory arrest directives. A screening process using German tribunals, with their actions subject to Military Government approval, has been established. … There would appear to be no reason to continue mandatory arrests in categories not now under trial or to be placed under trial before International Tribunal. It is recommended therefore that authority be given immediately to limit mandatory arrests to active members of organizations being tried or to be tried by International Tribunal, dangerous security suspects, and those individuals against whom specific evidence is available as to their participation in war crimes. If this authority is granted, it is proposed also to release those individuals under arrest who do not fall within these categories."[34] In addition to this change, in February 1946 Law No. 8 was changed and was not to apply to businesses with less than 10 persons. Once again the pendulum of change began its swing in the opposite direction.

The *Fragebogen* and the *Meldebogen*

In January 1946 the Offices of Military Government began administration of the three military government districts in the U.S. Zone of Occupation.[35]

With the adoption of the Law for Liberation from National Socialism and Militarism on March 5, 1946 everyone who was eighteen years old or older living in Germany was required to fill out a questionnaire regarding his or her political history. There were two types of questionnaires: the *Fragebogen* and the *Meldebogen*.[36] In each German *Stadt* (city) or *Landkreis* (county) *Spruchkammer* were organized and public prosecutors appointed. Those seeking public employment had to prepare the lengthy *Fragebogen*. It was necessary for all other Germans to file the *Meldebogen* forms with the prosecutor's office. Next, the investigative staff would conduct an investigation to determine if the person had been truthful in preparing his or her questionnaire and had honestly stated his or her political background. Armed with the results of the investigation and the questionnaire, the public prosecutor either found in favor of the individual and cleared him or her under the law, not subject to any penalties, or charged him or her as belonging to one of four classifications. The classifications were: major offender, offender, probationer or follower. The prosecutor had the option of placing a person in class IV (follower) without tribunal intervention. In the next step the tribunals then were presented with witnesses for the prosecution and defense and any other relevant evidence. Then the tribunal either exonerated the individual or placed the person in one of the four classes. Next, the tribunal applied the penalty, which ranged from a prison term of 10 years to property confiscations, special labor, details, employment restrictions, or in cases of a follower, it could levy a fine. The operation of the *Spruchkammer* fell on the Ministry for Political Liberation. The Military Government would exercise "merely an observatory supervision"[37] and couldn't order the court to make a particular decision in any case. Military Government activity was limited to referring cases for retrial where a decision was considered incorrect.

The Military Government sought to fill civil service positions to take over the administration and legal procedures within the new German government. To ferret out the Nazi elements an elaborate and detailed questionnaire, the *Fragebogen*, was used. To ensure honesty in the answers, falsification or the deliberate withholding of information had severe penalties. Due to the Germans' meticulous record keeping, crosschecking against Nazi party records reduced the risk of placing former Nazis in key positions in the new German government – even at a small village level. It was only a matter of time to discover those who had lied on their questionnaires. In the U.S. Zone alone, over 300,000 government employees were needed to effectively operate the government.[38]

The *Meldebogen*, a registration form, was prepared on about three-million people in the U.S. Zone, including prisoners of war. It was much shorter and hence faster to complete and review than its counterpart, the labor-intensive and lengthy *Fragebogen*. The longer form would eventually be phased out and the shorter *Meldebogen* adopted for exclusive use.

The military director of the Denazification Program in the U.S. Zone began evaluating the wisdom of sorting through millions of questionnaires that bogged down the program and tribunals. In August 1946 the Military Government granted an amnesty to Germans born after January 1, 1919. The rationale was that younger people were swayed by the National Socialist doctrine that was thoroughly embedded in their schools and everyday life. They were not volunteers to National Socialism, compared to adults who willingly joined and initiated programs to indoctrinate young children. By December of 1946 amnesties were granted to disabled persons and those with low income. The income restriction clearly showed these people hadn't profited from the Nazis.

The *Länderat* and Denazification

During the twelve-year reign of the so-called thousand-year Third Reich, Hitler allowed only one party – his. Previously under the Weimar Republic the left had been, "composed of Social Democrats, Democrats, and Communists; the center, of the Catholic Center party and the Bavarian's People's Party; and the right, of the People's Party, the Nationalists and the National Socialists. In the new Germany after Hitler, the rightist groups practically disappeared, the Communists were a small leftist group, and the two great parties were both moderates: the SPD (Social Democratic Party), slightly left of center, and the CDU (Christian Democratic Union), slightly right."[39] Nazis were prohibited from voting; however, a process needed to be developed to identify the National Socialist elements in the population and in influential leadership roles.

Free elections, radio and press were among the priorities established by the Military Government with food, housing and clothing being the top priorities. A nation that was hungry, cold and living in rags was not one open to new ideas. Basic needs would have to be met first, and then the teaching of democratic principles would be more favorably received.

The German *Länderat* (Council of States) in the U.S. Zone accepted the responsibility from the Military Government to draft a law requiring registration of all adults. The review began with the purpose of purging "major Nazis" from political leadership. In a meeting in Munich in March 1946 the *Länderat* Minister Presidents of Bavaria, Baden-Württemburg and Greater Hesse accepted the responsibility for denazification. The "Law Number 104 for Liberation from National Socialism and Militarism," drafted by the Military Government thus became the responsibility of the German *Spruchkammer* (Tribunals). General Clay noted it was ironic that the signing of the Law took place in Munich's old *Rathaus* where it all began for Hitler.[40]

Defining "Real Nazis"

The purpose of the Law for Liberation from National Socialism and Militarism was to, "determine who the real Nazis were so that they could be excluded from places of public influence while new German leadership was developing."[41] What this meant needed more defining. Five classes were established: "Category I: major offenders, to be punished by as much as ten years' imprisonment, confiscation of property, and permanent exclusion from public office; Category II: offenders subject to imprisonment, fine, and exclusion from public office but entitled to release from restriction on probation; Category III: followers, or Category IV: nominal Nazis who, although subject to fine, could exercise their rights of citizenship; and those in Category V; people exonerated as a result of the investigation."[42] The Tribunal decision imposed classifications and sanctions which governed the eligibility for all public and private employment in the U.S. Zone.[43]

Who the "real Nazis" were versus those who had jumped on board later as protection insurance was based upon a series of dates from the March 1933 general election. In February, when Hitler became Chancellor, and after the Enabling Act passed by the German Parliament handed him veritable dictatorial powers, a great influx of membership applications flooded the NSDAP. The motivations appeared primarily job related, rather than a commitment to National Socialism ideals. The Party declared that no new applications would be accepted after May 1st, in order to catch up with the tremendous backlog. Their announcement resulted in another tidal wave of applications in April prior to the cutoff deadline. The Nazis who had been members for a long time referred to the newcomers as the *Märzgefallene* or the "March casualties."[44]

Even Fritz Bayerlein's convenient and long-time consort, *Fraulein* Johanna Huber, had joined the party; her NSDAP card was dated May 1, 1933.[45] After the war Hanna worked for a private orthopedic physician, so she was not required to prepare the detailed *Fragebogen*. She fell into the over-eighteen requirement for preparation of the bureaucratically lesser evil, the *Meldebogen*. Since Hanna had been a member of the Nazi Party, it was necessary for her to submit the shorter form. She assumed the duties of a "masseuse" and visited many patients in their homes. Hanna was good at her job, and many benefited from her care and devotion. Bayerlein was also a patient of her employer, and neighbors hanging out their laundry in the fresh summer sunshine raised a quizzical eyebrow as Hanna happily made her house calls at Fritz's apartment. She was fiercely loyal to Bayerlein, had defended him in the past in a *Gestapo*[46] investigation, and would also lend her support for him in his *Spruchkammer*.

A Formidable Tasking

The German *Spruchkammer* (Denazification Tribunals) were established to begin the monumental task of sorting through nearly 13,000,000 registrants in the U.S. Zone of Occupation alone to determine the class of offenders and place them on trial to answer for the charges against them. About 3,000,000 were chargeable cases. At its peak, there were 545 tribunals with a total organizational strength of over 22,000. The Public Safety Branch of the Military Government supervised the tribunals and had the authority to set aside verdicts and require new trials.[47] The OMGUS Internal Affairs and Communications Division Director, Dwight P. Griswold, protested and stated in a lengthy memo to the OMGUS Headquarters Chief of Staff that, "inadequate consideration was given to the excessive number of persons which would be incriminated under its [the Law's] provisions." The Military Government revised the law with amnesties and introduction of summary administrative procedures for meting out small fines to followers (*Sühnebescheid*).[48] The Director further cited the immense workload still before the *Spruchkammers* and the Military Government: "Of the total 964,041 persons in Class I (24,281) and Class II (939,760), only 68,799, or 7 percent, were tried as of 31 January 1947. Five years will be required to dispose of these cases if they are tried at the rate of 14,264 per month which is the highest rate experienced in any month to date (November 1946) … The task is further complicated and increased by the fact that practically every person who is found to be a Major Offender, Offender, or Lesser Offender by a Trial Tribunal takes an appeal to an Appellate Tribunal. There have been a total of 13,971 appeals, 12,367 of which are still pending. It can be anticipated that this backlog will increase enormously because the number of appeals each month is now approaching 5,000 whereas cases are being disposed of at the rate of less than 600 a month, an average of twenty-four per Appellate Tribunal."

Director Griswold criticized the original law, which he believed resulted in herding, "masses of unrepentant Nazis through a denazification machine in a manner which breeds contempt and ridicule on the part of the German population and the other occupying powers. Cases of important Nazis are neither investigated nor adequately considered and are lost in the sheer mass of small fry. The American Military Government is laying itself open to the charge that it is only going through the motions and is not really carrying out the directives of its own government nor its quadripartite commitments."[49]

The Internal Affairs Director sought to narrow the scope of the numerically intimidating mountain of paperwork and trials. He pointed out the Law for Liberation goes "far beyond the requirements" of the original JCS 1067 and Potsdam Agreement in the number of persons it incriminated. This, Director Griswold noted, made the Law, "administratively impossible and politically unacceptable to the German people."[50] He reminded the OMGUS Headquarters Chief of Staff that the objectives were, "the punishment of war criminals as established by the International Military Tribunal; internment sanctions on Nazi leaders, influential Nazi supporters, high officials of Nazi organizations and institutions dangerous to the occupation or its objectives; removal and exclusion from public office and positions of responsibility in important private undertakings those persons having more than nominal participation in Nazi activities; those hostile to Allied purposes; and those who, by their political and moral qualities, are deemed incapable of assisting in developing genuine democratic institutions in Germany."[51]

Director Griswold pointed out the obvious – which sometimes is lost in the enthusiasm of policy initiation and the realities of dealing with over-optimistic program goals. He stated: "With the best of intentions, we have attempted through the Law for Liberation to exceed the [JCS 1067 and Potsdam Agreement] objectives by registering every person over eighteen years of age with the intention of adjudicating the case of every Nazi in the U.S. Zone. In doing so, we are sacrificing the objective enumerating by the paragraph 6 [of the JCS and Potsdam Agreement] because of the administrative impossibility of such a task. Moreover, we are encountering more and more resistance on the part of the Ministers of Political Liberation and their subordinates who are constantly concocting new schemes which amount to thinly veiled sabotage of the Law. For these acts they are not entirely at fault because any sincere effort on their part to enforce the Law as written is tantamount to political suicide, not only for themselves but for their political parties." In his criticism of the Law for Liberation's strict policies, he did propose suggestions. The suggestions were taken into account and implemented by General Lucius Clay, now the Military Governor of the U.S. Zone. However, Director Griswold pointed out that the Directors of the Regional Offices of Military Government for Bavaria, Baden-Württemberg, Greater Hesse and Land Bremen should be granted plenary [absolute] authority and direct operational control to "get things going." He cautioned that with the granting of an amendment the German authorities might construe their "civil disobedience" as a weakness on the Military Government's side and further seek to extract yet more concessions by using the same tactics.[52]

To address the deficiencies noted by Director Griswold, General Clay stated his decision in a strongly worded letter to the *Länderat*[53] in Stuttgart. The Military Governor stated:

> It is a fair criticism to state that in the past year we have been seriously diverted from our mission by an attempt to thresh too much empty straw. As a consequence, the investigation necessary for the adequate preparation of cases involving the principal offenders has been neglected. What is perhaps more important, public prosecutors and Tribunals have not had time to give due consideration to cases involving persons who are more than nominal Nazis and whose eligibility for appointment or reinstatement

in public office or positions of responsibility in important undertakings is a threat to the development of genuine democratic institutions in Germany.

"Experience has shown that the Law for Liberation incriminates too many people who were not sufficiently import adherents of the Nazi regime to be worth our concern unless they aspire to public office or a position of responsibility in an important undertaking. As the Law now stands, those people are barred from unimportant employment and activities in which no threat to the development of democratic institutions appears to be involved. At the suggestion of the Ministers of Political Liberation amnesties to large groups of persons have been granted, but the administrative load is still too heavy to permit the proper preparation and prosecution of the cases against those Nazis leaders who are really guilty. One of the prime objectives of the Law for Liberation is to make it impossible for such persons again to lead Germany to destruction; and it is feared that if the law in not amended, many of them will be cleared because of lack of time and proper preparation on the part of the public prosecutors and Tribunals.

"With these amendments … public prosecutors will be able to confine their charges to highly incriminated persons including (a) persons who are within Class I categories … (b) members of organizations found criminal by the International Military Tribunal, and (c) persons against whom the public prosecutors have evidence upon which they feel they can substantiate a finding of Major Offender or Offender.

"With the enactment of the Law for Liberation, the governments of the *Länder* entered into a solemn obligation to accomplish denazification with justice and sincere purpose. But Military Government did not thereby divest itself of its ultimate responsibility for denazification in the U.S. Zone. Our quadripartite commitments and our obligations to the people of all democratic nations, including the democratic elements within Germany itself, preclude this. Military Government must therefore continue to exercise as much control and supervision over denazification as may prove necessary to get the job done. Directors of Regional Offices of Military Government have been granted plenary authority in this matter. Whether occasion may arise necessitating the use of this authority rests entirely with you, in that it depends upon the sincerity and efficiency with which you administer and enforce the Law for Liberation.

"The amendments to the Law necessary to a more thorough and expeditious accomplishment of our mutual objectives are attached. I fully expect that with their adoption you will attack the denazification problem with renewed vigor and redoubled effort. Much has been learned during the past year, and great progress has been made in developing leadership and democratic government in your war-torn land. Our ultimate objective is democratic self-government for Germany. But a democratic house cannot be built with Nazi bricks. Certainly you must administer and enforce this law in letter and spirit or you will postpone your day of freedom and full acceptance into the family of peace loving nations.

Signed: Lucius D. Clay
General, U.S. Army
Military Governor"

German Commanders' "Ordinary Labor" versus Work for the Historical Division

The Office of Military Government for Germany (U.S.) directed the Greater Hesse office to allow the employment of former German officers working for the U.S. Army Historical Division. The Division's work was classified at "more than ordinary labor" and an exception to policy was necessary to complete the Army's work. The August 1947 directive from OMGUS to the director of the military government office in Greater Hesse read:[54]

> The Office of the Chief Historian, EUCOM has been charged by a directive dated 27 May 1947 with completion within a set period of the historical record of German operations against U.S. forces which is being compiled at Allendorf (Greater Hesse) through exploitation of German commanders and staff officers, now discharged into civilian status. Those former officers who have been previously engaged on the Historical Project as prisoners of war are not to be employed as indigenous personnel.
>
> Virtually all the former general staff officers, however, whom it is desired to employ on this project, are limited to ordinary labor by Article 59 and Paragraph L of the Appendix to the Law for Liberation from National Socialism and Militarism, and it is the opinion of this headquarters that the writing of history on behalf of a U.S. agency may not be classed as ordinary labor.
>
> It is nonetheless concluded, in view of the importance of the U.S. interest involved, that the demands of the Historical Project in this instance overrule the requirements of the denazification program and that an exception to the general employment policy must be made. It is furthermore anticipated that many of the former staff officers who are to be retained in connection with this project may adopt a reluctant and uncooperative attitude toward their work when they observe that others of their fellow staff officers, who did not cooperate with U.S. forces by service on the project, are now released and in some cases denazified and are free to resume a normal life, whereas they themselves are required to continue service on a program in the interest of the U.S. with the threat of denazification proceedings postponed to fall upon them at a future date.
>
> For the purposes, therefore, of avoiding interruption of the Historical Project and forestalling discontent on the part of the former general officers to be employed therein, you will:
>
> Issue Military Government approval for employment of subject former German staff officers and commanders on the German Historical Project at more than ordinary labor.
>
> Instruct the Minister for Political Liberation to establish a special tribunal in the Allendorf Community for the sole purpose of carrying out investigation and processing of the denazification cases of the former German officers there employed. The denazification proceedings of subject persons will be carried out as expeditiously as possible but in full accordance with the Law for Liberation and no special consideration of favor will be shown the respondents in these cases because of their connection with the Allendorf project. Neither is it desired to suggest condoning of careless haste nor superficial investigation in the handling of these proceedings, and the

tribunal will be required to prepare and investigate these cases with the thoroughness normally requisite under the denazification law. Sanctions, such as a confinement in a labor camp or employment restrictions, which may be imposed by Spruchkammer verdicts and which would interfere with an individual's work on the project may be held in abeyance on the request of the Office of the Chief Historian until termination of employment of employment of the respondent.

Your implementation of this plan will be closely coordinated with the Office of the Chief Historian, EUCOM.

BY DIRECTION OF THE MILITARY GOVERNOR

G.H. Garde
Lieutenant Colonel, AGD
Adjutant General

In Summary

The U.S. Army was of the opinion that, "all officers of the *Wehrmacht* contributed money towards some organization of the NSDAP, and these were monthly contributions which they were more or less bound to give."[55]

By February 1947, the OMGUS Greater Hesse Denazification Section, Public Safety Branch chief reported that the backlog of chargeable cases totaled 145,277. The number of cases filed totaled 51,487 of which 39,233 had been disposed. The Branch chief forecasted that at the rate of 10,000 cases each month, the backlog would take approximately fifteen months to complete. In January, for example, the output of disposed cases was about 5,000.[56] The Hesse prosecutors were holding approximately 700,000 *Meldebogen*. Progress was slowed by the fact that many cities in Hesse had no coal, which resulted in a decrease in the work output of the *Spruchkammer*.[57]

Bayerlein Prepares for his *Spruchkammer*

An Army decision was made to reduce the size of the Military Intelligence Service Center (MISC) at Oberursel. The MISC had held many general officers for nearly two years. With the closure of a nearby camp, the Army decided to relocate all General officers to Camp Allendorf. They could still work on their projects for the U.S. Army's Historical Services Division, which was also nearby. While a POW at the MISC, Bayerlein felt safe and protected, since the Americans liked him, and he was a favorite of the camp commander, Colonel Philp. With his surrender in the Ruhr and his pro-American and cooperative attitude, Bayerlein was hated by many of his peers and former superiors. He was threatened by the other generals who were looking forward to his arrival at Camp Allendorf. Forewarned by a sneering and gloating General Walter Botsch, Bayerlein cleverly thwarted their plans and appealed to the commander of the MISC to keep him. Bayerlein's plan worked, and the Americans held him at the MISC until his release.[58]

After his release from captivity on April 2, 1947 *Generalleutnant a.D.* Fritz Bayerlein[59] was employed as a civilian by the European Command Intelligence Center (ECIC) at Oberursel. This organization was the former MISC, and as in an old army tradition, it was renamed. As with many other former General officer POWs, Bayerlein worked on home projects for the U.S. Army Historical Services Division, under the direction of *General a.D.* Franz Halder.[60] Bayerlein was extremely worried about a possible imprisonment in a civilian internee camp until his *Spruchkammer* hearing scheduled for September 1947. Just before he was released, Bayerlein wrote the ECIC commander, imploring him to keep him interred at the ECIC compound, which was a more favorable environment than what he would face in an unknown civilian camp. Bayerlein feared fanatical Nazi elements would learn via the rumor mill of his traitorous (to them) surrender in the Ruhr. However, to his great relief, Bayerlein was released and was not placed under automatic arrest.

In the meantime Bayerlein had yet another problem. The Military Government *Landkries* office at Hesse called for Bayerlein's removal from ECIC. His entry into the *Reichswehr* prior to 1935 had placed Bayerlein as at least a Class II category offender.[61] He was a general officer from his promotion to *Generalmajor* in Africa, and a *Generalleutnant* as commander of Panzer Lehr Division. He had served as a General Staff officer under Guderian – acted as his operations officer during the attack on France and the invasion of Russia. Not only did Bayerlein face a witch-hunt among his former peers and superiors – now he faced a civilian tribunal. As the German expression clearly states – Bayerlein found himself "*zwischen Feuer und Hölle*" [between fire and hell].

The man was very worried.

Chapter 1 Endnotes

1. The NSDAP, *Nationalsozialistische Deutsche Arbeiterpartei*. The term 'Nazi' is an acronym compromising *Nationalsozialistische*. (Reference: James Taylor and Warren Shaw, "*The Third Reich Almanac*", World Almanac, New York, NY. 224.)

2. P.A. Spayd, "*Bayerlein, from Afrikakorps to Panzer Lehr, the Life of Rommel's Chief of Staff, Generalleutnant Fritz Bayerlein*," Schiffer Publishing, Ltd. Atglen, PA. 2003, 250.

3. The SS (*Schutzstaffel*) were the original bodyguard of Hitler, but later Himmler transformed it into several branches: the Waffen SS, concentration camp personnel, execution, extermination groups (*Einsatzgruppen*) and Hitler's bodyguards. The SD (*Sicherheitsdienst*) was the Nazi party's intelligence and security body. At the Nuremberg war crime trials the SD was declared a criminal organization, as was the Gestapo, and its members were under automatic arrest and subject to prosecution. (Taylor and Shaw, *Almanac*, 298-299)

4. Franklin M. Davis, Jr., *Come as a Conqueror, The United States Army's Occupation of Germany 1945-1949*." New York: The Macmillan Company, 1967. 178

5. The Control Council consisted of representatives from the French, British, Americans and Russians. Also, a U.S. Group Control Council was established in order to have one staff for military government in Germany; it was part of the Control Authority. Details and problems establishing and continuing the "Allied" Control Council are available in "*The US Army in the Occupation of Germany, 1944 – 46*," Earl F. Ziemke; 222, 223, 265, 267, 268, 342.

6. Davis, *Conqueror*. 251.

7. Zink, Harold, Former Chief Historian, U.S. High Commissioner for Germany. "*The United States in Germany, 1944-1955*." D. Van Nostrand Company, Inc. Princeton, New Jersey, 1957. 151.

8. Zink, *US in Germany* Ibid., 19.

9. Ibid., 21, 153

10. Ibid. 153.

11. Ibid., 21; and Ziemke, *US Army Occupation*, 37.

12. Ziemke, *US Army Occupation*, 130

13. Zink, *US in Germany*, 23

14. Lucius D. Clay, "*Decision in Germany,*" Garden City, New York: Doubleday & Company, 1950, 11-12.

15. Davis, *Conqueror*. 232.

16. Clay, *Decision in Germany,*. 8.

17. Ibid., 13.

18. Zink, *US in Germany* Ibid., 30.

19. Ibid., 157.

20. Ibid., 156.

21. Jean Edward Smith, (editor), *The Papers of General Lucius D. Clay, Germany 1945 – 1949*, Bloomington: Indiana University Press, 1974. Document Number 80. Denazification, 148.

22. Davis, *Conqueror*. 178.

23. Ibid., 61-62.

24. Zink, *US in Germany*," 150.

25. Ibid.

26. OMGUS, Office of the Deputy Military Governor, Lt. General Lucius D. Clay Subject: Law for Liberation from National Socialism and Militarism, to: Minister Presidents for Bavaria, Baden-Württemberg, and Greater Hesse, dated 5 March 1946, NARA RG 260, Box 1114.

27. Ziemke, *US Army Occupation*, 384, 385.

28. Ibid.

29. Ibid., 386, as quoted from the New York *Times*, 23 September 1945.

30. Ibid., 386, as cited from HQ Diary, XV Corps, 8 Oct – 10 Dec 45, 12 Oct. 45, in XV Corps, 215-0.3.

31. Smith, *Clay Papers*, Document 168 Denazification, 15 December 1946.

32. According to Earl F. Ziemke, Schaeffer was elected to the Bundestag of the Federal Republic of Germany in 1949, Finance Minister from 1949-1957, then Minister of Justice until 1961. Reference: Ziemke, *US Army Occupation*. 385.

33. Ziemke, *US Army Occupation*, 383, 386; HQs, USFET, Administration of Military Government in the U.S. Zone, Law, No. 8, 26 September 45, in OMGUS 411-2/3.

34. Smith, *Clay Papers*, Document 68. Minor Nazis and other Germans, 8 December 1945, 130.

35. Davis, *Conqueror*. 252.

36. Per Gary Wilkins, the term "*Meldebogen*" is a registration form, though in more contemporary usage the term is "*Anmeldeformular*". The verb "*melden*" itself means, "to report something/someone" and the verb "*anmelden*" means to announce or to declare, thus "officially register."

37. Office of Military Government for Greater Hesse, Subject: Operation of the Law for Liberation from National Socialism and Militarism, dated 9 December 1946, National Archives and Records Administration.

38. Clay, *Decision*, 67-68.

39. Ibid., 91-92.

40. Ibid., 99.

41. Ibid., 258.

42. Ibid., 258.

43. OMGUS, Greater Hesse, Denazification Division Letter to Public Safety Branch, dated 18 June 1947. Subject: Right of Military Government to disapprove certain classes of officials. NARA RG 360, Box 1114

44. Fitzgibbon, Constantine, *Denazification*, Michael Joseph London, Ltd., 1969, 39. From: William Sheridan Allen's *"The Nazi Seizure of Power."*

45. Spayd, *"Bayerlein"*, 21-23; Author's note: Johanna Huber, nicknamed 'Hanna', was born October 16, 1901. She lived her entire life in Würzburg, remaining a single woman. She died on June 6, 1981. Her occupation in 1938 was a *Sportlehrerin*, or sports instructor. In 1941 she served in the Reich Labor Service as a leader (*Arbeitsdienstführerin.*) (Stadtarchiv Würzburg) Her National Socialist card number was 3437327. (NARA Microfilm Branch).

46. The Gestapo, or *Geheime Staatspolizei*, was the secret political police of the Third Reich. The Gestapo was one of six organizations indicted for crimes against humanity at the Nuremberg trial. These six organizations were the leaders of the Nazi Party; the OKW (*Oberkommando der Wehrmacht*), the SS, the SA (*Sturmabteilung*), the *Reichs* cabinet and the Gestapo. (Reference: Taylor and Shaw, *Almanac*, 130-131.)

47. Fitzgibbon, *Denazification*, 259.

48. OMGUS Office of Military Governor, dated 1 April 1947; Subject: Amendment of the Law for Liberation from National Socialism and Militarism of 5 March 1946. To: Länderate. NARA, OMGUS – Records of the Denazification Division 1945-1947; Intelligence Reports, RG 260/390/48/30-231/6-2, Box 168.

49. OMGUS Internal Affairs and Communications Division, dated 1 April 1947, Subject: Desirable Changes in the Law for Liberation from National Socialism and Militarism and in Denazification Procedures in the U.S. Zone, To: The Chief of Staff, OMGUS Records of the Denazification Division, 1945-1947 Box 168, RG 260/390/48/30-31-6-2.

50. Ibid, page 2.

51. Ibid.

52. Ibid., 4.

53. The collective name for the German Council of Minister Presidents for Bavaria, Württemberg-Baden, Greater Hesse and Land Bremen in the US Zone of Occupation.

54. OMGUS (US) Memo dated August 1947, Subject: Employment of Former German Commanders and Staff Officers on Historical Project. AG 014.311(IA), NARA, OMGUS Records of the Denazification Branch, File: Field Instructions, RG 260/390/49/27/5-7, Box 1114.

55. Liaison & Security Office for Landkreis Buedingen, OMG Greater Hesse, memo dated 22 November 1946. NARA.

56. Public Safety Branch memo, dated 13 February 1947, OMG Greater Hesse, NARA RG 260, Box 1114.

57. OMGUS, Greater Hesse, memo dated 7 February 1947. To Director, OMGUS. Subject: Classification of Meldebogen. NARA, RG 260, Box 1114.

58. Spayd, *"Bayerlein"*, 246-248.

59. Due to Bayerlein's retirement from active service after 27 years in the German Wehrmacht he is correctly referred to as *Generalleutnant außer Dienst* abbreviated as *"a.D."*

60. Upon their release from the POW camps, many German generals and other senior officers were asked to complete their unit histories and personal combat experiences at their home, and under the supervision of General Franz Halder. The US Army Historical Division referred to these projects as "home projects", or "home work." Bayerlein, as well as his colleagues, also received food and sundry parcels periodically to supplement their meager rations. While working on these home projects, Bayerlein also worked for the European Command Intelligence Center (ECIC) at Oberursel, Germany. He was given an automobile for his business use. Such a prestigious allowance from the US Army to the General showed the high esteem in which he was held.

61. Under the Law for Liberation from National Socialism and Militarism, Chapter 1, Article 8, Section II, Paragraph 2. Per NARA Liaison & Security Office, Greater Hesse, Public Safety Branch.

2
The Gestapo File

"By the late-1930s it was a brave German who risked his career, his family, even his life, for speaking his mind. We might wish that more had opposed Nazism; we should recall the fate of those who did." — Doctor Richard Overy, Reader of History, University of London[1]

The Gestapo, Organization of Terror

The *Geheimestaatspoliezi*, or Gestapo, was the Third Reich's secret state police. A month after passage of Hitler's "Enabling Act" on April 26, 1933, the first German law establishing and governing the Gestapo was enacted. Hitler began his police state with the establishment of the Gestapo which took the role, in part, of a national political police force. Although an alien concept to Americans, the political police provided crowd control for strikes, riots and demonstrations.[2] Coordinated by Himmler, the complex marriage of the SS, SD and Gestapo created many overlapping areas of responsibility. As with any bureaucracy, competition among the various departments for leadership, power and authority was rampant. As with the SS and SD, the Gestapo had complete freedom to impose their version of protective custody upon anyone it wanted under the guise of subverting undesirable political activities. The Gestapo also had the power of automatic arrest and was responsible for investigating denunciations, many of which were petty complaints based upon revenge or personal gains.[3]

More often than not, the concept of due process and freedom of speech was subjugated for the sake of public interest. Manfred Rommel recalled, "Dependence on the official propaganda grew considerably; anyone listening to foreign radio programs was declared liable to severe punishment, especially if the news was disseminated. This strange act of government was declared necessary in order to protect German morale from being undermined by hostile influence. Another law provided that each criticism of the government should be severely punished for the sake of the public spirit, which should not be troubled."[4]

The public at large feared denunciation by personal enemies who were nursing old grudges or rivalries. Nazi *Blockwart* (block wardens) were used as spies who kept a close watch on their neighborhoods for signs of any non-conformists and potential enemies. Any slight, or perceived slight, against the Third Reich, its policies or leaders, could be reported. Germany became a police state, keeping its citizens in line through the exercise of denunciation and terror. However, even the Gestapo needed local support, which aided the overall repression of German citizens.[5]

Bavaria was predominately an agricultural state, with fewer Communists and Socialists for the Gestapo to track down. In particular, the Würzburg Gestapo office "could devote more time and energy to petty prosecutions."[6]

The Transfer Transition – Home Leave

During early September 1941, after fighting in the war for two years from the invasion of Poland, France, and Russia under the command of *Generaloberst* Heinz Guderian, *Oberstleutnant* Fritz Bayerlein faced a transfer to the western desert in North Africa. Guderian was rapidly falling out of favor with Hitler for failing to capture the coveted prize of Moscow and bring a quick and conclusive end to the war in the East before winter set in. Whether or not it was a coincidence, it appeared that Guderian's loyal command staff cadre would be relegated to the wastelands of the African continent. *General* Walter Nehring[7], Guderian's Chief of Staff, was ousted into the desert; and along with him, came another one of Guderian's staff officers, *Oberst* Kurt *Freiherr* von Liebenstein.[8] Other than their affiliation with and loyalty to Guderian, why three officers with extensive Russian fighting under their belt should be transferred to the western desert and not used to greater advantage in Russia was only known to Hitler and his throng. To serve under Rommel in the desert was considered by some officers as tantamount to punishment by career banishment. [9] Others, such as loyal friends like Fritz Bayerlein, would fare exceedingly well.

Newly promoted to the rank of *Oberstleutnant*, in September 1940, Bayerlein hadn't enough service time in rank, nor age, to fill the vacant Chief of Staff position to the Commander of the *Deutsches Afrikakorps (DAK)*. The resourceful Bayerlein did fare well, as his new appointment was requested by *Generaloberst* Rommel and arranged by Guderian. With such formidable career backing Bayerlein was secure in his new post and looked forward to serving under Rommel, who was a former instructor in the old Infantry School training days in the late-1920s. As an *Oberleutnant*, Bayerlein had served as *Hauptmann* Rommel's assistant instructor at the *Infantrieschule* at Dresden. The two men had forged a strong friendship, with Bayerlein visiting the former *Hauptmann*, his wife Lucie and young son, Manfred. When they worked together, the two men enjoyed both walking the countryside and driving Rommel's small car. Bayerlein openly admired his superior's affectionate and chivalrous treatment of his wife.[10]

Between his transfer from Russia to Africa, *Oberstleutnant* Bayerlein was enjoying a 30-day home furlough. He looked forward to the beautiful autumn days in September visiting his hometown of Würzburg, Germany. Bayerlein walked the streets and byways, accompanied by his attractive, long-term girlfriend Hanna Huber, his lively sister Ellen Dittmar and her handsome son, Friedrich. Accompanied by friend Walter Schmidt, the group took long walks through the vineyards and paths among the hills along the Main River. Ellen's little terrier trotted at their heels. The former Bavarian Kings' fortress, *Festung Marienburg*, overlooked the river valley and presided over the town of Würzburg and the small village of Heidingsfeld. Visiting his home, untouched by the war, the campaigns in Poland, France, and Russia seemed a distant memory for Bayerlein. This idyllic setting with magnificent *Tannenbaum* trees, fall foliage of wine country, would be overshadowed by an incident soon to face Bayerlein and his small group.

An Unknown Russian Prisoner

Waiting at a suburban train station, Fritz, Hanna, Ellen, Friedrich and Walter were witness to an unfortunate incident that would be repeated many times throughout Europe in the years to come. A detail of Russian prisoners of war were working on a nearby train track. One of the prisoners fell to the ground, and a camp guard attempted to get him back to his

Bayerlein photographs his sister, Ellen Dittmar (left): her husband, Matthäus: and Bayerlein's smiling girlfriend, Johanna Huber (right), on an overlook of the Main River. "Hanna had a lot of hope for Fritz," recalled a family friend. Photo was taken in September 1941 during his furlough between his transfer from Russia to Africa. (Photo courtesy of the Dittmar-Bayerlein Family Collection)

A younger Bayerlein enjoying a rooftop view of a neighboring village. The Bayerleins and their friends enjoyed hiking and traveling in Bavaria. Prewar photo. (Photo courtesy of Dittmar-Bayerlein Family Collection)

Bayerlein and sister Ellen relaxing on vacation. They frequented the ski slopes of Garmich-Partikirchen in the Bavarian Alps, and hiking the countryside's in the spring and summer months. (Photo courtesy of the Dittmar-Bayerlein Family Collection)

feet by beating him with an ox whip. Other prisoners dragged the man to his feet, and they were loaded onto the train. Bayerlein noticed this, although his sister noted that he said nothing. He frowned, watched the incident and was silent. Boarding the same train, the party arrived at the main *Hauptbahnhof* [11] in Würzburg.

De-boarding the train amid a crowd of people, Bayerlein and his group noticed the same Russian work party. His comrades were dragging the same hapless prisoner through the station to the main road as the guard continually beat him with his ox whip.

Bayerlein provides the details of his subsequent actions in a Gestapo report:[12]

Fritz Bayerlein
Oberstleutnant in the General Staff
Of the German Afrikakorps

Feldpost 40 800

To
The Chief of the Gestapo
Würzburg

Time: (up to noon on 9/23)
Würzburg, Sept. 20, 1941
Kürschnerhof 17

On September 19th at 18:45 in front of the main train station, I stopped the German escort man for a troop of Russian POWs, as he was using an ox whip to beat a prisoner who was not capable of walking on his own and who was being dragged along the road by two fellow prisoners, and since he was unable to get the troop of prisoners moving and a large crowd of people had formed around them.

I myself, as the senior officer present, stepped in, in order to ensure that the unpleasant, unmilitary images were quickly removed from public view, and arrange for the immobile prisoner to be carried away by several fellow prisoners.

The public was of mixed opinion over my measures, which were of a purely military nature, and which I undertook on my own official authority. In no way had the public any right to criticize my purely military measures, which were directed solely against the unprofessional behavior of the inexperienced escort man – a *Landesschützen* [*local militiaman*] – directed toward helping him out of an unpleasant situation.

I am informing the Chief of the Gestapo of the incident however, as I have learned that persons from the public inevitably became involved in the affair and I want to prevent these [individuals] from encountering any sort of detriment due to inaccurate representation of the incident. I state that the public could not take sides for, or against the prisoners, since the measures were directed solely at the conduct of the escort man. I must dispute any and all military understanding of any person with another view.

I am at your service for additional information; however, only until noon on 9/23, as I am departing for Africa in the evening. I have notified the commandant's office, Würzburg.

Heil Hitler!
Signed: Bayerlein

Bayerlein was careful to phrase his report to reflect his purely neutral military interest in the affair, and not demonstrate any perceived sympathy for the Russian prisoner. To do so would be tantamount to asking the Gestapo to transport him directly to a detention camp. A highly intelligent man, Bayerlein was aware of the repercussions of publicly showing any compassion for the enemy. In a report to the Americans after the war, Bayerlein recalled that he had "reprimanded the guard for his unmanly behavior, forbade further use of the whip and ordered the sick Russian carried away in spite of a hostile crowd of more than 100 people that had gathered around him and that hurled unspeakable curses at him." The American Army report cited that in the "melee that followed the ladies of Bayerlein's party were bodily threatened." His sister Ellen got in a heated dispute with the *Gauamtsleiter* and *Gau* judge of the NSDAP, Michael Langguth. Reportedly Langguth called "these ladies such names as 'whores' and '*Saumenschen*'[13] because they took sides with the Russian prisoner."[14] Summoned by the Gestapo two days later to report to their office, Bayerlein clarified his initial statement. He described his own measures and the Nazi *Gauamtsleiter* Michael Langguth's actions in greater detail.

Bayerlein's statement reads as follows:

Ellen, Fritz and nephew Friedrich pose for Hanna on the Löwen (Lion) Bridge. Behind them on the hillside is their favorite haunt, the Café Charlotten. Date of photo is September 1941, showing a happier activity during Bayerlein's furlough. (Photo courtesy of the Dittmar-Bayerlein Family Collection)

Downtown Würzburg Germany, a beautiful street scene. (Photo courtesy of the Dittmar-Bayerlein Family Collection)

The Würzburg Hauptbahnhof (main train station) – a scene of the infamous Russian POW incident. Photo taken at a happier occasion – returning from vacation sporting deep tans. (Photo courtesy of the Dittmar-Bayerlein Family Collection)

Uncle Fritz and nephew Fritz. The Main River in background. The family enjoyed hikes out of the town and into the surrounding countryside. (Photo courtesy of the Dittmar-Bayerlein Family Collection)

Young nephew Fritz Dittmar (left), Bayerlein, sister Ellen and a friend on one of their frequent walks around the Main River front. (Photo courtesy of the Dittmar-Bayerlein Family Collection)

Hanna Huber, Bayerlein's girlfriend, and his sister Ellen Dittmar. Fraulein Huber knew the Bayerlein Family for many years, from their former Blumenstrasse neighborhood located near the Main River. (Photo courtesy of the Dittmar-Bayerlein Family Collection)

At the Office of the *Geheime Staatspolizei*, in Würzburg, on September 22, 1941 State Police Office Nürnberg-Fürth

Local Office Würzburg

B. Nr. II A6 9392/41

Appeared the unmarried Oberstleutnant

Fritz B a y e r l e i n ,

of the German *Afrikakorps*, born 1/14/1899 in Würzburg, Army Field Post Office No. 40 800, and declared the following:

To my letter of 9/20/41, in which I described the incident with the Russian prisoners at the local train station plaza, I have the following to state:

I was in civilian clothing. With me/ in my company was

Sonderführer[15] Walter S c h m i d t in Army Uniform,

Arbeitsdienst Leader H u b e r and the salesman's wife D i t t m a r .

Miss Huber was also in uniform.

I had already observed the prisoner transport at the train station plaza in Seligenstadt, where the same incidents played out as in Würzburg. I did not step in there, however, because the time was too close to the train's departure.

With the arrival of the train at Würzburg, as the prisoner transport came to the train station plaza, the same deplorable state recurred with this I mean the prisoner who could not walk – that is, who had to be dragged by two other prisoners. A large group of people had already gathered at the plaza, which apparently – and as I learned later – had been awaiting the prisoner transport. In order to quickly remove this unflattering picture from public view, I introduced myself to the militiaman who led the column and gave him an order to have the prisoner carried, and this to be done by some of the other prisoners. At the same time, I demanded that he get the column moving and away from the train station plaza as quickly as possible. The Train Station Officer, who was present, I likewise ordered to see to it that the transport moved on as quickly as possible.

While I took these measures, I heard heckling, comments, and remarks from the public, part of which was for, part against, the prisoners. I later learned that among those gathered at the train station plaza was also a certain

L a n g g u t h

who, in response to the measures I had taken, apparently uttered:

"What is it with this civilian there – the malingerer ought to be right at the front."

The women who were accompanying me told me that they had responded to this remark by Langguth:

"He just came from the front – why don't you go there yourself?"

On Sunday, 9/20/41, in the evening at the Café Charlott, I learned that the incident with the Russian prisoners at the train station plaza had been reported to the Gau [*district – transl.*] directorate by a Herr Langguth, and that the Gau directorate had then passed the matter on to the Gestapo for further action aimed at both of the women.

Due to this knowingly false representation of the facts of the case by Herr Langguth, I wrote the letter of 9/20/1941 to the Gestapo, in order to rectify the facts. With regard to Prisoners of War and my measures, the two ladies did not need to say anything for or against the measures I took, or against the prisoners themselves. That Herr Langguth in his statement of the facts now mentions these specific two women as having behaved harmfully toward the State, or unfairly, is surely only attributable to the fact that the two women had bestowed on Langguth an appropriate rebuff and rebuke upon his insulting remarks with regard to my person.

I am an active officer, a WWI veteran, and since 9/1/1939[16] have been on unbroken duty at the front. For medals and badges I hold the EK II of the World War[17], the 1939 clasp to the EK II, the 1939 EK I[18] and the Wound Badge.

I will initiate measures against Langguth through my official channels for his insulting remarks.

In the near future I will not be available for questioning as I have been transferred to the German Afrikakorps and depart tomorrow.

The statement of facts given by me is correct. As witness I name the Sonderführer Walter Schmidt, Army Field Post Office No. 000 49 (co-owner of the Cafe Charlott

Würzburg); in addition, the two ladies, Arbeitsdienst Leader Johanna Huber, Würzburg, and Frau Dittmar, Kürschnerhof 17."

After reading the statement personally, signed
Fritz Bayerlein
Oberstleutnant

Recorded by:
Present:
Addendum:

As a precaution I am bringing a [*civil*] suit for affront against Herr Langguth, since at the time of said insult I was in civilian attire.

Würzburg, 22 September 1941
In accord with Signature:

Fritz Bayerlein
Oberstleutnant

The Gestapo Passes

An internal communication within the Gestapo office conducting the initial questioning, asked how the office intended to handle the case. It was apparently viewed as something the local Würzburg Gestapo office either felt was not worth pursuing, or else they felt it was too risky to handle and should be passed on.[19] The Gestapo memo reads as follows:

Gestapo Würzburg, Sept. 24, 1941
State Police Office Nürnberg-Fürth
Local Office Würzburg
B. No. II A 6 – 9392/41 – Sto.

U.gR. to

the Gestapo, State Police Office Nbg.-Fürth
in Nürnberg
with the request for notice and instructions. I intend to hand off the incident to the Attorney General in Würzburg after questioning the witnesses, including the accused, and direct a copy [*of the results*] to the office of the Commandant, Würzburg. Bayerlein is not a member of the Party. Langguth is a city council member, Gau Administrative Director and since 10/22/1925 a member of the NSDAP, member No. 20 967.

2) Registration card for Langguth is present, information questionnaire is attached.
3) W(ieder) v(orlage?). bei II A 6 [20]

On behalf of:

(Signature)

The Spirited Frau Ellen Dittmar

After her brother left for Africa, Ellen Dittmar was summoned to the Gestapo Office to answer the complaint filed by *Gauamtsleiter* Langguth. Langguth had chosen to directly attack Hanna by denouncing her to her superior and filing a complaint for insult against Ellen. Perhaps he had selected the women as easier targets, especially with the departure of Hanna's resolute boyfriend and Ellen's brother. Langguth had underestimated that Bayerlein was a force to be reckoned with and would not stand idly by while the two women in his life were threatened. With Langguth's denunciation of his girlfriend, Bayerlein had accurately forecast problems with the *Gauamtsleiter* that developed rapidly after his departure. Bayerlein attempted to thwart the brunt of Langguth's attack against Hanna by filing his own complaint. Expecting trouble, and warned by her brother and Hanna, Ellen was summoned to the Gestapo Office to recall the train station events:

Geheime Staatspolizei   Würzburg, Oct. 10 1941
State Police Office Nürnberg-Fürth
Local Office Würzburg

At summons appeared the married salesman's wife, Mrs.

Eleonore D i t t m a r , neé Bayerlein

born 4/22/1902 in Würzburg, resident in Würzburg Kürschnerhof 17, daughter of the City Senior Inspector Donat Bayerlein and Louise neé Denkmann, R.A. ev., was informed of the purpose of her questioning, and reported the following:

"Before the rise of National Socialism I was not a member of any political party or organization as a member. Long before the assumption of power I joined the NSDAP and since the 1920s have been a supporting member of the SS. From a political point of view I have never been faulted, nor have I ever, up to this point, been convicted of anything. Now to the story:

In the middle of September 1941, my brother Fritz Bayerlein, Oberstleutnant on the General Staff of the Afrika Korps, was spending some time on leave in Würzburg. In the evening hours of 9/19/1941 my brother, Fritz Bayerlein, the Sonderführer Walter Schmidt of Würzburg, the R.A.D. Leader Hanna Huber and myself stopped at the Main Train Station in Würzburg. My 16-year-old son, Fritz Dittmar, also happened to be accompanying us. As we left through the main entrance of the Main Train Station in Würzburg on this day, at a time between 6 and 7 o'clock PM, Russian POWs were being led through the train station plaza in the direction of Bismarck Street. If I remember correctly, there were 2 soldiers with the prisoners, who led the Transport [Troop]. Among the prisoners there was one who, for reasons not known to me, could no longer walk and was being dragged – to be accurate – by his fellows. The guard who had the lead duty carried an ox whip with him and struck the prisoner continuously as he was being dragged along. At this time, quite a large number of people had gathered. What position the collective crowd had taken with regard to the treatment of the prisoner by the guard, I cannot say for certain; there were some among them who had taken the prisoner's part; others, however, were against the POWs. In and of itself, the transport column offered a very poor military image. At first my brother had not expressed any opinion to us regarding the convoy, but rather went away from us, as he saw it, went over to the guard, identified himself, and conferred with him. My brother took *Sonderführer* Schmidt with him. While my brother and *Sonderführer* Schmidt spoke with the guard, Mrs. Huber and I were standing a bit to the side, watching the troop go by. My brother then also prevailed upon the Bahnhoff Officer to put a stop to the deplorable state of affairs. Mrs. Huber and I stood next to a civilian who was unknown to us in the Bahnhof plaza. While my brother was having a discussion with the *Bahnhof* Officer, the civilian, who stood just beside us, said in a quite loud tone of voice:

"What does this ridiculous civilian want – he belongs at the front"

When I heard these words, I turned my face toward the civilian and said:

"Why don't you go to the front?!"

The reason I said this was because my brother is an active duty officer and had been at the front since the start of the war. In addition, my brother had been in the World War as well. At my call to the civilian, he yelled this at me:

"What are you going on about, you bitches?!"

I did not respond to the civilian with anything at this insulting call. In response, Mrs. Huber said to the civilian:

"Please, we are with this gentleman."

In the meantime, my brother had finished his discussion with the Train Station officer, and together with Schmidt, had left. Frau Huber, I and my boy, joined my brother.

My brother likely did not hear the individual shouts from the civilian. I myself did not tell my brother anything about the incident immediately thereafter. Only when we moved onto *Kaiserstrasse* did I begin to tell my brother the details.

I then learned through Miss Huber on the following day, or the day after that, that a certain Mr. Langguth had inquired of her head office and had filed a denunciation. From this information I gained the certainty that the civilian who had called to my brother on the 19th of September at the train station: "What does this ridiculous civilian want then – he belongs at the front!" and at my retort "Why don't you go to the front?!" had shouted: "What are you going on about, you bitches?!", was this Langguth.

Likely at the end of September 1941, I was called to appear at the city Atonement Bureau in the case of Langguth, for personal insult. The first date I postponed, since I could not appear on that day. At the beginning of October 1941, I received a summons to the Würzburg Atonement Bureau but did not appear before the Bureau, having instead informed them that I had reconsidered the matter. In the meantime I spoke with Attorney Rothstein about the matter, and intend to file suit against Langguth himself for personal insult.

I am of the view that I did not insult Langguth with my response "Why don't you go first to the front?!" On the contrary I only stood up for my brother, who as an officer has been a long time at the front, and who Langguth identified as a ridiculous civilian and also made the remark that he ought to be at the front. So it is that I did not insult Langguth. On the contrary, Langguth insulted me as he shouted "What are you going on about, you bitches?!" at me.

I intend to direct Attorney Rothstein to execute on my behalf a private suit against Langguth for insult. To attest the fact that my testimony is correct, I call the Arbeitsdienst Leader Hanna Huber.

After reading the statement personally, signed
Eleonore Dittmar

Fraulein Johanna Huber, Lady Friend

Fraulein Hanna Huber, the first person that Gauamtsleiter Langguth had denounced, duly reported to the Gestapo office as ordered. She provided the following account of her memory of the event:

Geheime Staatspolizei Würzburg, Oct. 10 1941
State Police Office Nürnberg-Fürth
Local Office Würzburg

At summons appeared the unmarried Reichs Arbeitsdienst [*National Labor Service – transl.*] Leader.

Hanna H u b e r

born 10/16/1901 in Würzburg, currently with the RAD, Administrative District Leadership XIX, here at Hindenburg Street No. 34, and after being familiarized with the object of her interrogation, provided the following:

"On 9/19/1941 at about 6:30 PM I arrived at the Würzburg Main Train Station from a duty trip to Schweinfurt. After my arrival I met with Oberstleutnant Bayerlein, his sister Eleonore Dittmar and the Sonderfuhrer[21] Walter Schmidt.in the lobby of the Main Station. Dittmar's 16-year old son was also with Bayerlein, Schmidt and Mrs. Dittmar. The aforementioned persons are personally known to me. Oberstleutnant Bayerlein was wearing civilian clothes, while Sonderfuhrer Schmidt was in uniform. I left the station with the aforementioned persons, eastward of the construction fence erected at the train station. As I left the station's exit I saw on the street in front of the station building a halted column of Russian POWs. A large crowd had gathered around the immediate vicinity of the prisoners. I can no longer say exactly how many guards were with the column; I only saw one guard who struck a Russian prisoner – who apparently could not walk anymore – several times with an ox whip. I did not speak with Oberstleutnant Bayerlein about the treatment of the POWs by the military guards. After he saw the prisoner column, Bayerlein had moved away with Sonderführer Schmidt without a word to us and gone over to both of the guards. What Bayerlein and Schmidt spoke about with the military guards, I cannot say. I saw only that Bayerlein showed the guard an ID. Due to the fact that a large number of persons had gathered around the prisoner column, it was not possible for us to continue further in the direction of the city. While I then stood there at the station plaza, I heard a man who stood very close to Mrs. Dittmar, and who I didn't know, call out in a rather loud tone:

"What does this ridiculous civilian want? He should get himself to the Front!"

In response to this shout, Frau Dittmar, who was standing next to me, turned to the civilian in question and retorted:

"Why don't you go to the front yourself?!"

The response "Why don't you go to the front yourself?!" by Frau Dittmar doubtless resulted only because the shout by the civilian in question "What does this laughable civilian want – why doesn't he go the front!" had been meant for Dittmar's brother, Oberstleutnant Bayerlein. At Frau Dittmar's shout to the civilian in question "Why don't you go to the front?", the man turned to face us and yelled:

"What do you bitches want?!"

At this insulting catcall I responded to the person in question with the words:

"Please, we belong with this gentleman."

In the meantime, the Station officer had made his way to the plaza, and upon his arrival Oberstleutnant Bayerlein had immediately turned to him. What was said between the station officer and Bayerlein, I am again not able to say. After having spoken briefly with the Train Station officer, Bayerlein together with Schmidt [sic] left the plaza and we joined both gentlemen.

Bayerlein had not heard any of the individual jeers that had occurred while he had spoken with the guards and the Train Station Officer. Only as we moved into the Kaiserstrasse, even with the Hotels National, did Frau Dittmar describe the individual details.

I stress emphatically that Frau Dittmar as well as myself made no comments of any kind regarding the treatment of the Russian Prisoners of War, nor had we taken sides with them while we were standing in the station plaza. No insults were used neither by Frau Dittmar or myself; we merely replied to the civilian, with whom the cause of the whole incident rests, with the words already indicated. Who the civilian in question was that made the individual shouts, I cannot say. I only know that he had a gray hat on his head and there was a black band around the hat. It is questionable whether I would even recognize that person again were I to meet him. The matter seemed so unimportant to me, and for that reason I did not observe the individual in question any closer.

On 9/20/41, I then learned from the [*female*] district director of the RAD that at the administrative district office a certain Langguth had come by and had alleged that on 9/19/1941 at the Train Station Plaza in Würzburg I had taken sides with the Russian prisoners, and that for that reason a report had already been made to the Gestapo and to the Provincial Justice Ministry. I then gave an account of the facts of the case; and as my statements did not match those of Herr Langguth, the Ministry official had again conferred with Langguth. During the consultation it was explained to the Director that a case was pending.

I do not have any intention of seeking a suit against the civilian in question for insult, since the affair seems insignificant to me and since the person in question is not known to me.

After reading the statement personally, signed
Hanna Huber
Recorded by: Present (or Attorney)[22]

Gauamtsleiter Michael Langguth

After Langguth's sneak attack on Hanna, denouncing her to her supervisor, then learning of Bayerlein's preemptive strike on him, Gauamtsleiter Langguth retaliated with a civil suit against Bayerlein's sister, Ellen. Not content with accusing Hanna, Langguth turned his attention to Ellen Dittmar and filed a civil lawsuit:

Civil Suit Registry No. BS 181/ Copy   Würzburg, October 11, 1941
Office of the Ministry of Justice Würzburg
Before the civil official of document records noted below, appeared today

Michael Langguth

and lodged
against

Dittmar, Eleonore, salesman's wife in Würzburg,
Kürschnerhof 17

a civil suit
for libel
in which he declared:

On 19 September 1941 between 6-7 o'clock in the evening, Russian prisoners were unloaded at the main train station. Many people were standing there. One of the three guards had an ox whip with him so he could step in, if it became necessary. One of the Russians fell to the ground. The guard ordered him to get up, and gave him a jolt with his foot so that he would stand up. I had just come from my work post and went over there. I saw 2 women, a gentleman in civilian clothes, and 1 man in the uniform of a Sonderführer rush to the guard in order to take him to task for his behaviour. Many workers and others as well had gathered around this group.

The two women, among them the accused, Frau Dittmar, felt sorry for the Russian POWs and took a stance against the guard. Since now there was a danger that the workers might take sides against the guards, I saw myself obligated, as an Amtsleiter[23] of the Movement, and as city councilman, to effect an explanatory and calming mood on the crowd. I explained to the women that the Russians pretended to be ill and had shown themselves in the war as beasts, and that they were not humans, and that they needed no sympathy from the women. The accused, Frau Dittmar, now screamed at me in an agitated manner so that all the people standing around could hear "You belong at the front yourself!" The workers then took sides against the women and described them as whores and bitches.

From August 1914 to March 1920 I did my duty as a soldier with distinction for the people and the Fatherland. I also joined in the Polish campaign in the year 1939. In late autumn of 1939, I was released from duty due to my age, on a disposition of the Führer.

For just this reason, and as an Amtsleiter, I cannot allow the serious libel of the accused to pass without suitable atonement.

As evidence I name as witness:

Richard Popp, employee at the health insurance office in Würzburg, Textorstr. 6;

The administrative leader of the district group for the Haug Foundation, whose name I will also impart, and whose deposition is also at the Kreisleitung, Würzburg.

The oral-written remarks/observations indicated [above]

substantiate the facts for
the offense of libel, in accordance with
§§185 200 of the Penal code
StGB[24])

Against Frau Dittmar I hereby file a

Petition

and bring before the **Ministry of JusticeWürzburg**, a

Civil Suit

I propose the decision on opening of the main proceedings, before the Ministry of Justice, Würzburg, be made after preparatory actions have been carried out, and in the appointed/fixed/Trial *Defendant* ... be sentenced to an appropriate punishment as well as fined the costs of the case and carrying out the punishment.

I hand over

1. Testimony [Deposition] of the local Reconciliation Bureau of 10 October 1941 that the attempted reconciliation remained unsuccessful,

2. Testimony of the Public Relief (Social Welfare) League here of /from _____ _____ and request on the grounds of the latter to make application for the right to sue in **Forma Pauperis** [Armenrecht][25]
Read through, approved and signed:
Signed Michael Langguth.
Signed Müller JOS.

Finding

I.   Copy of the Private Suit is to be delivered to:
1. The Chief Prosecutor at the State Court of Würzburg.
2. The accused for eventual deposition within one week from being served.
II. [Paragraph stricken]

Würzburg, on 30 March 1942

Ministry of Justice:
Signed **Hohmann**
For notarization by the records official

[Stamp]   **Müller Jos** (signature)

Herr Richard Popp, the *Gauamtsleiter's* Reluctant Brother-in-Law

Since Gauamtsleiter Langguth felt the need of reinforcements to make his point and validate his account of the POW event, he brought what he determined was a trustworthy and independent source – as nepotism would undoubtedly work to his benefit – his brother-in-law, Richard Popp, to testify for him. His statements may have helped muddle up the situation even more than it was, but he said that Langguth was not shouting insults at the two women, phrasing it, "I did not hear Langguth using such an expression." Popp's statement to the Gestapo:

Geheime Staatspolizei Würzburg, December 11, 1941
State Police Office Nürnberg-Fürth
Local Office Würzburg
At summons appeared at the local office, the married employee
Richard P o p p

40 years old, resident in Würzburg, in Würzburg Pexterstr. No.6 and after being made aware with the object of his interrogation, provided the following:

"In the middle of September 1941 – I can no longer remember the exact day – I went at about 6:30 with the *Gauamtsleiter*[25] Michael Langguth from Würzburg in the direction of the train station plaza from *Bahnhofstrasse*.[26] As we were moving along to the North of the Kilian's fountain, we saw a column of Russians coming from the eastern exit out of the Main Train Station in Würzburg in the direction of the train station plaza. We intended to let this column march past us. After the Russians had left this exit and had marched a bit in the direction of the Bismark Strasse, one of the Russians collapsed. The guard made a move to get this Russian to stand – to get him moving. In this the guard was unsuccessful at first. The second guard, who was still with the column, had the column come to a halt, and then an attempt was made to have the Russian lying on the ground lifted up by the other Russians in the column. While the column's escort personnel were occupied with the Russians, the Café owner Schmidt, who was in Wehrmacht[27] uniform, came out of the station's main exit. Accompanying him were a civilian, two women and a young lad. The civilian went to the guard who was involved with removing the Russian. Whether the civilian had identified himself to the soldier, I cannot say, nor do I know what the civilian spoke about with the guard. However, I saw how the guard reached in his breast pocket and pulled out his *Soldbuch*.[28] In the meantime, a large crowd of people had gathered around the halted column. Due to the intervention of the civilian, and in particular, because the two women who were with the civilian had taken sides with the prisoners, it came to shouts from among the people gathered there. As regards the two women, I learned later, it concerned a Frau Dittmar and a *Fräulein* Huber. From Dittmar I heard how she expressed herself to the effect that, even if they were prisoners, they should not be beaten. On the basis of this remark, Herr Langguth replied that they should think about how our people were being handled. He also said that the Russian in question would dissemble if the guard did not act accordingly. I cannot repeat word for word the expressions that Langguth used. They were delivered in the sense that I have indicated. The gathered people then took a position against Frau Dittmar and Huber, and expressions such as "sluts", "bitches", and others came out. I did not hear Langguth using such an expression.

From Dittmar I also heard how she shouted at Langguth, who was standing right by her, "Why don't you go to the front?" or something similar. What preceded this, I do not know.

While the incident was transpiring, the station officer[29] came down from the station and looked after the column of Russians POWs. Through the station officer, the Russian who had been lying on the ground was then laid to the side and later evacuated with a wheelbarrow.

Dittmar and Huber then sifted themselves out of the crowd and made their way over to the civilian who had taken the guard to task, but who in the meantime had now taken up a position along the side of the building.

That Huber made use of any expression, or shouted anything while she stood in the station plaza, I can't say. I can't say that I heard her say anything at all.

I did not observe that Langguth, as the civilian questioned the guard, had used the expression, "what does this idiot civilian want then? He should go to the front". That Dittmar yelled something to Langguth, and that it was along the lines of: "Why don't you go to the front yourself?" I did hear; however, I do not know what preceded this shout. At the train station plaza, insulting expressions like: 'bitches', 'whores' were used. However, to Langguth having responded to Dittmar and Huber with: "What do you want, you bitches?" I cannot attest. I am of the opinion that these insults were called out in general from the gathered crowd of people.

On the day in question Langguth was in civilian clothes. Langguth is my brother-in-law; he is married to a sister of mine.

Among the people gathered there I saw the business director of the NSDAP Local Group "Haug" in Würzburg, Herr Truckenbrodt, resident in Würzburg, Reisgrubengasse, house number unknown. Truckenbrodt, too, may be able to provide information about the incident at the station plaza.

After reading the statement personally,
signed

Popp (Signature)
Notes:

• • •

Herr Ernst Truckenbrodt, the Witness

Drawing yet another witness into the fracas, the Gestapo then summoned Mr. Ernst Truckenbrodt, who was also identified at the train station. His testimony was of no particular help to either the Bayerlein group or to Langguth in enlightening the Gestapo as to who was throwing about insults at whom. Uncomfortable in his role as a witness, Mr. Truckenbrodt diplomatically weaseled around the issue and provided the following ambiguous statement:

Geheime Staatspolizei   Würzburg, December 11, 1941
State Police Office Nürnberg-Fürth
Local Office Würzburg

At summons appeared at the local office the single salesman

Ernst T r u c k e n b r o d t ,
46 years old, resident in Würzburg, in Würzburg Reisgrübengasse No. 3/1 and having been informed of the reason for his interrogation made known the following:

"On 9/19/1941 at about 6:30 PM I walked along the Bahnhof Street and wanted to go to the business office of the NSDAP Local; Group "Stft Haug", which was located at the premises on Bahnhof Street No. 26. As I neared the place specified, I saw a column of Russians stopped at the train station. A large crowd had gathered around the column. Out of interest I wanted to see what was going on there and went over to the train station plaza. As I reached the area of the column, I saw how one of the guardsmen was engaged with a Russian who lay on the ground. I also saw him kick the Russian. Since the Russian made no preparations to get up, the guard had a coat spread out, the Russian in question placed upon it, and in that manner carried away by the other prisoners.

Among the people gathered there I saw the business owner Eleonore Dittmar and a Miss Huber, who was in RAD uniform.

I also became aware that both of these women had used abusive language. What they said individually, I cannot say, in particular due to the reason that I had arrived a bit later at the train station and I was lacking the individual context. Through the people standing around there I learned that it appeared both these two women had taken the Russian's side due to the mishandling of the prisoner by the guard. Whether this conforms to the facts, I do not know.

Nor can I confirm that the guard who led the Russian had been spoken to by the brother of Dittmar, the Oberstleutnant Bayerlein, and challenged. When I arrived at the train station plaza, Bayerlein was already standing with Sonderführer Schmidt a bit to the side of the plaza near the [construction] of the Hauerrings

That Dittmar yelled to Langguth, who was also at the main train station – that is, had stopped at the main train station plaza – "Why don't you go to the front?" I did not hear. I only noticed that among the people gathered there came the expressions "Bitch! Whores" and similar thing as well, which were thrown about. From whom these expressions came, I cannot say; there was such confusion at the plaza that a person couldn't be certain who had called out what. There's nothing more I can say about it."

After reading the statement personally, signed
Truckenbrodt

The Solution

In a post-war interrogation Bayerlein relayed to the American interrogators that he was told by the Gestapo that he "had shown entirely the wrong attitude; the guards had acted only as instructed, and he would be court-martialed."[30] His senior commander in Africa, *Generaloberst* Erwin Rommel, in the spring of 1942, reportedly carried out this pseudo court-martial. Rommel ordered Bayerlein to end the affair. On military matters and battle decisions, Rommel had a habit of ordering court-martials for his staff, but usually the storm of his temper would blow over and he would forget about it.

Ordered to resolve the drawn-out and over-blown issue, Bayerlein wrote the Attorney General's office and stated that he would drop his charges against Langguth, if in turn, Langguth would drop his charges against his sister, and if he paid Bayerlein's legal expenses. Sister Ellen Dittmar's fashion shop was "reportedly boycotted and subsequently closed in April 1942" as a result of her support for the unfortunate Russian. Bayerlein stated that he was court-martialed in February 1942, his "attitude was reprimanded, but he was acquitted."[31]

Oberstleutnant Bayerlein, although ordered to end the affair with the words, "there are more important issues", was not one to give up easily and couldn't resist one last dig, once last time to kick the proverbial dog, aimed at the Nazi *Gauamtsleiter*. For the record, in his dismissal statement he mailed from the field in North Africa, Bayerlein wrote:

Oberstleutnant Bayerlein March 17, 1942
Feldpost (Army Field Post Office) 40800

To the
                        State Attorney General
Würzburg

I am ready to withdraw my suit against Herr Langguth so that the matter incited by Herr Langguth, which is at variance with the seriousness of the times, can be quickly cleaned up.

This is on condition that Herr Langguth himself bears all the court, Atonement Bureau and attorney fees of the opposing party as well.

I would, however, like to take the opportunity in closing to state the following about the whole affair:

Herr Langguth acted in an irresponsible manner against society and hurt the cohesiveness of the home front by attempting, without justification, to falsely attribute an anti-state character to two women. This is even more reprehensible as the husband of the first woman has stood continuously in the front lines since the first days of the war, through the Polish, French, Russian and African campaigns, and in so doing has earned the highest military awards. What both women actually did in the train station incident was simply indignation and defence against the unjustified, irresponsibly shouted rebukes and insults of Herr Langguth against me, a person who has to lay his life on the line many times a day in this war.

If Herr Langguth belatedly maintains that it was not he who said anything against me – rather that it was someone else – then he also cannot take the replies of Frau Dittmar as meant for him. Rather, they applied to the person who made the insults. His suit against Frau Dittmar for insult thereby becomes unfounded in and of itself.

The behaviour of Herr Langguth is even more incomprehensible to me since he holds an important position in the party and the city council, which cannot grant him any special privileges, but rather must be for him an even greater obligation toward irreproachable conduct.

Bayerlein

Copy to :
The Province Directorate
The District Directorate [Seal of receipt (& date) by Gestapo Office Würzburg]
The Würzburg City Council
The Gestapo [Secret State Police]
Herr Langguth
[Gestapo reference Number to Dittmar file]

• • •

So ended the Russian prisoner of war incident. Fritz, Walter, Ellen, Hanna and young Friedrich, demonstrated personal courage in the face of brutality brought home and its retribution. They were fortunate, because the event could have unfolded in a vastly more unpleasant manner, had the local Gestapo been of a more fanatical and vengeful mind. The four adults knew the danger, and young Friedrich understood that his elders had jeopardize the course of their lives for an unknown, sick and fearful man.

The children of Donat and Louise (Denkmann) Bayerlein: Fritz Herman Bayerlein (right), younger sister Eleanore and eldest brother Richard. Richard Bayerlein was killed in World War I, disappearing into the night in a trench, never to return. Their father made many attempts to have him located. (Photo courtesy of the Dittmar-Bayerlein Family Collection)

Lovely Eleanore Bayerlein, born 22 April 1901. Nicknamed as a child as 'Noon', then shortened to a modern 'Ellen'. (Photo courtesy of the Dittmar-Bayerlein Family Collection)

Ellen Bayerlein at age sixteen. (Photo courtesy of the Dittmar-Bayerlein Family Collection)

The good son – Fritz Herman Michal Bayerlein, born 30 January 1899. Prewar photo. His dream of becoming a math teacher never realized after World War I, Bayerlein stayed in the army in the between war years for the steady income it provided the family in the post-war shortages. (Photo courtesy of the Dittmar-Bayerlein Family Collection)

Chapter 2 Endnotes

1. Rupert Butler, "*An Illustrated History of the Gestapo*," MBI Publishing Company, Osceola MI, 1993, 10.

2. Browder, George C. "*Hitler's Enforcers, The Gestapo and the SS Security Service in the Nazi Revolution*," Oxford University Press, New York, 1996. 18, 20, 21.

3. Ibid., 69.

4. Manuscript from Herr Manfred Rommel to author, Patricia Spayd, of a speech given on July 20th, 1994 to the German Embassy in London.

5. Browder, *Hitler's Enforcers*, 68-69

6. Ibid., 66

7. Generalleutnant Walther K. Nehring served as Chief of Staff in Panzergruppe 2 under General Heinz Guderian. Bayerlein was the First General Staff Officer, Ia, (Operations) at the same time. Nehring was transferred to Africa and commanded the Deutsches Afrikakorps from March through August 1942 at which time he was wounded. He recuperated in Germany and returned to Africa in November 1942. After his service in Africa, Nehring was transferred to Russia.

8. Kurt Freiherr von Liebenstein was born on February 28, 1899 in Jebenhausen, Germany. He was the Ia (First General Staff Officer; similar duties to an Operations Officer) of the 10th Panzer Division then in the invasion of Russia in 1941, he was Chief of Staff of Panzergruppe 2 under Guderian.(per Franz Kurowski, "*Knights Cross Holders of the Afrikakorps*", Schiffer Military History, Atglen, PA. 208-209.) Von Liebenstein served as Guderian's Chief of Staff, along with Major Bayerlein, who served as the First General Staff Officer (Ia, Operations).

9. Remy, Maurice Philip, "*Mythos Rommel*", List Verlag, Ullstein Heyne List GmbH & Co. KG, 2002.

10. Spayd, "Bayerlein," 27.

11. Main train station in town.

12. The following statements and reports were obtained from the Staatsarchiv, Würzburg, Akten der Geheimen Staatspolizeit, über Langguth, Michael, Signatur 5640 Gestapo file. Coauthor Gary Wilkins translated the entire file verbatim from the original reports. They are provided here in the same format, as were the typed reports.

13. The women were called "*Huren*" and "*Saumenscher*" – translated as "whores" and literally "sow-sluts" – at the time a vile insult for women.

14. Spayd, "*Bayerlein*", 56-58; Source: Dittmar-Bayerlein family papers, US Army Report noted as "Appendix I", undated.

15. The Sonderführer was an "occupational specialist" within the German Army, sometimes holding officer equivalent rank, but with no command authority. Certain insignia on the uniform differed from regular Army personnel.

16. Date of the opening attack on Poland (start of WWII).

17. Iron Cross 1st Class, 1939 version

18. Iron Cross 2nd Class Spange indicates a second award of the EK II, to someone who had won the WWI Imperial version first. In this case, the new award of the EKII was the Third Reich version, which was dated 1939 on the cross bottom. Instead of being awarded another Iron Cross, the person received a small silver eagle clasp and bar with the date 1939, which clasp was worn affixed to the original WWI version award ribbon – transl.]

19. Clarification note by author Gary Wilkins.

20. The abbreviations are uncertain (even for German friends); possible meaning in parenthesis, would mean "presented again" in II A 6 (no indication as to what the designation represents).

21. Technical Specialist in a particular field; these individuals held an equivalent military rank, wore a military uniform but with w/distinctive shoulder boards and collar tabs. Despite the equivalent military rank, they did not have the command authority of a "line" officer and thus were roughly similar to the US warrant officer in that sense. – transl.

22. It is uncertain whether the German abbreviation "Anw:" in this case refers to "Anwesend" – i.e. 'present' as in an observer, or a witness to the proceedings – or perhaps "Anwalt", which would mean 'Attorney'. – transl.

23. A *Kreis* was the District, or County level of government within the German political/governmental system. The lowest level in this system was the *Block* [Block] consisting of 30 to 40 households; next, the *Zelle* [Cell] consisting of 4 to 6 city or town blocks; above this was the *Orts(gruppe)*. The *Orts* level was responsible for between 1500 to 3000 households. Above the Orts level came the *Kreis*, which was equivalent to a US district, or county, then the *Gau* (province), topped by the highest level, *Reichs*, which was equivalent to Parliamentary (national) level. At each level, there was an administrative (bureaucratic) section that represented government offices at that level. The administrative section handled all of the operational details (paperwork) at that operational level. The *Kreisleitung* generally referred to the administrative (bureaucratic) section of the Kreis level administration. The highest political position at the Kreis level was the *Kreisleiter* [Kreis Leader].

24. *Strafgesetzbuch* = Penal Code (Strafe= punishment/sentence)

25. *Gauamtsleiter* – a *Gau* was the largest German political/administrative entity short of the National level. It was roughly equivalent to the Canadian "Province" (though not as large in physical territory). *Amtsleiter* was a general title for a government employee within the *Gau* level administration, handling administrative matters, and Langguth was basically a senior department leader/ director of some sort.

26. *Strasse*, usually abbreviated "Str.", means "Street". This word can be used independently as a separate word, e.g.: *Bismark Strasse* (or *Straße*), or combined with a name, as in *Bahnhofstraße* (Train Station Street). Another address term is *Gasse* which is "Lane", or "Alley".

27. *Wehrmacht* – the Armed Service (military) – Schmidt was in military uniform – in this case the uniform of an Army Sonderführer, which was an Army style uniform with national breast eagle, but distinctive collar tabs (not the military pattern) and shoulder boards. This was a specialist position with equivalent officer rank, but no command authority.

28. *Soldbuch*, "Paybook" This was a small booklet with the soldier's photo ID and personal information, as well as limited details of unit assignment, promotions, awards, service history, leaves and pay receipts.

29. Station Officer – this probably refers to an officer in the *Bahnschutz Polizei* – the Railway Protection Security Police. This was a paramilitary organization with its own uniform and headgear, which maintained and coordinated security operations at railway stations and associated facilities.

30. Spayd, "*Bayerlein*", 56-58; Source: Dittmar-Bayerlein family papers, and NARA POW File; US Army Report noted as "Appendix I", undated. Subject: Details of an Incident Pertaining to the Mistreatment of Russian PW's and Bayerlein's Intervention. Cited sources as based upon interrogations and German court records. Bayerlein's Army Personalakte (personnel file) was purged of almost all the documents except his *Nachweiss* (chronological service, award and promotion file), so this information could not be cross checked to German Army records. It is noted by author P.A.Spayd that Bayerlein's claims could generally be cross checked and ultimately supported, though difficult, although at times it could take several years searching to verify information. Author attempts to collect and analyze any information on Bayerlein to present an unbiased portrayal.

31. Ibid.

3

Spruchkammer Obertaunus –
September 1947

"...a democratic house cannot be built with Nazi bricks."
— General Lucius D. Clay, U.S. Army, Military Governor

Definitions of the law, Nazism and militarism.
The Tribunal's chargeable case against Bayerlein

Considered a "militarist" i.e. member of the career military in the Wehrmacht and Reichswehr and served as a General Staff Officer.

Criteria for judgment: Rebuttal of the Criteria – how Bayerlein didn't fit the typical mold of the German officer class.

Preponderance of Evidence shown by Bayerlein's attorney, Ernst Wahl.

What we see in Bayerlein's file are his attempts to clearly demonstrate: he was a field commander only; not a *Junker* or Prussian; from a middle class family and retained these values; not a policy making part of the General Staff, although before the war and with Guderian and Rommel he served as a general staff officer.

Bayerlein demonstrates no enrichment to himself during his military career. Although he handily omits any reference to receiving an apartment building in October 1944 in the town of Heidingsfeld for his decoration the Swords to the Ritterkreuz. This was a standard policy in the German Army based on the high level of one's rank and the award. Usually given the choice of a farm, or in most cases, confiscated Jewish property, both Rommel and Bayerlein refused a farm. The apartment Bayerlein was given from the Heidingsfeld mayor. The building housed 4 apartments and was built as part of the expansion of the village by the town. It was not Jewish property and never had been, according to Würzburg and Heidingsfeld town records. Many village and town records were destroyed – downtown Würzburg was left in rubble. Heidingsfeld was across the Main River from Würzburg. When awarded the apartment building in Heidingsfeld in October 1944, Bayerlein kept all his four tenants, then converting the attic to his private living space. *Fraulein* Helga Mortstein was six years old at the time. Her brothers remember the general's arrival – everyone was excited to see the new landlord. Frau Morstein cautioned her six children not to bother the man. However, her older brother and a neighbor's boy escaped their parents' oversight and dashed to look into the staff car windows. Bayerlein got out, asked, 'Where do you boys live?' They pointed to the apartment building. To their great surprise and joy, the general gave them each an American Hersey candy bar. Their other siblings were a bit sour over this treat as they had obeyed and stayed indoors.

Bayerlein provides another photo session to Life magazine photographers, who seemed to enjoy watching a former high-ranking German general do "ordinary labor" as defined by the military government Laws against Nazism and Militarism. Bayerlein gave the photographers a good show and stated that he "wished to work his way up and perhaps one day own his own garage." Good Spruchkammer Tribunal publicity for the clever Bayerlein, demonstrating his understanding of American ideals of hard work and non-militarism. Photo dated March 1947. (Photo copyright and permission from Time-Life, photographer Walter Sanders/TimePix)

Prisoner of War and "Automechaniker" Fritz Bayerlein, former Generalleutnant, Commander of the LIII Armee Korps, Panzer Lehr Division, and Field Marshal Rommel's former Chief of Staff, works at the U.S. Army Camp King Motor Pool to escape the ire of his general officer colleagues for his surrender in the Ruhr Pocket. An Associated Press photographer and a journalist were shown to the motor pool by camp officials to witness a unique event – a German general getting his hands dirty in manual labor. Date of photo is March 1947 – one month before Bayerlein was released from two years of captivity on April 2nd, 1947. (Photo courtesy and copyright of the Associated Press, Frankfurt, Germany)

Wartime mayor of Würzburg, Herr Memmel, and Generalleutnant Bayerlein. For his award of receiving the Swords to the Ritterkreuz, Bayerlein was given the gift of a city-owned apartment in Heidingsfeld, located across the Main River, and became an immediate landlord of four rented apartments. Bayerlein didn't see the need to report this real estate gift on his Spruchkammer financial forms. Photograph timeframe is September 1944. (Photograph research courtesy of Herr Peter Hulanski and the Stadtarchiv, Würzburg.)

Bayerlein, as with all military members, didn't belong to the *Partei* (traditionally *Wehrmacht* officers and soldiers were prohibited from joining the NSDAP prior to July 20, 1944 the date of Hitler's attempted assassination). In March 1933 Party membership became mandatory for certain types of employment. All government workers were required to join and pay dues, and business owners were strong-armed into Party membership. Referred to as "March Hares" most people waited until employment party membership was mandatory. (Per records at the NARA II, Bayerlein's sister Ellen was summarily dismissed from party membership due to her support and sympathy to the Russian Prisoner of War in September 1941).

Bayerlein didn't donate money to the *Partei*. His nephew, Friedrich Dittmar, refused to attend the mandatory Hitler Youth program, and in spite of its many letters to his parents his absence continued.

Bayerlein's family was of non-Aryan descent – meaning his unknown, or at least undocumented, maternal grandfather was a Jew and didn't marry his grandmother, Emilie Denkmann. This fact was relayed to Bayerlein by his mother, Louise (Denkmann) Bayerlein, prior to her death. Bayerlein had also told Field Marshall Rommel and his wife Lucie. Lucie Rommel was accused of also being of non-Aryan descent, due to her hair and eye color. Mr. Manfred Rommel recounted that his mother was under close scrutiny, as was Bayerlein, based upon their appearance as they both had similar black coloring in both hair and eyes.

• • •

The Chargeable Case Against Fritz Bayerlein
The Trial Begins

Bayerlein's *Meldebogen* (Registration)
MISC, USA Historical Division & ECIC Support of POW Bayerlein
Support from General Hans Speidel – Field Marshal Rommel's Chief of Staff in Normandy
Financial Statement

Prozessvollmacht (Power of Attorney)

Power of Attorney
Attorney Ernst Wahl of 9 Henricus Street, Oberursel Ts. is hereby granted power of attorney to defend me before the De-nazification Tribunal.
Oberursel Ts., May 1, 1947

(signed) Fritz Bayerlein
Signature

Request from Bayerlein's attorney, Ernst Wahl, to expedite his trial. This is an advance narrative with attachments providing evidence to expedite the verdict through a written process.

Akten-Inhaltsverzeichnis

9l. 3. 3. 8. 6.

Des Absenders		Des Schriftstücks		
Name	Wohnort	Inhalt	Datum	Blatt-Nr.
Bayerlein,Fritz Herm.	Oberursel Ts.,	Meldebogen	2.4.47	1
Kammer Obertaunus	Bad Homburg	Der Bürgermeister	17.7.47	2
Kammer Obertaunus	Bad Homburg	Polizei	17.7.47	2
Kammer Obertaunus	Bad Homburg	Polit.Ausschuss	17.7.47	2
Kammer Obertaunus	Bad Homburg	Milit.Regierung	1o.7.47	3
Kammer Obertaunus	Bad Homburg	Finanzamt	9.7.47	4
Ernst Wahl RA.,	Oberursel Ts.,	Schreiben an Kammer	2o.5.47	5
Bayerlein Fritz	Oberursel Ts.,	Prozessvollmacht/ Wahl Ernst RA., 6o.	1.8.47	6
Hauptquartier 77o7 Mil.Nachr.Dienst Zentr.	Hauptquartier	An Mil.Regierung/ Entnaz.Abteilung	6.2.47	7-8
Hauptquartier 77o7 Mil.Nachr.Dienst Zentr.	Hauptquartier	Erklärung	6.2.47	9-1o
Streitkräfte d.Europ. Kriegsschauplatzes	Hauptquartier	Erklärung	6.12.45	11-15
Ernst Wahl RA.,	Oberursel Ts.,	Schreiben an Kammer	23.6.47	16
Dr. Hans Speidel	Freudenstadt	Erklärung	4.6.47	17
Willy Schulte	Hagen/Westf.	Schreiben an Bayerlein	9.6.47	
Karl H .Heile	Ludwigsburg	Schreiben an Kammer	17.7.47	19-2o
Ernst Wahl RA.,	Oberursel Ts.,	Schreiben an Kammer	19.7.47	21
Lieb Johann	Würzburg	Kindest.Versicherung	1o.7.47	22
Bayerlein Fritz	Oberursel Ts.,	Ins Akte von Blatt 1 - 19o separat		

Table of contents for the first denazification letter submission by Bayerlein's attorney.

Sphi 12011

6

Prozeßvollmacht.

Herrn Rechtsanwalt Ernst W a h l, Oberursel Ts., Henricusstr.9

wird hiermit zur ~~XXXXXXXXXXXXXX~~ meiner Verteidigung vor der Spruchkammer

Vollmacht ~~XXXXXXXXXXXXX~~ erteilt.

Oberursel Ts., den 1.Mai   1947

Fritz Bayerlein

Unterschrift

Oberursel (Taunus)

Henricusstraße 9

Telefon 776

Eingegangen

5

Spruchkammer Ober...
Der öffentliche Klä...

Spruchkammer
Obertaunus
z.H.des Herrn Öffentlichen Klägers K o c h
Bad-Homburg v.d.H.
Promenade

Betr: Automechaniker Fritz B a y e r l e i n, Oberursel Ts.
Hohemarkstrasse 4
Nr.d.Meldebog.: 12011

Ich überreiche anliegend Vollmacht.

Ich bitte um beschleunigte Durchführung des Verfahrens gegen
Bayerlein und nehme dieserhalb Bezug auf die Vorsprache des
Herrn Colonel W.R.P h i l p, Kommandeur der Militär.Nachrich-
ten-dienst-Zentrale der US-Streitkräfte (Oberursel Ts.),die
u.a.die Untersuchungen gegen Nationalsozialisten,Militariste
und Kriegsverbrecher führt.Bayerlein hat schon vor 1 1/4 Jah-
ren begonnen sich als Automechaniker einen neuen Beruf zu er-
arbeiten.Er wird nunmehr als Mitarbeiter des US-Oberkommandos
Historische Abteilung,tätig werden.

Ich überreiche als Anlagen weiter
1.Entlassungsantrag der Militär.Nachrichtendienst-Zentrale
vom 6.2.47 an die Denazifizierungsabteilung der Militär-Reg.
2.Begründung zu diesem Antrag.
3.u.4. weitere 2 Anlagen zu diesem Antrage.
5.Beurteilung Bayerleins durch die Militär.Nachrichtendienst-
Zentrale als der für die Untersuchung gegen Nazis,Militariste
und Kriegsverbrecher höchsten zuständigen Stelle der US-Stre
kräfte vom 25.4.46.

Aus diesen Urkunden ist zu ersehen,dass diese maßgebendste
Stelle Bayerlein eingehend untersucht und beobachtet und
seine Vergangenheit nachgeforscht hat.Dabei lag ihr auch
umfangreiches Material offen,das seitens der Alliierten be-
reits während der Nazizeit von den Nachrichtendiensten der
Alliierten zusammengetragen worden war.Das Ergebnis dieser
Untersuchungen ist: Bayerlein hat mit den Nazis nicht einmal
sympathisiert;er ist kein Militarist im Sinne des Gesetzes;
er ist ein einwandfreier Mann,der ein Gegner der Nazis war
und für seine Person die beste Gewähr für ein demokratisches
Deutschland bietet.

Auf diesen sicher festgestellten Tatsachen beruht die Entlassung Bayerleins unmittelbar aus Kriegsgefangenschaft -ohne
Internierungslager- in Freiheit.Diese Entlassung hatte gerade
das zur Voraussetzung,was die Militär.Nachrichtendienst-Zentr
trale festgestellt und die Denazifizierungsabteilung der
Militär-Regierung erneut geprüft und als vorliegend entschieden hatte: was sich mit den Anforderungen des Befreiungsge-
setzes deckt.

Ernst Wahl letter of May 20, 1947

Ernst Wahl   Oberursel Ts., May 20, 1947
Attorney at Law
9 Henricus Street
Oberursel (Taunus)
Telephone 776
(stamped: Received May 22, 1947, Denazification Tribunal Obertaunus, Public Prosecutor)

Denazification Tribunal
Obertaunus
Attn.: Public Prosecutor Koch
Bad-Homburg v.d. H.
Promenade
RE: Auto mechanic Fritz Bayerlein, 101 Hohemark Street, Oberursel Ts., File no. 12011
I hereby grant power of attorney:

I request that the case against Fritz Bayerlein be expedited and therefore refer to the statement of Colonel W. R. Philp, Commanding Officer of the Military Intelligence Service Center of the United States Forces (Oberursel Ts.), which among other things is conducting investigations of Nazis, militarists and war criminals. Bayerlein started a new career as an auto mechanic fifteen months ago and from now on will be employed with the Historical Division of the US High Command.

I am submitting the following supporting documents:

1. the request for Bayerlein's release submitted by the Military Intelligence Service Center to the Denazification Department of the Military Government

2.the statement explaining the reasons for the request

3. and 4. : two other documents pertaining to the request

5.the verdict on Bayerlein's case made on April 25, 1946 by the Military Intelligence Service Center, the US Armed Forces' highest authority in the investigation of Nazis, militarists and war criminals.

These documents show clearly that this highest authority investigated and observed Bayerlein and examined his past. In its investigation of Bayerlein, the authoritiy had access to ample material, which had already been collected by the Allies through the Allied News Services while the Nazis were still in control. The investigations led to one conclusion: Bayerlein was not even a Nazi sympathizer; he is not a militarist according to the law; he is an irreproachable man who opposed the Nazis and who in himself presents the best guarantee for a democratic Germany.

These well-established facts were the reason why Bayerlein was released as a free citizen directly from the prisoner of war camp and without further incarceration in an internment camp. His release was based on what the Military Intelligence Service Center had concluded and what the Denazification Department of the Military Government had examined once again and judged to be as here stated: which is in compliance with the liberation law.

For the liberation law, it is a question of the same criteria which were determined by the US Military Intelligence Service and examined and pronounced upon once again by the

Denazification Department, i.e.: Bayerlein did not belong to any Nazi organization; he did not even sympathize with Nazism; he was not a militarist; he was an opponent of Nazism and militarism and proved his objections to both by unequivocal acts of resistance.

For this reason and alone on the basis of the enclosed documents, which are irrefutable proof, I request that:

1. the case be concluded through written procedure
2. the case against Bayerlein be dismissed because this law does not apply.

Without intending to cause a delay to the conclusion of the case, I inform you that I will be submitting more evidence to the file.

(signed) Ernst Wahl
Attorney at law

. . .

ARBEITSBLATT (worksheet)

De-Nazification Tribunal, Obertaunus
Bad Homburg v. d. H. 6/24/47
Office of the Public Prosecutor
Tel: 2179
File No. 3366 Mo./Kö

Worksheet

Bayerlein Fritz Hermann		Auto Mechanic
(Last Name)	(First Name)	(Occupation)

Oberursel Hohemark
(Town) (Street)
1/14 /1899 Würzburg
(Date of Birth) (Place of Birth)

Spruchkammer Obertaunus
(Der öffentliche Kläger)
Telefon 2179

Bad Homburg v. d. H. 24.5.47

Aktenzeichen Ot 3366 Mo./Kö._   **Arbeitsblatt**

Bayerlein	Fritz Hermann	Automechaniker	
(Zuname)	(Vorname)	(Beruf)	
Oberursel	Hohemark		
(Wohnort)	(Straße)		(Haus-Nr.)
14.1.99	Würzburg		
(Geburtsdatum)	(Geburtsort)		

Die Auskünfte in diesen Spalten müssen auf **Tatsachen** beruhen. Meinungen und Vorschläge sind zu vermeiden.
Die Eintragungen sind so beschleunigt vorzunehmen, daß das Arbeitsblatt **binnen 24 Stunden** weitergegeben werden kann. Deshalb sind die Rückfragen bei anderen Stellen zu **vermeiden**.
Die Vollständigkeit und Richtigkeit der Angaben in Spalte 1 sind auf Grund der vorhandenen Unterlagen nachzuprüfen.

1. Auszug aus dem Meldebogen	Gruppe *II*	Datum u. Unterschrift des Bearbeiters.
1.5.44 Generalleutnant, Panzer Lehr Division 1922 – 45 Berufs-Offizier·		26.6.47.

The information in these columns must be based on facts. Opinions and suggestions should be avoided. The entries are to be resolved quickly enough that the worksheet can be handed over within 24 hours. The completeness and accuracy of the statements in Section 1 are to be verified on the basis of existing records.

1. Excerpt from the Registration Form. Group II 6/26/47
        Date and Signature of the Clerk:
        5/1/44 Generalleutnant, Panzer Lehr Division
        1922-45 Career Officer
        [Signature]

ARBEITSBLATT (reverse of worksheet – opinion of local police department in Oberursel.)

Information

Of : Judgment <u>not possible,</u> since only a few months in Oberursel.
The person named on the reverse has been registered with the Police since April of this year.
Particulars of a political nature are therefore *not possible*.
Of: Judgment <u>not possible</u> since only a few months in Oberursel.

        Signatures:
        Mayor 7/17/47
    Police 7/7/47
    Political Parties 7/7/47

• • •

HEADQUARTERS
7707 MILITARY INTELLIGENCE SERVICE CENTER
APO 757   US ARMY

6 Febuary 1947

SUBJECT ; POW Fritz BAYERLEIN

TO   : Whom It May Concern

1. The following in brief is the known record of Lt. Gen. BAYERLEIN.

a. B. has never been a member of the Grand General Staff, but only occupied Staff position in the field.

b. Racially he was considered unsound by the Nazies on acount of partly non-aryan decent and in accordance with the Nurnberger Laws of 1934 he was to be discharged from the army. This, however, was not carried out in view of his recognized ability.

c. In government elections he voted Social-Democratic ticket and contributed several articles to the Social-Democratic newspaper "Fraenkischer Volksfreund" formerly published in Wuerzburg.

d. His open fight against mistreatment of Allied prisoners of war cost B. a court martial in 1941 and his family the loss of their business.

e. On 15 April 1945 B. surrendered with his troops, the justly famous Panzer Lehr Division. He was not absolutely compelled to do this at that time but his well-considered action undoubtedly saved many lives on both sides even though it did not appreciably effect the final outcome.

f. Since his surrender B. has been exclusively in the hands of US intelligence agencies. Going greatly experienced in armored warfare in all theaters of fighting he is extemely knowledgeable. He has contributed many technical, tactical and intelligence papers upon request. He appears honest, open, industrious and cooperative at all times.

2. The undersigned has the fullest confidence in BAYERLEIN and recommends he be given every consideration by all U S and Allied agencies.

s/s   W.R. Philp
T/S   W.R. PHILP
       Colonel, FA
       Commanding.

7707
Military Intelligence   CERTIFIED TRUE COPY :
Service Center
APO 757, U. S. ARMY
SONER PROCESSING   HARRY KAIN
        &   CAPTAIN QMC
EVACUATION SECTION   OIC   PP

Letter of support for Bayerlein from U.S. Army commander of 7707 Military Intelligence Service Center.

HEADQUARTERS
7707 MILITARY INTELLIGENCE SERVICE CENTER
APO 757   US ARMY

6 February 1947

SUBJECT: Release of German PW

TO   : Military Government Officer, OMG, Bavaria, De-nazification
          Section, APO 170, US Army

1.. It is requested that Prisoner of War FRITZ BAYERLEIN, formerly
Lieut.General, German Army, be released from U S custody and given the
status of a free citizen.

2. BAYERLEIN has rendered the U S Forces highly important services
as shown in attached statements.

3. BAYERLEIN is a resident of Wuerzburg and at present confined at
this post.

s/s W.R. PHILP
T/S W.R. PHILP
     Colonel, FA
     Commanding

2 incl:
      1 ltr Col Marshall
      1 ltr Col Philp

A CERTIFIED TRUE COPY:

HARRY KAHN
CAPTAIN QMC
OIC   PP&E

7707
Military Intelligence
Service Center
APO 757, U.S. ARMY
PRISONER PROCESSING
&
EVACUATION SECTION

Letter of Release of German PW, Fritz Bayerlein – released from captivity in April 1947. However, Bayerlein faced detention for the denazification trial in Hesse.

HEADQUARTERS
THEATER SERVICE FORCES
EUROPEAN THEATER

Office of the Theater Historian

(rear) APO 887
6 December 1945.

TO WHOM IT MAY CONCERN:

    1. On various occasions during the period from August-November 1945, Genlt· Fritz Bayerlein (PW), former commander of Panzer Lehr Division of the German Army, has worked with the War Department Historical Commission and USFET Historical Section. Genlt Bayerlein has prepared numerous studies on the St.Lo breakthrough, Ardennes Offensive, and Ruhr pocket. In addition he has willingly supplied oral information on German dispositions and intentions.

    2. These studies and information supplied by Genlt Bayerlein have been of great value in compiling an accurate account of American operations, and his cooperative spirit is commendable.

                    s/s l a marshal l
                    T/S L A MARSHALL
                    Colonel, GSC
                    Theater Historian

A CERTIFIED TRUE COPY:
ROBERT A DORAN
1st Lt, AUS
Asst Adj

7707
Military Intelligence
Service Center
APO 757, U. S. ARMY
PRISONER PROCESSING
&
EVACUATION SECTION

HEADQUARTERS
EUROPEAN COMMAND
OFFICE OF THE CHIEF HISTORIAN
OPERATIONAL (GERMAN) BRANCH   GJR/mg

APO 757
14 May 1947

TO WHOM IT MAY CONCERN :

    1. Since October 1945 Generalleutnant Fritz Hermann BAYERLEIN (PW) has worked directly with the Historical Division in compiling an accurate history of German counter-operations for the War Department. He prepared both written material and sketches for the Ardennes, Northern France, Rhineland and Central Europe Campaigns.

    2. His information has been of great value to this Division and his cooperative spirit is commendable.

                  C.V. PENCE
                  Col Inf
                  Deputy Chief

14

HEADQUARTERS
UNITED STATES FORCES EUROPEAN THEATER
MILITARY INTELLIGENCE SERVICE CENTER
APO 757

OFFICE OF THE COMMANDING OFFICER

25 April 1946

TO : Whom it may concern
Subject : Recommendation for Fritz BAYERLEIN

1. PW Fritz BAYERLEIN, Major General (Generalleutnant), and late commander of the justly famous Panzer Lehr Division and the 53rd Corps surrendered with his troops to the U.S. Forces on 16 April 1945 near Iserlohn, Germany.

2. Since 25 April 1945 BAYERLEIN has been with this center and its forerunner, Mobile Field Interrogation Unit No.4, respectively. During this year Bayerlein's past has been reviewed and he himself carefully observed.

3. The following remarks regarding his person appear justified:

   a. General BAYERLEIN has been a good and gallant soldier, whose fair way of fighting has gained him the respect of those, who opposed him in battle. There is nothing in his record that indicates that his conduct has not been proper at all times. He can by no means be regarded as a militarist in the sense attached to the term.

   b. It can be unqualifiedly stated, that he has no Nazi leanings; to the contrary, his views and behavior are definitely democratic to an extent not often found in an German Army officer of his rank.

   c. It is felt that if Germany had more men of the caliber and integity of Bayerlein, the country's future as a democratic nation would look much brighter.

   d. In the summer of 1945 BAYERLEIN was selected to participate in a course of instructions, which was to prepare him for a position in the civil administration of Germany. Because of illness at the time he was unable to attend this course.

4. It is strongly recommended and hoped that BAYERLEIN will be given all possible considerations in any matter regarding his person, fortune or employment.

W. R. Philp

W.R. PHILP

The Denazification Tribunal serves notice to Bayerlein of the hearing:

Zustellungsurkunde,
September 1, 1947

Denazification Tribunal Obertaunus
Bad Homburg v.d.H.,   September 1, 1947
          Fy/E
File No.: Ot. 3366
(stamped: Received: September 13, 1947, Denazification Tribunal Obertaunus, Office of the Public Prosecutor)

Affidavit of Service of Legal Process
Today Bayerlein, Fritz Hermann, auto mechanic of Hohemark, Oberursel was served the charges and the notification of charges dated September 1, 1947 by hand delivery.
(signed) Fritz Bayerlein

_____(Signature of the Recipient)

_____(The Servicing Official)
Oberursel (Taunus), September 9, 1947

• • •

The Public Prosecutor serves Bayerlien a copy of the charges & request for witnesses:

The Public Prosecutor of the De-Nazification Tribunal
Obertaunus
File No. OT **3366**   Fy/E
To Mr. Fritz Hermann Bayerlein
in Oberursel Ts.
Hohemark
You are hereby receiving a copy of the charges of 9/1/1947.
You are required to submit the testimony of witnesses (with exact addresses) or (any) other evidence, in duplicate, within the period of 14 days, and any petitions or pleas in accordance with Article 34 of the Law.
Bad _____ d.H. 9/1/1947

(*SEAL*)   (Signature)
The Public Prosecutor
Freyeisen

• • •

25

File No. **3366**   9/4/47

The official decision is to be reported to:

Charge Sheet*

1.Minister of Political Freedom (3 copies)

2. Police authorities in

3. Employment bureau in

4. Finance and tax authority

5. His/her superior office, namely:

6. Private employer, namely

7. Military government in

8. Income and assets authority (in the case of banned property)

9. Residence bureau

10. Prosecutor

* *(on A20 document)*

[**A20**   ]

De-Nazification Tribunal Obertaunus   Bad Homburg   9/12/47

file No. Ot. **3366**/Ko

Service of Legal Process Certificate

Today Bayerlein, Fritz Hermann, of Oberursel/Ts Hohemark

was served by hand delivery the written summons for an oral hearing on 9/15/47 at 11 o'clock.

_____(Signature of the Recipient)

_____(The Servicing Official)

Bad Homburg v.d.H.,

9/12/47

• • •

[**A21**]

The De-Nazification Tribunal Obertaunus in Bad Homburg v.d.H.

File Number: Ot **3366 Kö**

Summons to an Oral Proceeding

Fritz Hermann B a y e r l e i n

In **O b e r u r s e l / T s** . **Hohemark**

On the basis of the Charge sheet of 9/1/47 delivered to you on 9/9/47, an oral proceeding has been directed against you.

You are therefore ordered to report punctually, on **Monday morning 9/15/47 at**

11:00am before the De-Nazification Tribunal of **Obertaunus**, Council Chamber

Kreistags, of the **State Magistrate's Office, Bad Homburg** at **Luisenstrasse 88/90**, for an oral hearing.

The term of summons is reduced to **xxx** days.

You are simultaneously informed that:

1. The evidence is detailed on the reverse side of the **charge sheet**.

2. In the case of an unexcused non-appearance, action can be taken and a decision reached in your absence, or your presence can be forced by a subpoena or fine.

3. You can present to the chairman of the Tribunal an invitation for any witnesses,

or

Expert witness, or produce any other evidence with presentation of the facts for which proof is to be submitted, or bring along persons with you to the oral proceedings, who you wish to be questioned

Every communication is to be marked with the file number given at the upper left.

Bad Homburg v. d. H., 12 September 1947

Chairman of the Tribunal
Jellinek
Copy received:
The Concerned Party
The Petitioner

Meldebogen

Translator's note: In compliance with the Law for Liberation from National Socialism and Militarism, Bayerlein was required to file a *Meldebogen,* or registration form, with the office of the public prosecutor. This form and the more lengthy and detailed *Fragebogen,* required for those seeking public employment, were used to determine the level and nature of an individual's Nazi involvement. The following is a paraphrased summary of the information found in Bayerlein's *Meldebogen.*

In his *Meldebogen*, submitted on April 2, 1947, Bayerlein states that he did not belong to any National Socialist organization, nor did he receive any awards of any kind for services to the Nazi party, nor did he benefit in any way from a membership in a Nazi organization nor receive any funds from the Nazi party. (questions 1-5)

Bayerlein states furthermore that he was a career officer in the German Army from 1922 to 1945, serving finally in the Panzer Lehr Division as *Generalleutnant*, a rank which he attained on May 1, 1944. He was a general staff officer, not an officer of the NS and held no office in any NS organization. He lists the stages of his military career including detailed information about his rank, post, income, and overall private assets at each stage. He notes that a sudden increase in his assets was due to the fact that he had inherited proceeds from his mother's life insurance in 1936. (questions 6 – 8)

He asserts that he neither managed nor controlled a business, nor was he granted any titles or positions by the state, party, or other organizations. (questions 9 +10) He is not and was not a subject of an investigation and his employment was not approved in writing by the military government. (questions 11 + 12)

In question 13, Bayerlein states that, under the law, he falls into category 5 – those exonerated after investigation. At the prompt, "If you believe that the law does not apply to you, state your reasons here…," he explains, "I believe that I fall into the group of the exonerated because of the same reasons (active resistance against Nazism and Nazi warfare) that led to my early and preferential release from custody as a prisoner of war by the U.S. War Department.

• • •

[A11]

Headquarters of the Armed Forces of the European Theater of War
Office of the Historical Division
Amy Post Office Nr. 887
6 December 1945

1. Many times during the period from August – November of 1945 *Generalleutnant* (Prisoner of War) Fritz Bayerlein, previously commander of the Panzer Lehr Division of the German Army, worked together with the War Ministry Historical Commission and the Headquarters of the European Forces, Military Division. Gen. Bayerlein prepared a great number of studies on the breakthrough at St. Lô, the Ardennes Offensive, and the Ruhr Pocket. Furthermore, he voluntarily delivered oral reports about German plans and intentions.

2. These studies and information, as delivered by Bayerlein, were of great value to the compilation of an exact report on American operations and his spirit of cooperation is praiseworthy.

Signed S.L.A. Marshall
Colonel, General Staff

• • •

Headquarters of the European Command
Office of the Chief of the Historical Operations Division
Army Post Office Nr. 757
14 May 1947
December 1945

1.) Since October of 1945, *Generalleutnant* Fritz Hermann Bayerlein (Prisoner of War) has worked directly together with the Historical Division in the compilation of an exact history of the German counter operations, for the War Ministry. He presented written and sketched material on the Ardennes Offensive, northern France, the Rheinland and the battles in central Europe.

2.) His information was of great value for this Division, and his spirit of cooperation is commendable.

Signed G.W. Pence
Colonel, Inf.
Acting Commander

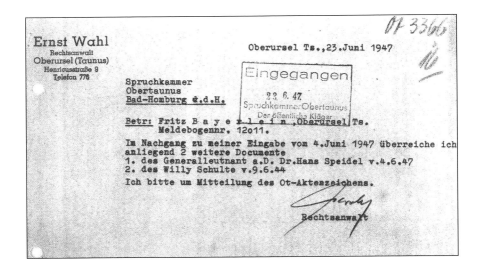

. . .

Herr Wahl, Bayerlein's attorney, submits witnesses statements to the Tribunal. Attorney Wahl attempted to dispatch the case through written proceedings rather than a hearing in person.

Oberursel Ts., July 19, 1947
Ernst Wahl dated June 23

Ernst Wahl
Attorney-at-law
9 Henricus Street
Oberursel (Taunus) Oberursel Ts., June 23, 1947
Telefon 776
(marked: Ot 3366 16)
(stamped: Received June 23, 1947, Denazification Tribunal Obertaunus , Office of the Public Prosecutor)
Denazification Tribunal
Obertaunus
Bad-Homburg v.d.H.
RE: Fritz BAYERLEIN, Oberursel Ts., Registration file no. 12011.

In addition to my submission of June 4, 1947 I am submitting the following two documents:
1. the first written by *Generalleutnant* (retired) Dr. Hans Speidel from June 4, 1947
2. the second written by Willy Schulte from June 9, 1944
Please inform me of the Ot file reference numbers.
(signed) (illegible)
Attorney-at-law

Dr. Hans Speidel

48 Katranft Street
Generalleutnant (retired)
Freudenstadt
June 4, 1947
(stamped: Received June 22, 1947, Denazification Tribunal Obertaunus, Office of the Public Prosecutor)
RE: Conduct of former *Generalleutnant* Bayerlein, as the commanding general of the 53rd Army Corps.

In the concluding statement of his report to the Historical Division USFET, General Bayerlein clearly depicted the hopelessness of the situation facing General Field Marshal Model's soldiers in the Ruhr pocket. "Hold at any cost, bleed to death", dig in to take up a position of all-round defense on a small scale and encircle on a large scale – this had been Hitler's motto since Stalingrad and what he considered to be the highest wisdom. In his blindness beyond measure, Hitler once again ordered a "fight to the last man" for the Ruhr pocket, although this tactic could not bring any military or political successes on German territory but would only bring death and destruction to the troops, the people and country; even the infrastructure that was crucial for supplying the bare necessities to the population was supposed to be destroyed.

In a display of great moral fortitude, true patriotism, and decisiveness, *Generalleutnant* Bayerlein went against this order, although doing so would pose a most terrible threat to Bayerlein himself and his men, as the judgment against the commander of Königsberg,* which was known to all in those days, had made clear.

As far as the documents regarding the events of April 1945 were available to me, I can make the following assessment:

Through General Bayerlein's surrender of the 53rd Army Corps at Iserlohn on April 16, 1945, not only were 30,000 men saved from destruction but German civilians and land were kept from harm. With this deed, General Bayerlein showed a rare degree of civil courage. His decision to oppose and take action against Hitler's criminal warfare is an exceptional deed in every respect.

(signed)   Dr. Hans Speidel
            Retired *Generalleutnant*
Last Chief of General Staff for General Field Marshal Rommel,
political prisoner from September 7, 1944 until liberation by the French Army on April 29, 1945.
Signature attested by: City of Freudenstadt   Mayor (signed) (illegible signature)
(stamped with official stamp: City of Freudenstadt)

Translation of letter from Willy Schulte:

(*Translator's note: the copy of the original handwritten document was illegible in some spots. I have reconstructed the text to the best of my ability. The missing information does not detract from the letter's tone and intent.*)

Willy Schulte   61 Allee Street, Hagen, Westphalia 1216 *(? Illegible postal code)*
June 9, 1947
(Stamped: Received, June 23, 1947, *Spruchkammer Obertaunus*, Office of the Public Prosecutor)
Esteemed Mr. Bayerlein,

It seems very strange to me to address you in this way, but since I don't know whether you'd like to be addressed by your former title, I'll begin like this. Please don't hold it against me or take offense.

If I mention: invasion, Schulze, von Hauser, perhaps you'll remember this little lieutenant more easily.

I came across your address in a roundabout way, after having heard about your sad fate some time ago from …(?) who expressed much approval of your latest decision. I can only hope and wish that you are doing well under the circumstances and that you will be completely free very soon. With this wish, I act as the spokesman of my old comrades. Now that we can *glimpse (illegible)* behind the scenes of recent *events, (illegible and missing text, translator's suggestion)* – we all look back on that difficult time with gratitude and only now can we truly appreciate what you did for us, because you stayed at your post, against your own convictions, and in doing so were able to overturn a murderous order of sheer madness and save a lot of bloodshed. As men and as soldiers, we were able to put our trust in your leadership, and this spared us from a lot of hardship in the last phase of the war. For this, I would like to thank you in the name of all of my comrades, both friends and strangers, who I know (all – *illegible*) agree with me. We will always be there for you, as you were there for us then.

In gratitude, yours faithfully

Willy Schulte
P.S. I correspond with Baron Hauser, who is presently in Vienna trying to get admitted to the university, as well as with most of my old comrades. If you'd like, I could write to tell you more about what's become of them.

• • •

Another letter submitted for the Tribunal:

Karl H. HEILE
32 Favoriten Gardens
Private Scholar   Ludwigsburg
Author
July, 17, 1947
(stamped file number: Ot. 3366) (stamped: Received July 21, 1947, Denazification Tribunal Obertaunus, Office of the Public Prosecutor)
To: Denazification Tribunal Obertaunus
Oberursel a. Taunus
RE: Tribunal Case Fritz Herm. Bayerlein, presently auto mechanic, formerly General of the Panzer Troops, 101 Hohe Markt Street, Oberursel am Taunus

As a surviving victim of fascism with one of the longest terms of confinement and more than 12 years of persecution, nine of which were spent in actual imprisonment (duly registered by the Regional Board of Political Persecutees of National Socialism, 16 Uhland Street, District Office Ludwigsburg, Wuerttemberg),

With the view that in reaching a verdict in the cases of former National Socialists, purely character-based factors are of as great importance as facts,

And further taking into consideration that my personal opinion as a true victim of Nazi Fascism will be of some value, if I can fulfill my democratic duty as a citizen in the cause of loyally re-building the state by supporting worthy Germans, who in their various and individual circumstances were ensnared by the brown* (Nazi) stranglers of our people, in their attempts to restore their civic honor,

I request permission to state the following facts in the Bayerlein case:

I made Bayerlein's acquaintance at Camp King in Oberursel in the first days of May of this year. We lived in the same house for six weeks and I had ample opportunity to observe Bayerlein, even if he was not aware of being observed. I will summarize my main observations as follows:

1. Bayerlein was clearly and honestly making every effort to dutifully fit back into the community at large, even as a manual laborer.

2. Socially, that is, principally in his manners and in his conduct, vis à vis his work companions from the simpler, not intellectual, classes, Bayerlein distinguished himself and very strikingly from such pompous characters, such as former General Kessler or former Lieutenant Häusing (both of whom were notorious in the administrative offices of Camp King for their arrogant and caricature-like demeanor among all the Germans held there). Bayerlein socialized easily and openly with his work companions and was very well-liked for it. For example, I will quote the words of a simple worker who in the presence of many of his colleagues stated: "If the Americans think that we'll march under guys like Kessler and Häusing, they've got another thing coming. Under someone like Bayerlein, we'd fall in again any time." (This was in reference to a war against Soviet Fascism.)

3. In his conduct and speech to me as a political persecutee, Bayerlein showed an equally frank and obviously honest regret. This regret was not tinged by any of the theatrical pathos that we see so often in the usual, poor, "innocent" Nazis. I consider myself to be a fairly good judge of character; but with Bayerlein, I've always had the strong feeling that: he is an honest German man, who is ashamed of Germany's and his own past under the Nazi regime and who with conviction and sincerity, will do his utmost to become a valuable member of the greater community.

I have no knowledge of General Bayerlein's past as a National Socialist and military commander and therefore can make no objective assessment in this matter. But I cannot imagine that a man like Bayerlein, of such a candid nature, could have acted any differently ten years ago than he does today.

If this, my statement, could do a little to sway the Denazification Tribunal in favor of a German man and former National Socialist, whom I admire despite the fact that I am a victim of the harshest Nazi persecution, then the purpose of my statement will have been served.

Mr. Bayerlein himself has no idea in the least that I have submitted a written testimony. He does not even know that I am aware of the fact that he is being called before the Denazification Tribunal for a summary trial.

I authorize the Denazification Tribunal to use this statement in any way that it finds expedient under the German law.

KH HEILE (signed)

• • •

Lieb
Text 21:

Ernst Wahl   Oberursel Ts., July 19, 1947
Attorney-at-law
9 Henricus Street
Oberursel (Taunus)
Telephone 776

(stamped with Ot. File No. 3366)
(stamped: Received July 21, 1947, Denazification Tribunal Obertaunus, Office of the Public Prosecutor)

To: The Public Prosecutor/ Obertaunus
           Bad-Homburg v.d.H.

In the case against Fritz BAYERLEIN <u>Ot. 3366</u>
I further submit to the file the following affidavit made by Johann Lieb.
(signed)

Johann Lieb statement
<u>Affidavit</u>
I, the undersigned Johann Lieb, after being first duly sworn and informed of the consequences of making a false affidavit and furthermore informed that this affidavit is to be presented to the authorities, namely to the Denazification Tribunal, do depose and say that:

a. I, Johann Lieb, 46 years old, salaried employee, residing at 23 Wörth Street, Würzburg, am not affected by the Denazification Law.
b. I have known Mr. Fritz Bayerlein since 1919.

Eight days ago I met Mr. Fritz Bayerlein by chance at the Würzburg/Frankfurt train station, after having not seen him for many years. Bayerlein told me of his pending denazification. In the course of our conversation, I offered to make the following statement on his behalf of my own free will – Mr. Bayerlein had not asked me to do so nor indicated in any way his desire that I do so:

In 1919 and 1920, Mr. Bayerlein was a non-commissioned officer in the same company of Würzburg Regiment 45 in which I was also serving. I was in the orderly room. Bayerlein was very popular with the men whose trust he had won, so he was elected representative of the company several times. Bayerlein engaged in Social Democrat politics and expressed his socialist views and convictions openly. He often kept company with Sergeant Büttner, who was a member of the Social Democratic Party.

In the spring of 1920, Bayerlein wrote several articles that were published in the SPD newspaper, the *Fränkischer Volksfreund*, in Würzburg. In these articles he opposed the actions and the excesses of the *Freikorps* and spoke out against the reactionary tendencies of the *Freikorps*. Because of this, Bayerlein's superiors hounded and monitored him and tried to get him discharged. He was later transferred.

I know that Bayerlein ...*(missing text)* ...his social and democratic ...*(missing text)* ...about him the whole time right up to the most recent past has remained favorable.

Würzburg, July 10, 1947
(signed) Johann Lieb

• • •

Klageschrift

Bayerlein's *Klageschrift* is a request to be moved to Group III, Lesser Offenders, from Group II, Offenders. Group I is Major Offenders. Each group has specific imprisonments and fines, lesser by group.

Mitteilung Klageschrift
Hessian State Ministry   G.Fy/E   Bad Homburg v.d.H.   September 9, 1947
Minister for Political Liberation
The Public Prosecutor of the Denazification Tribunal Obertaunus
File No. Ot 3366
To the Denazification Tribunal Obertaunus
Bad Homburg v.d.H

Charge Sheet
I charge BAYERLEIN, Fritz Hermann, presently auto mechanic and formerly *Generalleutnant*, born on January 14, 1899 in Würzburg, resident in Oberursel Ts. Hohemark in compliance with the Law for Liberation from National Socialism and Militarism of March 5, 1946 with the request that he be placed in group 3 Lesser Offender.
      Legal Grounds:
The party concerned belonged neither to the National Socialist Party nor to any of its organizations. He is legally incriminated for the fact that he was a career officer of the German Armed Forces after June 1, 1936 and attained the rank of *Generalleutnant*.

For this reason, he falls into the group of persons listed in Part A of the Law's Appendix and must be considered an incriminated person according to Article 10 of the law by virtue of refutable assumption.

The body of evidence presented by the party concerned in order to refute the legal assumption weighs strongly in his favor.

In order to come to a fair decision in this matter and to find a verdict befitting the party's conduct, a hearing is necessary, in which we will examine first and foremost

HESSISCHES STAATSMINISTERIUM   G.Fy/E   Bad Homburg v.d.H., den 1.9.4?
Der Minister für politische Befreiung
Der öffentliche Kläger bei der Spruchkammer

Obertaunus

Aktenzeichen: Ot 3366

An die Spruchkammer   O b e r t a u n u s

Bad Homburg v.d.H.

Klageschrift

Ich erhebe Klage gegen   früher   Generalleutnant a.Zt.

B a y e r l e i n   Fritz Hermann   Automechaniker
(Beruf)

geb.   14.1.99   in   Würzburg

wohnhaft O b e r u r s e l Tn.   Hohemark

auf Grund des Gesetzes zur Befreiung von Nationalsozialismus und Militarismus vom

5. März 1946 mit dem Antrag   ihn   in die Gruppe   3

der   Minderbelasteten   einzureihen

Begründung:

Der Betroffene gehörte weder der Partei noch einer der Gliederungen oder Organisationen an.

Seine gesetzliche Belastung besteht darin,dass er als Berufsoffizier der Deutschen Wehrmacht nach dem 1.6.1936 den Rang eines Generalleutnants erreichte.

Er fällt damit unter die im Teil A des Gesetzanhanges aufgeführten Personen und muss demnach gemäss Art.10 des Gesetzes kraft widerlegbarer Vermutung als Belasteter angesehen werden.

Das von ihm eingereichte Entlastungsmaterial zur Widerlegung der gesetzlichen Vermutung scheint weitgehend zu seinen Gunsten.

Um eine einwandfreie Beurteilung zu erzielen und einen tatsächlichen Verhalten entsprechenden Spruch finden zu können, ist mündliche Verhandlung erforderlich. In dieser wird vor allem zu untersuchen sein ob er als Militarist anzusprechen ist und welchen Widerstand er Zielen und Methoden des Nazismus entgegen setzte.

Klageschrift request to be moved to Group III lesser offenders.

whether he is to be considered a militarist and what type of resistance he mounted against the aims and methods of Nazism.

The circumstances of this case justify the charge according to Article 11 of the law.

The local jurisdiction of the Denazification Tribunal is determined by Article 29 of the law.

I request that a hearing be conducted.

Evidence

1. Documents: Registration form (Meldebogen) 12011 Oberursel Ts.
2. Witnesses
3. Experts
4. Further evidence: Information from the public authorities, the committee of the political parties, trade associations, the finance and employment bureaus.

The Public Prosecutor

(signed and typed) Freyeisen

(stamped: Greater Hessian State Ministry, Minister for Reconstruction and Political Liberation, Denazification Tribunal Obertaunus)

• • •

Zustellungsurkunde: (Summons)

Zustellungsurkunde September 1, 1947

Denazification Tribunal Obertaunus Bad Homburg v.d.H., September 1, 1947

Fy/E

Spruchkammer Obertaunus

Aktenzeichen Ot 3366

Fy/E   Bad Homburg v. d. H., den 1.9.47

Zustellungsurkunde

Heute wurde (mir) dem   B a y e r l e i n   Fritz Hermann   Automechaniker
(Name)   (Vorname)   (Beruf)

O b e r u r s e l   Hohemark
(Wohnort)   (Wohnung)

d   ie Klageschrift und die Mitteilung zur Klageschrift v.1.9.47
(Bezeichnung des Schriftstückes mit Datum)

zugestellt durch Aushändigung an

Eingegangen

1 3. 9. 47
SpruchkammerObertaunus
Der öffentliche Kläger

F. Bayerlein
(Unterschrift des Empfängers)

(Der Zustellungsbeamte)

Oberursel (Taunus), den   - 9. Sep. 1947

K/0160   8 47 8000 588

Die Spruchkammer Oberfaunus in Bad Homburg v. d. H.

Aktenzeichen: Ot **3366 K8.**

Ladung zur mündlichen Verhandlung

Herrn/Fräulein X

Fritz Hermann B a y e r l e i n

in **O b e r u r s e l / Ts.**
Hohemark

Auf Grund der Ihnen am **9.9.47** zugestellten Anklageschrift vom
1.9.47 wird mündliche Verhandlung gegen Sie angeordnet.
Sie werden deshalb auf

M o n t a g , den 15.9.47 **vor** mittags **11** Uhr

vor die Spruchkammer **Obertaunus Kreistags** Sitzungssaal **des Landratsamtes Bad Homburg,**
zur mündlichen Verhandlung geladen und zu pünktlichem Erscheinen aufgefordert **Luisenstr. 88/90**
Die Ladungsfrist ist abgekürzt auf **XXXXXXX** Tage.

Zugleich wird Ihnen eröffnet: **der Klageschrift**

1. Die Beweismittel sind auf der Rückseite xxxxxxxxx verzeichnet.

2. Im Falle eines unentschuldigten Ausbleibens kann in Ihrer Abwesenheit verhandelt und entschieden werden, jedoch kann Ihr Erscheinen durch Vorführungsbefehl oder Ordnungsstrafen erzwungen werden.

3. Sie können die Ladung von Zeugen oder Sachverständigen oder die Herbeischaffung anderer Beweismittel unter Angabe der Tatsachen, über die Beweis erhoben werden soll, bei dem Vorsitzenden der Spruchkammer beantragen oder Personen, deren Vernehmung Sie wünschen, zur mündlichen Verhandlung mitbringen.

Jede Zuschrift ist mit dem links oben angegebenen Aktenzeichen zu versehen.

Bad Homburg v. d. H., den **12.9.47** 194

Der Vorsitzende.

[signature]

Ausfertigung erhalten:

Der (die) Betroffene

Der Antragsteller

Ladung zur mundlichen Verhand lung (summons to tribunal oral proceedings).

File No.: Ot. 3366
(stamped: Received: September 13, 1947, Denazification Tribunal Obertaunus, Office of the Public Prosecutor)

Affidavit of Service of Legal Process

Today Bayerlein, Fritz Hermann, auto mechanic of Hohemark, Oberursel was served the charges and the notification of charges dated September 1, 1947 by hand delivery.

    (signed) Fritz Bayerlein

(Signature of the Recipient)
(The Servicing Official)
Oberursel (Taunus), September 9, 1947

. . .

Ladung zur Mündlichen Verhandlung
(Summons to Tribunal Oral Proceedings)

Ladung zur Mündlichen Verhandlung (27)
The De-Nazification Tribunal Obertaunus in Bad Homburg v.d.H.

File Number: Ot **3366 Kö**
Summons to an Oral Proceeding
Fritz Hermann B a y e r l e i n
In **O b e r u r s e l / T s .**
Hohemark
On the basis of the Charge sheet of 9/1/47 delivered to you on 9/9/47, an oral proceeding has been directed against you.

    You are therefore ordered to report punctually, on **Monday morning 9/15/47 at 11:00am** before the De-Nazification Tribunal of **Obertaunus**, Council Chamber **Kreistags**, of the **State Magistrate's Office, Bad Homburg** at **Luisenstrasse 88/90**, for an oral hearing

    The term of summons is reduced to **xxx** days.

    You are simultaneously informed that:

    1. The evidence is detailed on the reverse side of the **charge sheet**.

    2. In the case of an unexcused non-appearance, action can be taken and a decision reached in your absence, or your presence can be forced by a subpoena or fine.

    3. You can present to the chairman of the Tribunal an invitation for any witnesses, or Expert witness, or produce any other evidence with presentation of the facts for which proof is to be submitted, or bring along persons with you to the oral proceedings, who you wish to be questioned

    Every communication is to be marked with the file number given at the upper left.

Bad Homburg v. d. H., 12 September 1947
Chairman of the Tribunal
Jellinek

**Minister
für politische Befreiung
Spruchkammer Obertaunus
Telefon 2179**

Ot 5366.

Bad Homburg v. d. H., den 10.9.47. 194..

Vermögensübersicht des Betroffenen
gemäss dem Gesetz zur Befreiung von Nationalsozialismus
und Militarismus vom 5. März 1946.

1. Name: Bayerlein

2. Vorname: Fritz, Hermann

3. Geburtstag: 14. Januar 1899.

4. Wohnort: Ober Ursel/Ts. Hohemarkstrasse 101

5. Geschäftszweig, Beruf oder Beschäftigung: Automechaniker

A. Vermögen :	Beschreibung oder Kennzeichnung des Vermögensgegenstandes. Name und Anschrift des Besitzers, Ort, Art und Weise der Verwahrung	Betrag bezw. Verkehrswert (Realisationswert) in Reichsmark am Tage des Inkrafttretens des Befreiungsgesetzes vom 5. 3. 1946
1. Unbebaute und bebaute Grundstücke (möglichst genau nach Gemeinde, Grundbuchblatt, Katasternummer, Strasse- und Hausnummer zu bezeichnen).	Siedlungshaus im gemeinsamen Besitz von mir, meiner Schwester und Neffen. Würzburg, Heidingsfeld, Taschen-Ackerweg 9	Gesamtwert: 26075 RM. [Hiervon Anteil meine Schwester 5000 Rm, meines Neffen 9000Rm
2. Gewerbliches Vermögen (Handels- oder Handwerksbetrieb usw.) Letzte Jahresschlussbilanz u. wenn möglich, Geschäftseröffnungsbilanz, sowie die letzte Vermögenssteuererklärung beifügen. keines	Verwaltet von meiner Schwester Frau Ellen Dittmar, Würzburg-Heidingsfeld, Taschen-Ackerweg 9 . Das Haus steht gem. Entschei-dung der amerik. Mil. Reg. nicht unter Ver-Mögenskontrolle.	
3. Banknoten, Münzen, andere Zahlungsmittel (Wechsel, Scheck) Postscheckguthaben, Guthaben bei Geldinstituten, Sparkassen- u. sonstige Einlagebücher, Wertpapiere, (soweit nicht in Geschäftsbilanz aufgeführt).	Bankkonto 4775.- Rm.	1775.- Rm.
4. Ausstehende Forderungen (namentlich Hypotheken-, Grund- u. Rentenschuldforderungen, Forderungen aus Kauf- und Darlehnsverträgen, Rentenforderungen, Forderungen aus Versicherungsverträgen und gegen Sterbekassen, Gehalts- und Lohnforderungen unter Angabe des Namens u. Wohnortes des Schuldners oder der Zahlstelle, sowie bei eingetragenen Forderungen: Bezeichnung nach dem Grundbuch (soweit nicht in Geschäftsbilanz aufgeführt).	keine	
5. Beteiligung, Geschäfts- u. Genossenschaftsanteile, (soweit nicht in Geschäftsbilanz aufgeführt).	keine	
6. Handwerkzeug, Maschinen, landwirtsch. od. zum gewerbl. Betrieb bestimmte Geräte (soweit nicht in Geschäftsbilanz aufgeführt).	keine	

Vermögen sübersicht des Betroffen (financial and property statement, page one).

Copy received:
The Concerned Party
The Petitioner

• • •

Ladung des Rechtsebeistandes
Denazification Tribunal Obertaunus in Bad Homburg v.d.H.
File Number: Ot 3366 Kö
Summons
Of the Petitioner's Legal Council
Attorney Ernst WAHL
9 Henricus Street
Oberursel/Ts.
A hearing against Fritz Hermann Bayerlein, Oberursel will take place before the Denazification Tribunal in the District Assembly Courtroom of the administrative district office Bad Homburg, 88/90 Luisen Street on Monday, September 15, 1947 at 11:00 am.

You are therefore summoned to appear before the court as legal council of the party in question.

The evidence is detailed on the reverse side of the charge sheet. Every communication is to be marked with the file number given at the upper left.

Bad Homburg v. d. H., September 12, 1947
Court Registry of the
Denazification Tribunal

• • •

Vermögensübersicht Form (Financial Statement) Prepared by Bayerlein

Minister for Political Liberation   **September 12, 1947**
Bad Homburg v.d. H.
Denazification Tribunal Obertaunus
Telephone 2179

Asset statement of the Party Concerned
Pursuant to the Law for Liberation

1. **Last Name:** Bayerlein
2. **First and Middle Names:** Fritz Hermann
3. **Date of Birth:** January 14, 1899
4. **Place of Residence:** 101 Hohemark Street, Ober Ursel/ Ts.
5. **Profession: Auto Mechanic**

A. Assets:
1. Land or Building: Description and Value:
Apartment building owned in common ownership with my sister and nephew.
Address: 9 Taschenackerweg, Heidingsfeld Total Vale: 25,075 RM
Of this value of my sister owns 5,000 RM and my nephew 9,000 RM

2. Business Property: Apartment building managed by my sister, Mrs. Ellen Dittmar, The house is not under property control according to the American Military Government.

3. Bills, coins, and other means of payments, postal funds, bank deposits, savings bank deposits, stocks, securities: Bank account: 4,775 RM

4. Outstanding Debts (mortgages, land, rent debts, purchases or loans, insurance policies, death benefit funds, salary pay demands, including name and address of debtor or the paying agent: NONE

5. Shares or stakes in companies or consortiums: None

6. Tools, equipment, machinery used for agricultural or commercial purposes: NONE

7. Missing Data

8. Animals: NONE

9. Unused stock, agricultural or commercial supplies/ stock: NONE

10. All household effects and all personal effects including linens, clothing, etc, in an itemized list:
All of my personal property was destroyed in the bombing. In possession now: only a worm out suit, coat, 2 sets of wash and 2 American work suites – 80 RM

11. Art work, jewelry, gold and silver, carpets etc. in an itemized list.
None

12. Other objects, items or rights of value not listed above.

Total A:
None

30,930

B. Debts:

13. Mortgages, land or property charges, rent charges (not listed in business balance sheets) Share of the house's value belonging to my sister and my nephew and spent for the cost of repairing damage to the house caused by bombing

5,000

9,000

1,500

15. Bank loans (not listed in business balance sheets)

16. Other liabilities (not listed in assets balance sheet)

Total B:

15,500

A. Assets	(Items 1 – 12)	=	30,930	RM
B. Debts	(Items 13 – 16)	=	15,500	RM
C. Net assets		=	15,430	RM

• • •

A Vermögen :	Beschreibung oder Kennzeichnung des Vermögensgegenstandes. Name und Anschrift des Besitzers, Ort, Art und Weise der Verwahrung	Betrag bezw. Verkehrswert (Realisationswert) in Reichsmark am Tage des Inkrafttretens des Befreiungsgesetzes vom 5. 3. 1946
8. Haustiere (Pferde, Rinder, Schweine, Esel, Schafe, Hühner, Hunde u. dergl. (soweit nicht in Geschäftsbilanz aufgeführt).	Keine	
9. Warenvorräte, landwirtschaftliche oder gewerbliche Vorräte (soweit nicht in Geschäftsbilanz aufgeführt).	keine	
10. Alle Haushaltungsgegenstände und alle Gegenstände des persönlich. Bedarfs einschließlich Wäsche, Kleidung usw. nach **besonderer** Aufstellung der Einzelgegenstände.	Durch Bombenschäden alle bewegliche Habe verloren. Im Besitz nur ein abgetragener Anzug, Mantel, 2 Wäschegarnituren und 2 amerik. Arbeitsanzüge.	80.-Rm.
11. Kunstgegenstände, Schmucksachen, Geld- und Silbersachen, Teppiche usw. nach **besonderer** Aufstellung der Einzelgegenstände.	keine	
12. Sonstige, vorstehend nicht aufgeführte Werte, Sachen und Rechte.	keine	
— Zusammen A :		30930
B. Schuldverpflichtungen :		
13. Hypotheken- und Grundschulden, Renten- schulden oder Reallasten (soweit nicht in Geschäftsbilanz aufgeführt).	Anteile meiner Schwester 5000 und Neffen, Hypotheken 9000 und Kosten für Wie- 1500	
14. Verbindlichkeiten auf Grund von Warenlie- ferungen und Leistungen (soweit nicht in Geschäftsbilanz aufgeführt).	derinstandsetzung des bombenbeschädigten Hauses	
15. Bankverpflichtungen (soweit nicht in Ge- schäftsbilanz aufgeführt).		
16. Sonstige Verbindlichkeiten (soweit nicht in Vermögensbilanz aufgeführt).		
Zusammen B :		15500

A. Vermögen . . (Ziff. 1—12) = 30930 RM

B. Schuldverpflichtungen (Ziff. 13—16 = 15500 RM

C. Reinvermögen . . = 15430 RM

Vermögen sübersicht des Betroffen (financial and property statement, page two).

View from the Schwartzbock Hotel, Weisbaden, Germany showing a bombed section of the city, dated April 27, 1947. (NARA, U.S. Army Signal Corps Photo SC 284989)

Chapter 3 Endnotes

1. Frau Helga Woods and her older brothers recounted this story to the author on her travels to Würzburg in October 2000.

2. *Meldebogen* literally means 'Registration Form'.

3. Members of the NSDAP wore brown uniforms and were known as *Braunhemden* or Brownshirts.

4. The SPD was banned by Hitler through the Enabling Act of 1933.

5. *Freikorps*: paramilitary groups often formed after World War I by disaffected soldiers. In the spring of 1919, *Freikorps* members killed SPD members whom they believed to be Communists. Many Nazi leaders were formerly in the *Freikorps*.

4
The General's Defense

"We are fighting to defeat and wipe out the Nazis who started all this goddamned son of a bitchery." — Patton.[1]

Open Court Session – Minutes of the Case (Protokoll)

Protokoll

Translator's Note: The Protokoll was a preprinted form. Sections of the form that were not filled out because they did not apply were not translated.

Open Court Session of the Denazification Tribunal Obertaunus
File No. Ot: 3366
Record of Proceedings
of the open court session of *September 15, 1947*
Present at the hearing in the case against auto mechanic and former Generalleutnant Fritz Hermann BAYERLEIN, born on January 1, 1899 in Würzburg and resident in Hohemark, Oberursel/Taunus, were:

    1. Johann Jellinek , Chairman
    2. Jean Dinges and Johann Krimmel, Members
    3. Gustav Freyeisen, Public Prosecutor
    4. Margot Plebuch, Court Recorder

Summoned and appearing in person before the court in this matter were: the party concerned as well as his legal counsel, Attorney Ernst Wahl of 9 Henricus Street, Oberursel/Taunus. Witnesses were not summoned.

Under examination, the party concerned stated that: he is the auto mechanic and former *Generalleutnant* Fritz Hermann BAYERLEIN, born on January 1, 1899 in Würzburg and resident in Hohemark, Oberursel/Taunus, and unmarried.

The charges were then presented by the public prosecutor –

The party concerned was asked if he had anything to say to refute the charges. He stated that:

He came from a family of very modest means and was able to attend Gymnasium with the help of a scholarship stipend. His father was an old Social Democrat and was well read in the subject of politics which he tried to introduce his son to. From the age of eighteen in the year 1917 until the end of the war, the party concerned took part in the serious action in the West; the hardship of that time and the terrible toll it took on his fellow sufferers are indelibly etched in his memory. At that time he served as a simple infantry soldier, declining from the outset to become a candidate in the officers' corps whose elitist nature was repellent to him. After his discharge from the army, he wrote several articles published in the newspaper, the *Fränkischer Volksfreund*, in which he spoke out against the National Socialists' reactionary tendencies in the Freikorps. He was, at the time, the company leader of the 3rd company of the 21st regiment of the Reichswehr. This company was neither involved in the "Black Reichswehr" nor in the training of NS groups. In fact, unlike other companies, it rejected any connection with such groups. During the so-called "Hitler (or Beer Hall) Putsch" on November 11, 1923, this company was one of the few companies in northern Bavaria considered to be loyal to the constitution of the Weimar Republic and reliable enough to be sent to Munich-Grosshadern to put down the putsch. Company members were jostled and verbally abused by Hitler's supporters during this incident.

He himself had always been an ardent Social Democrat and opponent of National Socialist views. For him the *Reichswehr* was solely a military instrument, and as such, was subordinate to the state and existed to serve the state, rejecting "tradition" and establishing itself on the basis of the Weimar constitution. For this reason, he had no connections with the "Black Reichswehr" and refused to train its members.

In response to the chairman's question as to whether it had been possible for him as company leader to refuse to train the "Black Reichswehr", he responded: "This training was a voluntary thing" and that is why he could just refuse to do it. He had other views and wanted nothing to do with Hitler officers. Even after the Nazi takeover, none of these basic conditions had changed for him. He rejected any connection to the ideology of the Third Reich and avoided party members in any way he could. He never belonged to the NSDAP or any of its organizations. Moreover, he was a devout Catholic and always attended service. Against all National Socialist rules, while he served in Hungary in 1944, he stayed with Cardinal SEREDI who was later killed by the Gestapo. While he was there, he appeared with the Cardinal in public and also attended his church services. He even urged his troops to attend camp services and gave the camp clergymen his full support. Nazi sentiments were not tolerated under his command. He retained opponents to the Nazi on his staff, for example HARDEGEN, KAUFMANN, and VON HEYDEN, who had all been noted as untrustworthy in their files. He did many things and always opposed the policies of the Hitler supporters.

In 1941 he was in Würzburg on furlough, recovering from an injury. He was out for a walk with his sister and nephew and dressed in civilian clothes when he reprimanded some camp guards at the Würzburg train station because they were mistreating a few of the Russian POWs they were accompanying; as an officer, he ordered the guards to carry a sick prisoner into the camp despite the protests from the crowd of onlookers. His intervention and rebuke of the guards resulted in a court martial for him and the loss of his sister's store which was forced to close its doors after this incident. At his court martial, he found out that the mistreatment of prisoners was promoted by Himmler. He was accused of sympathizing with the prisoners.

Furthermore, he issued strict orders on the treatment of prisoners of war on the front, prevented the evacuation of the local population in Russia, and in addition saved POW Camp HEMER (250,000 men) by sending over an American major who was a POW at the camp to the American units that were mistakenly firing on the camp. He had also provided this camp with food from his supplies and later handed it over to the Americans.

He refused to support Nazism in any way and also refused to enrich himself through Nazism. When he was awarded the Oak Leaves to the *Ritterkreuz*, he turned down a further offer of land, explaining that he did not want to secure advantages through this system and did not want to be counted among the landowning military "gentry".

His rank as a general enabled him to do everything to bring an end to the war. He did not carry out the *Führerbefehle* (Hitler's own orders) and tried again and again to lead his troops out of the war. Against Hitler's orders, he tried repeatedly to save what could still be saved. "Fight to the last man" was a motto he neither recognized, nor followed.

As Rommel's Chief of Staff in 1942, he deliberated with Rommel on how to bring about a speedy end to the war, renouncing a final victory for Germany. Rommel went into the Führer's Headquarters where he put forward his suggestions. All of Rommel's suggested plans were brutally and forcibly rejected. The party concerned was at that time deployed to Russia and Rommel lost his post as commander on the invasion front. Later Rommel was sent to the western front by Stülpnagel, who was involved in the plot of July 20, 1944; there, Rommel informed the party concerned in a private meeting about the state of the resistance movement on the Western Front and the plot to get rid of Hitler. He stayed in further contact with Rommel. All of the plans made with Rommel failed. In a state of delirium, Stülpnagel, who had injured himself seriously after the failed assassination attempt, disclosed Rommel's involvement in the plot. After a car accident, Rommel was forced to commit suicide in front of Hitler's adjutants because of all of his links to the assassination plot. After Rommel and he had decided to try to put an end to the war, Bayerlein tried again and again to put up resistance in strategic and/or tactical areas and made it possible, as far as it lay within the reach of his command, to lead his troops out of the war and keep them from certain destruction. When he and his division, along with two other German divisions, were surrounded in the Ukraine near Kirovograd where they were ordered by Hitler himself to stay and defend to the last man, he disobeyed this order and acting on his own initiative, he escaped with his division, and apart from two wounded men, he brought them out unharmed and saved them all from certain destruction.

In August, 1944 he did not carry out the order to lead the Panzer Lehr Division out of the pocket of Argentan-Falaise to mount an attack on Avranches and once again, in disregard of Hitler's order, he brought his division out of the pocket and into safety. This resulted in another court martial and a harsh rebuke from the V. Panzer Army.

Furthermore, he did not follow Hitler's orders to mount a counterattack in November of 1944 in the Saar Territory for which he was threatened to be removed from the troop. He surrendered the city of Winterberg against strict orders to hold it. Because of this, the city was handed over to the Americans undamaged.

On April 16, 1945 he handed himself and his 30,000 men over to the Americans at Iserlohn/Ruhrgebiet and surrendered. This was the first and only capitulation by a higher commander in the West. Through his surrender, he not only saved the lives of many German and American soldiers but also kept a lot of German property in the war zone around Iserlohn from being destroyed and completely demolished. He evacuated the city of Dortmund without a fight and against orders and surrendered the city of Winterberg to the Americans against Hitler's strictest order and without a fight. He always lived modestly and shared both joy and sorrow with his soldiers on the front line. He stayed in dugouts and temporary command posts just like his soldiers and only wore his medals, decorations and badges of rank in rare cases and on special occasions.

For this reason, he remained in close contact with his soldiers up till the day of his surrender and even later, earning their great esteem as a commander and a man. After the war when he was released from American custody, he began to work as an auto mechanic in order to start a new life and help his German fatherland rebuild.

After each witness____expert____ was examined and each document was read, the party concerned was asked if he had anything more to state…

The Public Prosecutor and the party concerned as well as his legal counsel – -received the judgment on their statements.

The Public Prosecutor requested that the party concerned be placed in the category of exonerated persons according to article 13 of the law of March 5, 1946.

The party's legal counsel stated that the law did not apply to the party concerned and therefore the party concerned has to be considered cleared of all incrimination.

The party concerned was given the opportunity to have the final word.

He had nothing more to say.

After closed deliberation by the tribunal, the chairman pronounced the following verdict by reading the sentence, giving the grounds for the sentence and explaining the rights of appeal.

Verdict:

The party concerned is not incriminated according to the law. The proceedings against him are dropped.

The costs of the proceedings will be assumed by the state.

The Members

The Chairman

(signed)Krimmel, Jean Dinges

Jellinek

• • •

Official Verdict

• • •

Original Document

This verdict is legally valid on November 2, 1947

The Denazification Tribunal Obertaunus   Bad Homburg v.d.H., September 15, 1947

File No. Ot 3366 Je/Pl   Delivered to the Public Prosecutor on October 1, 1947

Receipt confirmed: (signed) Koch

On the basis of the Law for Liberation from National Socialism and Militarism of March 5, 1946, the Denazification Tribunal <u>Obertaunus</u> consisting of

1. Johann Jellinek   as Chairman
2. Jean Dinges as Member
3. Johann Krimmel   as Member
4. Gustav Freyeisen   as Public Prosecutor
5. Margot Plebuch   as Court Recorder

pronounces in the case against the auto mechanic and former *Generalleutnant* Fritz Hermann Bayerlein, born on January 14, 1899 in Würzburg, and resident in Hohemark, Oberursel/Taunus on the basis of the hearing the following:

Verdict:

The party concerned is not incriminated by this law.

The case is dismissed.

The costs for the proceedings will be assumed by the state.

Grounds for verdict:

The party concerned did not belong to the (National Socialist Party) nor to any of its organizations.

    The party in question was able to clear himself of all and any incrimination; already in his childhood, through his upbringing in his parents' home, he developed a pronounced sense of justice and decency in his social attitude. In the war of 1914-1918, in which he took part as a common soldier, he rejected a career path as an officer out of his conviction that he would only offer his services as a soldier to a democratic state. After the war he spent a few more years working in the demilitarization process which was then taking place. When the Republic demanded a safeguard for its state structure, the party in question signed up for twenty-five years of military service, guided by his socialist ideals. Because of his exemplary leadership of his troops and the trust he had earned among his subordinates, he was often chosen as the representative of the troops he led. In further illustration: Bayerlein's company, which was considered to be particularly true to the constitution (of the new Weimar Republic), was the one given the order to suppress the Putsch of November 9, 1923 in Munich. After 1933, the defendant was promoted to higher military ranks because of his exemplary conduct and abilities.

    He participated in the Poland campaign in 1939 and the fight against France in 1940 as a staff officer of the 10th Panzer Division. It was in this group, that the hopelessness of this war due to the vast superiority of the Allied forces was first recognized and discussed in detail by Rommel and his colleagues. After his unsuccessful attempts to end the war in a respectable manner, General Field Marshal Rommel took Bayerlein into his confidence, discussed and initiated the preliminary preparations of an indirect resistance. On the Africa front, the defendant failed to carry out a *"Führersbefehl"* (or strict order given by Hitler himself) for the first time when he withdrew the troops serving under him near the town of Fuka, although Hitler had commanded that no troops retreat. This saved the lives of many soldiers. Another episode which took place in Würzburg, when Bayerlein was home recuperating from an injury, clearly shows the defendant's character: At a train station in

Würzburg, Russian POWs, who were being transported, were beaten with ox whips by the escort soldiers. The defendant, dressed in civilian clothes at the time, saw this and took action – giving the soldiers the order to put a POW, who had collapsed, on a stretcher and have him carried. The angry crowd of onlookers spoke out vehemently against the intervention by the defendant and his sister – (one of them) going so far as to file a lawsuit which eventually led to the closing of the subject's sister's clothing shop. In his later actions on the Russian front, the party concerned once again displays his social-minded attitude toward the less fortunate as well as his troops. As he did in Africa, he tried once again in Russia to protect the property of the local population. On the front at Kirovograd, Bayerlein refuses to carry out a *Führerbefehl* for the second time. Of particular note, is his conduct in Hungary where he stayed with Archbishop Seredi, Furst Primas of Hungary at his Palace in Esztergom, where he supported the Archbishop in his efforts to protect the local Jewish population. Seredi later became a victim of the SS. When he is called to the Atlantic front by Rommel, who places great trust in him, the subject once again offers his services to the resistance movement building within the military. Rommel, Stülpnagel, Speidel work together on these plans. After the failed undertaking of July 20, 1944, Stülpnagel attempts suicide but only succeeds in wounding himself. In his delirium, he discloses Rommel's involvement. Rommel, who must also depart from this life shortly after, and the party concerned agree that each will play his own part in trying to bring an end to the war with the aim of saving many lives. On the retreat, Bayerlein finds several opportunities to avoid engaging the enemy until he finally surrenders without the permission of his superiors in April 1945. On the entire length of the march from France back to the Ruhr, he makes sure that the orders for the destruction of factories and utilities are not carried out. By sending an American POW who was a major, the subject saved a POW camp in his sector that held 25,000 Allied soldiers. Thanks to him, the cities of Winterberg and Iserlohn remained undamaged because he refused to defend them in flagrant disregard of a direct order.

All of this is clear evidence that the party concerned put up resistance far beyond his powers by sheer force of personal courage. There is absolutely no incrimination and the Tribunal was able to pronounce the aforementioned verdict.

Pre-war Frankfurt am Main – Major i.G. Fritz Bayerlein behind the wheel of a Mercedes-Benz staff car. He was the Logistics Officer (Ib) in the General Staff of the XV Armee Korps in 1938. (Photograph courtesy of the Dittmar-Bayerlein Family Collection.)

Commissioned as an officer in the Reichswehr and promoted to the rank of Leutnant on January 1st, 1922 Bayerlein sits for a formal portrait to record the event. He was assigned to the 21st Bavarian Infantry Regiment in Würzburg. (Photograph courtesy of the Dittmar-Bayerlein Family Collection.)

Pre-war photograph: Always fond of wearing a M43 Einheitsfeldmütze instead of the officer's usual Schirmmütze visor or Dienstmütze service cap, Bayerlein smiles for the photographer. He is standing next to a woman. Other women are standing among the men, watching a parade. (Photograph courtesy of the Dittmar-Bayerlein Family Collection.)

Bayerlein (front row, 3rd from left) and fellow officers are enjoying their sports training. Bayerlein is wearing his utility uniform. (Photograph courtesy of the Dittmar-Bayerlein Family Collection.)

Early photos of officers at a field exercise: Leutnant Bayerlein is on the left. The men are eating bread, evidently not taking much of a meal break from their apparent lively discussion. This photo may be of a training exercise during this timeframe. Village houses are in the background behind the tree row, location and date unknown. (Photograph courtesy of the Dittmar-Bayerlein Family Collection.)

Leutnant Bayerlein (right) listens as the field discussion continues among the other officers. A civilian joins the group. Date estimated between January 1922-1927 from Bayerlein's rank in the Reichswehr during this time. He was assigned to the 3rd company of the 21st Bavarian Infantry Regiment during these years, with training assignments with the 7th Pionier Battalion (Engineer). In April 1927 he attended the Infantry School, but for an unknown reason was recalled to his company, perhaps due to more political unrest. Location is unknown. (Photograph courtesy of the Dittmar-Bayerlein Family Collection.)

Oberleutnant Bayerlein turns to confront the photographer. (Photograph courtesy of the Dittmar-Bayerlein Family Collection.)

An older Major Bayerlein, as the Chief of the 2nd Company, Machine Gun Battalion 6. He was promoted to Major as of June 1st, 1938 and served as the MG Company Chief from October 12th 1937 (as a Hauptmann) until November 12th, 1938. (Photograph courtesy of the Dittmar-Bayerlein Family Collection.)

Leutnant Bayerlein and contemporaries in the field training. Photo dated between 1922-1927, based upon his rank. (Photograph courtesy of the Dittmar-Bayerlein Family Collection.)

Promoted to Hauptmann (Captain) on March 1st, 1934. Bayerlein (3rd man from right) served four years in this rank until his next promotion to Major on June 1st, 1938. In August 1934 all military members had to swear a mandatory personal oath of allegiance to Adolf Hitler, rather than to the German state. (Photograph courtesy of the Dittmar-Bayerlein Family Collection.)

Major Bayerlein enjoying his Abendessen (evening meal) with his fellow officers. (Photograph courtesy of the Dittmar-Bayerlein Family Collection.)

Major Bayerlein working at his desk. One of his subordinate officers in the Panzer Lehr Division noted that his commander's lower lip would jut out "in a razz" when confronted with something particularly disagreeable, as his expression shows in this photo. (Photograph courtesy of the Dittmar-Bayerlein Family Collection.)

Operation Barbarossa – the invasion of Russia on June 1st, 1941. This photograph shows Oberstleutnant i.G. Bayerlein (right) as Ia, First General Staff Officer (Operations Officer) of Panzergruppe Guderian, facing Field Marshal von Kluge with Blumentritt nearby holding a briefcase. Photograph may have been taken in July 1941 near Minsk. (Photograph courtesy of the Dittmar-Bayerlein Family Collection.)

Major Bayerlein, watching a soccer game, sports a healthy profile, an image that would not last throughout the coming war. (Photograph courtesy of the Dittmar-Bayerlein Family Collection.)

Oberstleutnant i.G. Bayerlein hands reports to Field Marshal von Kluge. Photo believed to have been taken in July 1941, Russian front near Minsk. (Photograph courtesy of the Dittmar-Bayerlein Family Collection.)

Major Bayerlein drinking overtime at his sister's home – as he lists on the chair arm for support. (Photograph courtesy of the Dittmar-Bayerlein Family Collection.)

Oberstleutnant i.G. Bayerlein, July 1941, Russian front. His fellow officers seem to be joking behind his back. Bayerlein is wearing a fly net – rarely worn while photos were taken. (Photograph courtesy of the Dittmar-Bayerlein Family Collection.)

Oberst i.G. Bayerlein in Africa – around March 1943 – shortly before his promotion to Generalmajor. Bayerlein rescued an Arab's flock of sheep and goats from hungry German and Italian soldiers. He was rewarded with a little pet that he adored. (Photograph courtesy of the Dittmar-Bayerlein Family Collection.)

Bayerlein (center) turns over command of the 3rd Panzer Division to his successor, Oberst Helmut Lang (standing in doorway) on January 8, 1944. Guderian recommended Bayerlein for the command of Panzer Lehr Division, removing him from the hell of frozen Russia. He would be thrown from one hell to the worst he faced during his entire career – the fighting in the West. (Photograph courtesy of the Dittmar-Bayerlein Family Collection.)

Generalmajor Bayerlein on the Russian front in January 1944. He was the Commander of the Berlin-Brandenburg 3rd Panzer Division from October 1943 until January 8, 1944. Here his Aide-de-Camp in Africa, Oberleutnant Alexander Hartdegen (left), shares his friend's fate. Hartdegen met Bayerlein in March 1942, and the two men were transferred to Russia, then returned to Germany to prepare and organize the Panzer Lehr Division. Bayerlein and Hartdegen were life-long friends. (Photograph courtesy of Herr Otto Tenning, "Radio boy" of the 3rd Panzer Division.)

Training and fitting the Panzer Lehr Division for the impending Allied invasion near Budapest, Hungary: Bayerlein and Hungarian General Jeno inspect and admire their armor. The Panzer Lehr Division and the 16. SS Panzer-Grenadier Reichsführer Division were sent to Hungary for a twofold purpose – to reinforce the Hungarian Regent's faith in Germany and insure loyalty by force, if necessary. (Photograph courtesy of the Dittmar-Bayerlein Family Collection.)

Bayerlein and Hungarian General Jeno during their armor and workshop tour in March 1944. Bayerlein, appearing haggard after his Russian front experience, and illnesses in Africa, listens politely to his Hungarian host. Oberst Luxenburger (left), Commander of Panzer-Artillerie Regiment 130, lost one arm during World War I. (Bundesarchiv Koblenz, Bild 146/33/74/17)

The easy comradeship of two generals – Hungarian and German – is evident from the relaxed posture of the men. "General Bayerlein was an effective liaison with the Hungarians," Major Bernd Werncke, the Panzer Lehr Logistics Officer, recalled. "He was cordial, and we spent time with the Hungarians conducting training and training and yet more training!"

Bayerlein, Krüger, and subordinate staff officers follow Archbishop Serédi to the entrance of the enormous Esztergom Cathedral. Bayerlein and Excellency Serédi became friends to the extent that Bayerlein moved into the Esztergom Cathedral and stayed as a guest of the Archbishop. (Copyright Bundesarchiv Koblenz, Propaganda Kompanie Photographer)

His Excellency, Hungarian Archbishop Serédi Jusztinián, escorts his visitors – Generalmajor Bayerlein, Commander of the Panzer Lehr Division, and Generalleutnant Walter Krüger, Commander of the LVIII Reserve-Armeekorps – on a tour of the Esztergom Cathedral north of Budapest, Hungary. Hauptmann Alexander Hartdegen (2nd from right), Bayerlein's Aide-de-Camp, looks fondly at his friend. They remained friends after the war and until Bayerlein's death in 1970. Hartdegen was a staunch supporter of Bayerlein and provided witness testimony for Bayerlein's Denazification Trial. Photo taken in March 1944. (Copyright Bundesarchiv Koblenz, Propaganda Kompanie Photographer)

Hungarian Archbishop Serédi was an outspoken opponent of National Socialist deportation and persecution of Jews, his open criticisms in his Masses and leaflets in Budapest brought him under Sicherheitsdienst (SD) scrutiny. The SD killed dissidents in occupied territories under orders from SD leader Adolf Eichmann. It was General Bayerlein who protected the Archbishop in the Panzer Lehr Division's operating sector of Esztergom, an intervention documented and supported by the memoirs of the Archbishop, located and published postwar. In this photo Archbishop Serédi, Generalleutnant Krüger and Generalmajor Bayerlein attentively listen to their host. From the time Bayerlein and his Division left Hungary in early May 1944, the Archbishop's days were numbered. The courageous Archbishop Serédi Jusztinián was murdered by the SD in October 1944. (Copyright Bundesarchiv Koblenz, Propaganda Kompanie Photographer)

Krüger and Bayerlein enjoy their tour of the massive Esztergom Cathedral with the Archbishop as guide. Bayerlein was adept at switching religious practices from Catholic to Protestant – his father was Catholic and mother Evangelical (Protestant). Oberst Luxenburger (right) was brutally killed by being strapped to the hood of a Canadian vehicle in the fighting during the D-Day invasion. (Copyright Bundesarchiv Koblenz, Propaganda Kompanie Photographer)

Field Marshal Maximilion von Weichs, (3rd from left), was commander-in-chief of Army Group B in the East from 15 July 1942 until the beginning of February 1943. From July 1943 until the end of March 1945 von Weichs served as the commander-in-chief of Army Group F and commander-in-chief in the Southeast. In this photo von Weichs and Bayerlein (2nd from left) speak with Catholic priests at the Esztergom Cathedral. Bayerlein condoned the harboring of Jews by the priests and actively protected them from the SS and SD operations. Von Weichs was extradited to Yugoslavia on March 31, 1948 for the "commission of murder and other crimes." (Bundesarchiv Koblenz Bild 146/87/138/33A)

Generalleutnant Bayerlein speaks with a Hauptbahnhof official while his sister Ellen Dittmar, and her husband, Matthäus, stand nearby. (Photograph courtesy of Dittmar-Bayerlein Family Collection.)

LEBENSLAUF
Military Record & Part II (Entwicklung)
Bayerlein's Evidence & Testimony to the Tribunal (Note: D references – see next chapter details.) Bayerlein's attorney submitted the following testimony through his attorney Herr Ernst Wahl:

ERNST WAHL   9 Henricus Street
Attorney-at-law   Oberursel/Ts.
Tel.: 776
June 4, 1947

To:
The Public Prosecutor
Denazification Tribunal
Obertaunus
Bad Homburg v.d.H.

(stamped: Received June 6, 1947, Denazification Tribunal Obertaunus, Office of the Public Prosecutor)

RE: Fritz Bayerlein, 101 Hohemark Street, Oberursel, Registration Form No. 12011
In reference to my petition and supporting documents submitted and dated May 20, 1947, I am now putting forth the following evidence:

Curriculum vitae
1899: Born on January 14
1917: Called up for duty as an infantry soldier on the Western Front after graduation from *Gymnasium*
1918: Wounded as an infantry soldier, petty officer in October, company representative in the Revolution
1921: Enlisted into the 100,000 man army as professional military
1922: Officer with 25-year term of duty (until 1946)
1923: Infantry regiment in Würzburg, deployed to put down the Hitler Putsch in Munich
1923-1932: *Leutnant* (second lieutenant) and *Oberleutnant* (first lieutenant) ranks in Würzburg, Army Sports School in Berlin and Infantry School in Dresden.
1932-1935: Student in officers' training in Berlin
1934: *Hauptmann* (captain) rank
1935-1936: Staff in the Division in Frankfurt a.M.
1937: Company leader in Coburg
1938: Major rank, transfer to Jena
1939: General staff officer of the 10th Panzer Division, Polish campaign
1940: XIX. Panzer Corps, French campaign, *Oberstleutnant* (lieutenant colonel*)*, Panzer Regiment 8
1941: Russian campaign, Chief of Staff of the German *Afrikakorps* in North Africa, combat group leader, brigade leader, wounded.
1942: *Oberst* (colonel) rank

1943: Commander of the German troops in the 1st Ital. Army on the Tunisian Southern front, named (not promoted) *Generalmajor* (brigadier general), seriously ill.

1944: *Generalleutnant* (major general), invasion front, Normandy, eastern France, Lorraine, Ardennes, western Germany.

1945: March, command of the 53rd Corps, battles on the Rhein and Ruhr.

1945: March 16, surrenders with all troops as first and only higher commander on the Western Front to do so. Works with American authorities.

1946: Since March 2, employment as an auto mechanic

1947: Released directly from war captivity as a free citizen (without further captivity in interment camps) with the approval of the American War Department in Washington, still employed as an auto mechanic.

P. 2

I am submitting the enclosed supporting documents pertaining to Bayerlein's curriculum vitae with the request that they be returned when you are finished with them. [*Author's note*: Documents were located in the Librtary of Congress. Due to poor microfilm, they are not included].

1. *Army Talks* issue of July 1945
2. *Frankfurte Hefte* issue of June 1946
3. *New York Herald Tribune* issue of March 10, 1947
4. *Stars and Stripes* issue of March 10, 1947
5. *Neue Zürcher Zeitung* issue of April 1947

II.

Bayerlein's development and attitude were molded by:

1. the modest circumstances he came from
2. his family's political and religious attitudes
3. the impressions made on him by the First World War

Regarding point 1:

His father was the head inspector of the municipal gas works in Würzburg, who had married the daughter of a miller, and brought up his own three children as well as the two children of his dead brother on the modest income of a civil servant. Bayerlein attended *Gymnasium* with the help of scholarship money. His father died in 1933, his mother in 1936.

Regarding point 2:

His father, who had worked his way up to his position as head inspector, was a Social Democrat who was well versed in politics to which he tried to introduce his son. He was also a practicing Catholic.

Regarding point 3:

Away from his father, eighteen-year old Bayerlein lived through hard combat on the Western Front from 1917 to the very end of the war; the hardships and suffering of his fellow soldiers left an indelible impression on him. He served in this war as an infantry soldier refusing to join as a candidate in the officers' corps whose elitist nature and well-guarded distance from the enlisted men repelled him.

Because of this spirit of camaraderie with and feeling of social responsibility for his fellow soldiers he was made the representative of his company in the Revolution.

Reference

When he was discharged from the army, he did not join the *Freikorps* bands of militia but instead he attacked the reactionary tendencies of the *Freikorps* in articles that were published in the social democratic newspaper, the *Fränkischer Volksfreund*.

Reference

He was an enthusiastic supporter of the Weimar Republic and, like his father, a Social Democrat; he was an opponent of National Socialist and reactionary views of militarism as a goal in and of itself and a state within the state. For him, the army was solely an instrument of the state, and as such was subordinate to the state, which it must serve, rejecting "tradition" and establishing its purpose and identity in the constitution of the Weimar Republic.

That is why his was the only company sent to Munich by the military district of Munich to put down the Hitler Beer Hall Putsch in 1923, because the troops from Munich – with the exception of the Braun company – were not loyal to the Republic, whereas Bayerlein's troops were considered to be true to the constitution of Weimar.

Page 3 (of original text):

That is also why Bayerlein had no ties to the "Black Reichswehr", which he refused to train, and why he had no ties to "Deutsch Völkisch" supporters and avoided contact with Hitler's officers as well; in fact, he distanced himself deliberately and pointedly from these illegal movements and groups.

Reference

Even after Hitler had taken over power, nothing changed in this situation. Bayerlein rejected any connection to the ideology of the Third Reich, as he avoided any contact, personal or professional, to the organizations, groups and supporters of this ideology.

Bayerlein did not belong to any NSDAP organization, although this was in regards to the NSV very soon and in regards to the NSDAP etc. (beginning in 1944) generally permitted and even requested. Even his parents and his nephew and sister, who lived with him, belonged to no NS organizations (with the small exception of his nephew who was required to join the Hitler Youth for one year).

Reference

In his rooms, he had no pictures of high ranking Nazis or of the "*Deutschen Gruss*" or Hitler salute. He did not attend even one NSDAP meeting or event, nor did he pay one cent to any Nazi organization. It was generally known that Bayerlein attended Catholic church services. This he did even as a higher-ranked officer and general or in the field when such services were available. The army chaplains enjoyed his full support and he even urged the troops to attend service.

Reference

In 1944 he had quarters in Hungary in the residence of the well-known Nazi opponent, Cardinal Seredi, who was later murdered by the SS. He appeared with Seredi in public and attended his services openly as well. Through several proclamations, Seredi had made himself known as an opponent to the ideology of Nazism and declared himself a protector of the Jews. (although an SS division was nearby)

Reference

In his family home, in his quarters and with his people, Bayerlein constantly listened to foreign broadcasts although in no position he held was he ever granted permission to do so; even at a time when he was already under the control of the NS (National Socialist) field officer (in this case, an SA *Brigadeführer*).

Reference

He did not tolerate Nazi views in his private or military life. He undermined the NS commander or rendered him harmless by warning his own people or by hindering and ridiculing the NS officer and his work.

Reference

He retained men who were opponents to the Nazis on his staff (for example, Hartdegen, Kaufmann, v. Heyden), although their files bore the stamp "unreliable". In 1941, (while in civilian clothing and in the company of his nephew and sister) he took immediate action against the mistreatment of a Russian POW, when he happened to notice the abuse while at the train station in Würzburg. In spite of the protests of the crowd of onlookers led by the *Gauamtsleiter* Langguth, he ordered the guards to carry a sick Russian into the camp instead of forcing him to walk by beating him with a whip. The result of his actions: a proceeding against his sister (resulting later in the closing of her shop) and a court martial for Bayerlein.

Reference

In Hungary, strictest orders and their observation for the protection of the large local population of Jews – in agreement with Cardinal Seredi. (in contrast to the neighboring SS Division)

Reference

Strictest orders and their observation for the humane treatment of prisoners of war and local populations according to international law standards (in Russia as well, in spite of Nazi orders to the contrary).

Reference

Saving the prisoner camp Hemer (25,000 men) by sending over an American major who was a POW to the American units who were firing on the camp by mistake. The camp was not under his command but Bayerlein fed the starving camp from his own supplies and later surrendered it to the Americans.

Reference

On the retreat from the Battle of El Alamein, he personally safeguarded the herds of sheep that belonged to the Arab population from plundering by the German and Italian soldiers.

Reference

In the Ukraine, he prevented the evacuation of the local population which should have been carried out by attack units before the Russian Offensive (1943).

Reference

In the Ukraine he stopped the livestock belonging to the local population from being herded away.

Reference

He fed starving Russian refugees from German field kitchens (1943).

Reference

He prevented the local population from being evicted from their homes to quarter German troops.

Reference

All of this already clearly shows that Bayerlein was no Nazi, that, to the contrary, he rejected the Nazi ideology as much as he rejected Nazi actions, even when it went against orders; the following only goes to emphasize the point: Bayerlein not only refused to support Nazism in any way, he not only put up resistance to Nazism everywhere, he also refused to enrich himself through Nazism: when he was presented with the oak leaves to the *Ritterkreuz*, he refused the further offer of a piece of land. He did not want to profit from this system, and he did not want to enter the caste of the landed military gentry.

D 7
III.

As soon as Bayerlein had reached a rank and position with sufficient influence, he did what he could to

1. bring an end to the war, and if that was not entirely possible,
2. lead his troops away from the war as much as he could until he could surrender with all his troops, even at the price of giving up positions that by "highest order" or "Führer's order" were to be "defended to the last man"
3. save what cities and property he could, also in disregard of highest orders.

Regarding point 1:

As Rommel's Chief of Staff (October 1941), he deliberated with Rommel on how to put a quick end to the war, giving up the goal of an "*Endsieg*" or final victory (already before the landing of the Allies in North Africa). This resulted first in Rommel's decision to present the options at the Führer's Headquarters. His presentation was unsuccessful and his suggestions were brutally rejected by Hitler and Göring. Rommel and Bayerlein then agreed that they would have to resort to illegal means from this point on. As a result of his presentation in the Führer's Headquarters, Rommel was later removed from his post. Bayerlein was sent to Russia and Rommel became commander-in-chief on the invasion front, where he sent for his trusted co-planner, Bayerlein to join him on the Western Front.

There, Stülpnagel, who was the military commander in France and who later died in the plot to kill Hitler of July 20, 1944, called Bayerlein to a secret night meeting to brief him on the state of the resistance movement within the military in the West, which aimed at removing Hitler and bringing an end to the war by surrendering the Western Front. On May 7, 1944 Bayerlein promised Rommel that, in his command post on the Western Front, he would adhere to any orders that would help bring about their aims. For this reason, he continued to stay in contact with Rommel through his orderly. The plan failed after Rommel had issued Hitler an ultimatum on May 15, 1944 because of Rommel's serious car accident and the subsequent discovery of the plot of July 20, 1944. (Rommel was forced to take poison in front of Hitler's aides because of his involvement in the plot.)

Reference
Once Rommel and Bayerlein had decided to try to put an end to the war, Bayerlein began to put up strategic and/or tactical resistance and to keep his troops out of the war whenever possible.

The English had already won the Battle of El Alamein in North Africa, when Hitler's order came not to surrender an inch, but to hold, be victorious or die. As the Commander of the Corps, Bayerlein, in defiance of the order and completely on his own authority, led his troops out of the battle in retreat and by doing so saved all of them from certain destruction.

Reference
In 1943, Bayerlein's division and two other German divisions were surrounded in the Ukraine near Kirovograd. Hitler's order: hold the city at all costs to the last man. Bayerlein broke ranks and led his division out of the path of certain destruction against orders and once again on his own authority; only two of his men were injured.

Reference
In August, 1944 he did not carry out the order to lead the Panzer Lehr Division out of the pocket of Argentan-Falaise to mount an attack on Avranches and once again, in disregard of Hitler's order, he brought his division out of the pocket and into safety. This resulted in another court martial and a harsh rebuke from the V. Panzer Army.

Reference
In November of 1944, he did not follow Hitler's orders to mount a counterattack in the Saar Territory. Consequence: he was threatened with removal from the troop and received harsh rebukes from the 1st Army and the XIII. Corps.

Reference
Delayed advance in the Ardennes Offensive against the explicit order for a fast and ruthless thrust forward. Because of this, the division was spared being surrounded and destroyed (a fate which befell the neighboring division).
Consequence: Serious accusations by the V. Army that he was to blame for the failure of the offensive. Dismissal from his command post in this division.

Reference
Unauthorized withdrawal of regiment troops from his division which had been placed under another section near Hochscheid/Luxemburg in January 1944; once again acting against orders but saving the regiment troops from destruction.
Consequence: Court martial by the VII. Army, transfer. The trial was never concluded because of Bayerlein's deliberate delays and the length of the investigation.

Reference
Surrender of Winterberg against explicit orders to hold the city and refusal to recapture this transport hub in April 1945 which left the city completely unharmed.

Reference
Bayerlein surrenders with all of his 30,000 troops near Iserlohn in the Ruhrgebiet on April 16, 1945. This was the first and – in the West – only surrender of a higher-ranked commander. This surrender went against Hitler's strictest orders, which forbade any surrender, and was punishable by hanging and subject to *Sippenhaftung* or "kin liability". This surrender was carried out against the resistance of his own staff and a few troop commanders, who all had the right to shoot the surrendering officer. Through his actions, Bayerlein saved the lives and health not only of his 30,000 men but also of innumerable enemy soldiers as well as protecting a lot of German property in the battle zone near Iserlohn.

Reference
We reserve the right to submit the assessment of a military expert, the former *Generalleutnant* and political prisoner Dr. Hans Speidel.
Regarding point 3:
Disregard of Hitler's order to destroy all essential property and infrastructure:
In the Ruhrgebiet, no destruction (in agreement with the superior command)

Reference
Evacuation of the city of Dortmund without a fight and against orders;

Reference
(page 7 of original text)
Evacuation of the city of Winterberg without a fight and against orders; orders to recapture not carried out.

Reference
Iserlohn and surroundings completely unharmed because of his surrender.

Reference
A series of separate incidents when Bayerlein prevented the destruction of German property and possessions.

IV.
This portrait of Bayerlein is rounded out and completed:
1. by his own lifestyle
2. by his relationship in times of peace and war with the soldiers he led
Regarding point 1:
In his civilian life and as a soldier and officer, Bayerlein lived modestly. He avoided all extravagance in clothing, food and drink, appearance, housing etc. He refused to be quartered any differently than his troops and stayed like them in dugouts and fortifications. He seldom wore medals, decorations, or badges of rank, and never wore them on the front, on his few leaves home to convalesce, he wore civilian clothing. He never even possessed

the red general stripes. His refusal to enrich himself by accepting property is further proof of his character.

Reference
Regarding point 2:

In his lifestyle and personal attitude he was modest, in his attitude toward his soldiers during war time and in peace he was comradely. He helped his men whenever and however he could, and there was no difficult situation in which he himself, even as general, was not right there with and for his troops. In the most dangerous endeavors he was right at the front, leading his troops because he never expected anything from his men that he would not do himself, and because he also never wanted to see his soldiers brought into senseless or hopeless situations. He still considers his relationship with his soldiers, which he began as an eighteen-year-old infantryman in the battles on the Western Front in the First World War and continued right up to his surrender in the Ruhrgebiet, as his greatest achievement, placing it above his successes and honors. The experiences of the eighteen-year-old infantry soldier in the First World War were for him the most lasting impression of what it meant to live and suffer as a soldier among other soldiers; and that is why he chose to share the lot of his soldiers without sparing himself.

V.

For Bayerlein then the end of the war and his military career did not mean the end of his very self or the end of his fate. He turned his attentions immediately and decisively to the reconstruction of Germany; after his surrender he continued his efforts to bring the war to an end to the best of his abilities with as few further victims as possible; and, as soon as he was allowed to create a new life for himself as an auto mechanic, a job in which he could be of use to society. At present he is about to take the auto mechanic apprenticeship certification examination and will then work for some time in the Historical Department of the U.S. Armed Forces Headquarters

After the preceding account, there is no need to state once again that Bayerlein was neither a Nazi nor a Nazi sympathizer. From the preceding account it is also clear that he was no militarist. There are professional soldiers all over the world, in Sweden, Denmark, Holland, England, America, and Russia. What makes a soldier a militarist is his view of the military. The militarist sees the military as an end in itself, an autonomous power existing outside of the state's power and a tool for expansion and the exertion of control on the international stage. The non-militarist sees the military as a profession and a duty whose sole purpose is to serve the state, that is, a state which within the framework of international law seeks peace and the material and spiritual well-being of its citizens; to protect such a state is the purpose of the armed forces. If Bayerlein had been a militarist, he would not have refused to enter into the caste of landed military families, he would have rejected his moral duty to follow the paths that led other soldiers into the arms of the National Socialist regime, and on to actions, that complied with Nazi orders but went against international law, on to the senseless slaughter of people and the senseless destruction of property; he would have taken paths that led to the internment camp and to the Nuremberg Tribunal or to some other court.

(signed) Ernst Wahl, Attorney-at-law

Chapter 4 Endnotes

1. A high school with a challenging curriculum aimed at preparing students for higher studies and culminating in a university entrance examination.

2. Illegal paramilitary groups whose formation after World War I went against the Treaty of Versailles terms

3. A boycott of Ellen's boutique forced her to close.

4. Added by translator for clarification

5. Added by translator for clarification

6. Attempted assassination of Hitler.

7. German Revolution of 1918

8. Illegal paramilitary groups whose formation in the Weimar Republic went against provisions of the Versailles Peace Treaty

9. Right wing movement in the Weimar Republic

10. Straight-armed Nazi salute, often accompanied by the words Heil Hitler.

11. Family members were held liable for a person's actions and could be punished.

5

Witnesses for the Defense

"We are like the people in a boat floating down the beautiful river of fictitious prosperity and think that the moaning of the none too distant waterfall – which is going to engulf us – is but the song of the wind in the trees." — Patton.[1]

Witness Statements and Documents from the *Spruchkammershe (trial file)*

Dokumenten – Liste:

D1 – Angermann

D2 – Barth

D3 – Caesar

D4 – Enderle

D5 – Frisch

D6 – Fleischer

D7 – Hartedegen

D8 – Held

D9 – Hetzel

D10 – Huber

D11 – Hiltmann

D12 – Hegener

D13 – Huebner

D14 – von Heyden

D15 – Kauffmann

D16 – Maul, Automechaniker

D17 – Reitter

D18 – Suets

D19 – Straub

D20 – Speidel

D21 – Schmidt

D22 – Schwarz

D23 – Dietrich

D24 – Funke

D25 – Colonel Philp, Commander, MISC #4.

D26 – Amtsgericht Würzburg

D27 – Hitler Jugend

• • •

D-1

Dr. of Law Angermann Idstein i./Ts., February 19, 1947

Attorney-at-law and Notary Public

7 Weiherwiese, Idstein im Taunus

Bad Schwalbach Branch

5 Goetheplatz (Haus Tannenburg)

AFFIDAVIT

I hereby swear to the accuracy of my statement below on the character of the former *Generalleutnant* Fritz BAYERLEIN:

1.

I knew Mr. Bayerlein throughout the time that he served as division commander of the 3rd Panzer Division as well as the Panzer Lehr Division. The 3rd Panzer Division was in action in the East at that time (1943/44), the Panzer Lehr Division in the West (1944/45). As intendant of these divisions, in which I served at the same time as Mr. Bayerlein, I was in constant contact with both the division commander and the troops he led. I, therefore, know Mr. Bayerlein and his activity as division commander very well and know just as well how he was regarded by his troops.

2.

The personality and actions of former *Generalleutnant* Bayerlein are most strongly characterized by the fact that he sharply and unconditionally rejected all types of Nazi methods of warfare and held strictly to the principles of international law for warfare. This was shown through his energetic advocacy for ethical warfare and the ethical treatment of prisoners of war and civilians both in occupied areas as well as by the troops of the 3rd Panzer Division in the East and the Panzer Lehr Division in the West.

Mr. Bayerlein put up resistance to orders of the higher or highest ranks of leadership which went against the principles of humanity and decency by expressing his opinion to superior officers and higher command authorities openly and bluntly and by either ignoring or by changing orders to reflect his own principles, even when the orders came directly from Hitler himself. He never left it to his subordinate officers to deal with senseless or inhumane orders, instead in such cases he personally took responsibility for disregarding or altering the orders in question. That Mr. Bayerlein was not immediately called to task for this behavior, I can only assume had to do with the fact that his exceptional leadership skills were sorely needed and that his own decisions always turned out to be the right ones in the end.

In the same way Mr. Bayerlein insisted on the ethical treatment of prisoners and civilians in the occupied territories everywhere in his area of command, he also did all he could to ensure that the war against the enemy in the East and in the West was waged ethically. With this in mind, he trained his troops and his commanders, issued appropriate orders and saw to it that these orders were strictly enforced. For this reason, it was impossible that under Mr. Bayerlein's leadership in the East or in the West that unfair actions would be carried out against the enemy or that prisoners of war or civilians in occupied areas would be treated in any way that went against international law. Whenever civilians in the occupied areas came to him with their wishes or their complaints Mr. Bayerlein personally saw to it that the rights of the local population were protected. As the former intendant of the 3rd Panzer Division as well as the Panzer Lehr Division, I myself received Mr. Bayerlein's strict orders on the care of POWs, to provide prisoners with sufficient food and clothing and, at any time, to be able to provide immediate assistance when large numbers of prisoners arrived. In this way, the prisoners of war both with the 3rd Panzer Division and with the Panzer Lehr Division were always well provided and cared for; during the winter in the East, prisoners of war were even provided with blankets and warm clothing from the troops' own limited supplies.

3.

In the leadership of his troops, former *Generalleutnant* Bayerlein's first and foremost principle was to keep his troops from harm and avoid losing men as far as this was possible. He sharply criticized and rejected any success that was achieved with undue hardship on the troops or with more than the absolutely necessary number of casualties. Through appropriate training and strict orders, Mr. Bayerlein made sure that this guiding principle of leadership was completely ingrained in all of his subordinate officers. A decisive factor that led to the actual implementation of this principle in the war was the fact that Mr. Bayerlein himself was always in the middle of the action on the front line whenever his division was deployed and always led his own troops personally. Therefore, Mr. Bayerlein inevitably shared all dangers and hardships with his soldiers and was known to every last man in his division.

Both in the 3rd Panzer Division and the Panzer Lehr Division Mr. Bayerlein enforced these principles of leadership with such consistency and strictness that they were fully accepted and observed in both divisions. For this reason, every member of the division to the very last man knew without a doubt that he served under leadership with the keenest sense of responsibility. The result was that Mr. Bayerlein enjoyed the deepest respect and boundless trust of all the division members of the 3rd Panzer Division as well as the Panzer Lehr Division.

Apart from these leadership principles, Mr. Bayerlein considered it his most important duty to do everything possible for the care of his troops. As the former intendant of the 3rd Panzer Division and the Panzer Lehr Division, I myself know best that Mr. Bayerlein, like almost no other division commander, always showed the strongest interest for the mental and bodily well-being of his troops. He listened willingly to all the worries and troubles of his soldiers and helped them in word and deed like a father. In his selfless and fatherly manner, it often happened that Mr. Bayerlein helped needy soldiers at his own expense. He continuously asked about the state of supplies for the troops and kept abreast of the situation. Whenever any problems arose with the regular provisioning of the troops, he did whatever he could to ensure that these difficulties would be removed in the shortest time possible. When the troop faced particular struggles or hardships, he saw to it that extra rations or provisions were handed out and he personally took responsibility for such measures. At the same time, he refused on principle to be treated any better than the simple soldiers.

Just as Mr. Bayerlein enjoyed the absolute respect and boundless trust of the soldiers he led for his leadership style and the careful deployment of his troops, he was admired and liked by all for his personal modesty and his tireless care for the welfare of the troops.

4.

Mr. Bayerlein decisively rejected any kind of Nazi propaganda in his sphere of command. In closer circles he openly expressed his opinion on the sheer madness of the war. In keeping with this basic attitude, he also rejected the notion of a senseless "fight to the last man", which his deeds proved again and again, when he, on his own authority, surrendered positions that per orders were to be held, in order to pull his troop out of empocketed areas and avoid any unnecessary loss of lives. His rejection of the Nazi propaganda of "total victory" is clearly shown in his answer to a question he was often asked: when asked what he thought the eventual outcome of the war would be, he always answered: "I'll just let myself be surprised."

In conclusion it is clear that Mr. Bayerlein actively resisted the Nazi regime not only through his own free decisions in handling orders given by higher or even the highest leadership posts but also through his overall/personal conduct.

I am aware that making a false affidavit is punishable by law.

I declare emphatically that I was neither a member of the NSDAP nor am I in any other way incriminated by the Law for Liberation from National Socialism and Militarism.

/on the basis of my military service

(signed) Dr. J. Angermann

On this 20th day of February, 1947, appeared before me Attorney and Notary Public, Dr. Angermann, a person known personally to me to be the person who affixed his signature to this document above. I hereby place my hand and official seal of office to witness.

(signed, illegible)

(stamped: District Court, Idstein)

District Court Councilor

• • •

D2
Joachim Barth
Barth, Joachim
Südhämmer, February 20, 1947

AFFIDAVIT

I, Joachim Barth, resident at 137 Südhemmern, Kreis Minden/Westphalia make the following statement about Mr. Fritz BAYERLEIN of my own free will.

I have known Mr. Bayerlein since 1943. I was his subordinate in the Panzer Lehr Division.

1. As a division commander, Mr. Bayerlein personally strived to train his troops to conduct warfare ethically and fairly, and to treat prisoners of war and civilians properly.

2. For example, before the march into Hungary, he gave clear instructions for the troop directives in a speech he made in Bruck an der Leitha. He forbade the seizing of property and expressly stated that he wanted no harassment of the many Jews who lived in Hungary. Under his command there were no breaches and no crimes against humanity.

3. In his division he permitted every soldier to practice his religion and supported his army chaplains. He also personally attended religious services.

4. In his attitude toward the NSFO (Nazi field officer), he clearly showed that he was no Nazi general. When the NSFO arrived in his division, he said to his commanders, "Gentlemen, from this day on I will be under observation. I beg you all to be careful as well. I will see to it that this gentleman is not let loose among the troops." And that is exactly what he did. The troops never had to deal with the "snoop".

5. Mr. Bayerlein enjoyed the complete trust of his soldiers, whose most careful deployment he saw as his most important duty.

6. Mr. Bayerlein never supported the ideologies of National Socialism and he made no secret of his attitude in the sphere of his command.

I did not belong to the NSDAP or any of its organizations.

(signed) Joachim Barth
> This signature was duly witnessed:
> (signed: illegible)

· · ·

D3
Kurt Caesar
December 16, 1946

I was a subordinate of then Captain and later General Fritz Bayerlein from October 1941 to May 1943.

Although Mr. Bayerlein was by chance aware of my political views, he did not act against me in any way, but rather he let it be known to me in many private conversations that he flatly rejected the Nazi regime as a system and an idea. He hoped even then to find an opportunity to actively express his conviction.

His conduct and attitude toward prisoners of war and his treatment of his own soldiers are proof of his views. At every turn he did what was humanly possible to deflect or totally avoid hardships and difficulties.

His lifestyle – food and lodging – was as simple as that of the troops with which he shared all the dangers of the front.

Concerning my own person, I declare that:

I was never a member of the NSDAP or any of its organizations.

From 1929 to 1936 I was a correspondent for southern Europe for the *Zürcher Illustrierte*, Zürich. Since this publisher was anti-Nazi, I was excluded from the Reichsverband der dt. Presse (Press Association of the German Reich)

From 1936 on I was a member of the editorial staff of the central publisher for the Catholic World Youth Rome, Vatican.

In 1939 I belonged to the first active anti-fascist resistance cells in the province of Varese, Italy.

From 1943 on I actively participated in the anti-fascist underground movement (C.L.N. Comitato de Liberazione Nazionale and the C.V. L. Corpo Volontari Libertà). In the same year I was admitted to the Italian Communist Party and played a major role in preparing the uprising of April 25, 1945.

I was given the command of the 121st Partisan Brigade by the Brigade group B of the partisans.

I am willing at any time to give a sworn testimony for Mr. Bayerlein.

Kurt Caesar

• • •

D-4
Dr. Ernst Enderle
Würzburg, May 6, 1947
43 Zeppelin Street

AFFIDAVIT

From the end of 1944 to 1945, I, Dr. Ernst Enderle (medical doctor), was a subordinate of the former *Generalleutnant* Fritz BAYERLEIN in the Panzer Lehr Division. I served in the division staff as troop doctor (doctor of the reserves). I was with Mr. Bayerlein a lot then and often accompanied him on his drives to the front. Therefore, I am familiar with his views, his attitude and his life style.

Bayerlein never shied away from being in the hot (critical) spots of the fighting with his troops on the front so that he could spare them from senseless losses and take measures to prevent such losses at the right moment. His care for the troop was well-known. Bayerlein was not your typical general; instead he was always modest, affable and helpful. He was not typical in many ways. He often and openly expressed his views on the futility of the war and the necessity of ending it quickly to me and to all and in public.

Because of the views he held, he tried however he could to spare his troop.

After the unsuccessful assassination attempt on Hitler of July 20 – a failure he considered a true misfortune – he endeavored to save as many lives as possible in this futile war. For this reason, he never carried out a useless mission that senselessly sacrificed the troop.

This rule of his can be observed particularly in the division's action in the Saar Territory in November 1944, in the Ardennes Offensive of December 1944/1945 and in the fighting on the Remagen bridgehead in March 1945.

• • •

D-5
Dr. M. Frisch
Specialist for Surgery
17 Julius Promenade
Würzburg, May 17, 1947

AFFIDAVIT

I first met Mr. Fritz BAYERLEIN, presently resident in Ober-Ursel/Taunus, in the spring of 1943 when I was a ward doctor in the station hospital in Würzburg. At that time, he was a *Generalmajor* and recipient of the *Ritterkreuz*; he had come to Würzburg from the North African theater of combat to undergo an operation. From our very first meeting he made an extremely favorable and personable impression on me; his modest and undemanding nature and his easy-going manner were pleasantly not in keeping with his rank and high honors, and were in stark and welcome contrast to the manners of similarly ranked Nazi officers I had met many times before. In our daily meetings – Mr. Bayerlein received inpatient treatment for about 6 weeks – we soon came to speak of things that had nothing to do with his illness. A fellow Würzburger, he had seen me before and heard things about me; he also knew that already in December of 1939 my wife had been convicted by the Nazi special court of an offence against the *Heimtückegesetz*. This may, in fact, be the reason why Mr. Bayerlein trusted me enough to reveal his views. He was convinced of the utter futility of the war and sharply criticized the way the war was being conducted in Russia and in the Balkans. I also learned interesting details about the *Afrikakorps* and Field Marshal Rommel, Mr. Bayerlein's chief, for instance that already in 1942 at the *OKW* Rommel had called the continuation of the campaign in Africa useless and suggested that the troops be withdrawn. However, he was not able to convince anyone that his evaluation of the situation was correct and he had to put up with Göring's derision. Göring recommended that Rommel visit a cold water spa since he must be suffering from tropical madness because no one could tell him (Göring) that the Americans could make better airplanes and tanks than the Germans. If Rommel had said the Americans could make better razor blades, then he (Göring) may have believed him, but tanks and planes – that was just ridiculous.

If Mr. Bayerlein's opinion of the highest levels of command was withering, his opinion of the world vision and goals of the NSDAP was, if possible, even more scathing. I would like to emphasize that all of Mr. Bayerlein's comments and judgments showed complete objectivity and deep concern for the future of the German people.

In the summer of 1944, I treated Mr. Bayerlein for the second time, this time for a period of 4 weeks. He had come home from the front in North Africa with a foot injury. Our conversations continued. His worries about the outcome of the war had only grown. He considered all further resistance to be senseless because, whatever happened in the end, it would only lead to even greater loss of life and destruction of the homeland. For this reason, he thought it a crime to continue the war which had been lost long ago.

In conclusion, I would like to say that I consider Mr. Bayerlein to be a reputable professional soldier like the many who exist all over the world. He strongly rejected the ideology of National Socialism and just as strongly objected to the Nazi party's influence over the German Armed Forces, to which he belonged since 1917. The comments that he made to me, which I am willing to swear to at any time, must be given considerable weight coming as they do from an officer of his rank. It is of course right that he thought he could trust me, but on the other hand, he must have known that his remarks could have easily cost him his head, if I had been indiscreet. Therefore, I think that I am right to believe that Mr. Bayerlein is neither a militarist nor an active National Socialist in the sense of the Liberation Law.

I myself am not incriminated by this law according to the verdict reached by the Denazification Tribunal II in Würzburg.

The affixed signature was witnessed by the Police Department, Würzburg, May 19, 1947

(signed) Dr. Max Frisch
(stamped) Dr. M. Frisch, Specialist for Surgery,
17 Juliuspromenade, Würzburg

• • •

D-6
D 6: Fleischer
Rudolf Fleischer   Erbrach, January 20, 1947
No. 41 Erbrach/Obfr.

AFFIDAVIT

Of Rudolf FLEISCHER, born July 27, 1915.

Not a party member.

During the time that Mr. Fritz Bayerlein was the commander of the 3rd Panzer Division, I was the *Hauptmann Kommandeur* of the *Heeres-Flak-Artillerie-Abteilung* 314 in the 3rd Panzer Division and therefore a subordinate of former *Generalmajor* Bayerlein

The following statement was written from memory since all of my records have been lost. Therefore, I cannot guarantee the completeness of the statement.

1. Mr. Bayerlein joined the 3rd Panzer Division as commander near the end of 1943. Like any new commander he was received with a little skepticism. But soon after he took command, this skepticism turned into great esteem and boundless trust. At first in the officer corps, a bit later but much more firmly among the men; because he was the only division commander I have ever come across who was known, admired and loved by almost all of the front soldiers.

2. From the beginning, Mr. B. stressed again and again in his conversations and his command talks that he, as a front soldier, placed great value on the ethical and humane conduct of war. He often told us about the "ethical warfare" in the North African theater where he had come from, and he emphasized that he wished to continue at all events in the same manner in the Eastern theater of war as well.

3. His attitude to his subordinates was always very compassionate and kind. He treated civilians and prisoners of war in the same way because he always saw and respected them as people first. I know of no case – and it is in my opinion all together impossible – that Mr. Bayerlein ever gave an order that resulted in a subordinate tormenting or harassing a civilian or a prisoner in any way. In this, he always tried to instruct us and act an example to us all.

4. On his political views I can only say that I am not aware that he ever spread Nazi propaganda through the troop, because the Nazi methods, warfare and personnel policies went completely against his grain. Whenever he did, however, have to pass on an order from the higher levels of Nazi leadership which revealed their incompetence too obviously, he did it in such a cynical way that those who agreed with him were happy to hear him and sometimes even worried about him, because he risked his own neck with his open manner, if the wrong people ever got wind of it. For instance, it was fairly widely known that he listened to foreign radio broadcasts on an almost regular basis; so we spoke very openly about the latest news from London and Moscow.

5. In his leadership he always tried to spare his men. His motto was: always lead yourself, and always put yourself in the worst hotspots, and never risk a human life lightly. By following these rules he forced his subordinate officers as well to stay with their men and ensured in this way that his troops would be deployed as carefully as possible because they would never be led from behind a desk, over the radio, or through a telephone line. That is also why no senseless orders were given that were based only on heavy pencil lines drawn on a map and whose execution could mean the real loss of many lives. The lengths that he would go for his people is shown in the fact that he was also present – if only as an observer or advisor –

a.) When he had to send parts of his division to other groups. I can remember one incident in the area of southwestern Tscherkassy very well. Some troops from the 3rd Panzer Division were supposed to go with another division to mount an attack through a swampy area and into a wooded area. There were heavy losses, success was very questionable, and the troops already seemed to be lost. All of a sudden, Bayerlein turned up in the most dangerous spots and led his men back to safety; without his help they would have all probably been lost. I myself was an eye-witness to this event and can best testify as to how happy we all were to see him and how we were all filled with a feeling of safety, security and trust at the sight of him.

b.) His care for his troop is shown even more compellingly by the following example. We were near Kirovograd. When I brought him the message that we were being surrounded by 3 divisions, he thought a bit then said to me something along these lines: "Kirovograd sounds like Stalingrad, we'll break out of this encirclement before it's too hard to break through." Everyone who heard this order was overjoyed to receive this glimmer of hope. Then he ranted – which he often did – but this time with particular vehemence – about the senseless way the Nazis were waging the war and the "idiotic *Führerbefehle*" and stated that he was not willing to pay attention to them but instead would do what he had to for the welfare of his men. Everyone said that he broke contact with his superior commanders on purpose so that he would not even have to receive the stupid orders that he wasn't going to carry out anyway; besides, he was much better oriented anyway because he would get his information directly from Radio Moscow.

c.) Another example of the way he shared the hardships of the war with his men and did his utmost for their care is the fact that even in the cold nights of the winter of 1943/44 he stayed on the battle field with his troop instead of going off to warm staff quarters. When he got too cold on his haystack, he would move for a time into a hut that would then become his "division staff quarters". If he allowed himself this type of relief, then he granted his men any type of relief possible. And I am convinced that most of the soldiers in this war lived better than he did while he belonged to the 3rd Panzer Division.

6.) These few examples and lines should be enough to give you an impression of the attitude, lifestyle and leadership style of Mr. Bayerlein, who in my opinion was the most well-liked and admired commander of the 3rd Panzer Division.

In summary, I can say that to my knowledge no soldier nor for that matter any person was ever sacrificed because of the actions or deeds of Bayerlein but hundreds were saved from death or injury because of his leadership.

(signed) Rudolf FLEISCHER

The signature above of Mr. Rudolf Fleischer is hereby witnessed and notarized.

Erbrach, January 21, 1947

Mayor of the Markt Erbrach (Oberfr.)

Fee: 2 RM

Reg. No. 221/46

· · ·

D7

Alexander Hartdegan

Bonn/Rhein, 25 NOV 1946

Bonn/Rhein 22a

Baumschulallee 17 (British Zone)

Statutory Declaration

In recognition of the significance of a declaration made under oath and of the legal penalties and other consequences of misrepresentation, I give in the following a description of the personality of the former *Generalleutnant* of Panzer Troops

Fritz Bayerlein

The official declaration also includes details about my person, and my relationship to Mr. Bayerlein as necessary for a complete understanding of things.

I.) Concerning myself: After the assumption of power by National Socialism in 1933, I went to Spain and then to South America. In Rio de Janeiro, for the first time, I came into opposition with an NSDAP party functionary, in particular with regard to the fact that I had married a Brazilian citizen whose racial background I could not prove, in knowing disregard of the NSDAP's racial program. I responded to the conflict that ensued in connection with this question by marring my wife under Brazilian law, with total disregard of any caution concerning possible reprisals against my relatives back in Germany (who had already been threatened). This action led directly to the Party back in the homeland threatening to take recourse on the one hand against my brother, who worked in the Foreign Service, while on the other hand threatening a direct confiscation of my financial assets remaining in Germany.

When I was called up for the Army at the beginning of the war (at the time, I was on a European vacation), I was shunned by the local Party office due to my fundamentally negative stance and was only able to get out of being publicly prosecuted due to the fact that I was in service as an officer.

After being taken prisoner in 1944, I was flown over to a POW camp in North America, where I had a leading position in the Anti-Nazi officer's camp at Ruston, Louisiana, which had been co-founded by me.

I was constantly together in Service with Mr. Bayerlein in the years from September 1942 (El Alamein) to July 1944 (27 July 1944 St. Lô) and during this time held the following positions under his direct command:

A loyal and decisive witness: Generalmajor Bayerlein and his steadfast aide-de-camp, Hauptmann Alexander Hartdegen, on a walking tour of Budapest, Hungary in March 1944. Following the defeat in Tunisia in May 1944, the men were evacuated to Italy. Hartdegen followed Bayerlein to Russia; then he was assigned to the Panzer Lehr Division. After the war Hartdegen testified for Bayerlein's Spruchkammer and provided statements regarding his health during the flight out of Tunisia in order for Bayerlein to obtain a 60% disability rating with the German veterans' administration. (Bundesarchiv Koblenz Bild 146/2002/10/7a)

Oberleutnant Alexander Hartdegen and Oberstleutnant Fritz Bayerlein met in March 1942. Hartdegen was one of the few men with whom Bayerlein maintained a lifelong friendship. Both Hartdegen and Bayerlein aided German author Dr. Paul Carell Schmidt in documenting their experiences in Carell's books on the D-Day Invasion, Operation Barbarossa and Stalingrad. Bayerlein and Hartdegen relayed their first-hand accounts in these books in great detail. (Photograph courtesy of the Hartdegen family to author.)

Hartdegen married a young, pretty woman, Miss Edith Teichmann, of German parentage who lived in Rio de Janeiro. They married on December 24, 1938. Upon his return for a vacation in Germany a few weeks later to show off his new bride to his family, to his surprise, he was immediately drafted into the German Army and was not allowed to return to Brazil. He and Edith made the trip after the war was over, taking their baby daughter, Dolores, with them. They had a second daughter, Ivone, who was born in Brazil. (Photograph courtesy of the Hartdegen family to author.)

1942-1943	Personal Ordnance Officer (Adjutant)
1943-1944	(Winter) Division Adjutant, 3rd Panzer Division
1944	Personal Ordnance Officer (Adjutant), Panzer Lehr Division

Since I was bound to Mr. Bayerlein above and beyond official duty through shared political and ideological principles as well as the closest personal relationship, I am in a position to objectively and exhaustively comment on his personality and attitude toward the NSDAP and the 3rd Reich. Regarding my own person, the following individuals are prepared to provide information:

1. Dr. of Law Walter Peters, Assessor of the State Court of Bonn, Bonn/Rhein.
2. Herr Adolf Lackert, Political Prisoner, Bonn/Rhein
3. Mr. Allan Jones, Priory Close, Bridlington, Yorkshire
4. The witnesses that I gained in the USA from the successfully completed democratic educational training.

On the Person of Mr. Bayerlein:

The decisive impression or Mr. Bayerlein's personality I gained on the occasion of his award of the Oakleaves [to the Knights Cross] decoration. It was customary to bestow large gifts on the soldiers who won this high decoration, which was usually taken care of by presenting them with a large land holding in the German-occupied territories. Bayerlein refused such an offer, however, on the grounds that he could not justify such personal self-enrichment. This stance also marked the general attitude he held toward the conduct of the war and the application of all orders regarding measures to be taken toward the peoples of the German-occupied areas and in particular, his attitude toward the troops he led. Mr. Bayerlein, as an officer of highly recognized abilities, was not only a modest person in his lifestyle, but also looked after his troops in the same measure. Not only did he never commit any crimes against humanity, but rather had in addition always supported the view that despite the war, the basic tenets of human decency toward the local civilian population and foreign troops were to be upheld. In particular, he practiced an exceptional tolerance toward Jews; upon moving into quarters in Maab (Gyoer-Hungary), he called in a Jew as his translator – even though this action was noted and disapproved of by several other commanders. If, despite the many documented instances of his stepping in on behalf of the racially persecuted, no immediate penal action was taken against him, this was not attributable to any tolerance from his superiors or the highest Party offices [in the occupied territories], but rather to the fact that they could not do without him on account of his exceptional abilities. It was a natural consequence of this general attitude that he was personally fearless and did not avoid personal danger during combat. In contrast to the many frequently observed cases in the senior leadership he had neither secured any advantages from his position, nor had he ever enriched himself from the possessions of others. His strict orders within his area of command. The following facts, in detail, are worthy of particular emphasis:

1. At the command briefing (in which I took part) at Bruck on the Leitha prior to the entry into Hungary, he exposed himself to strong criticism – though not targeted against him personally – from his subordinate commanders, due to his strict prohibition of any excesses against the local population, particularly against Jews.

2. After entering Hungary, he gained the special trust of Cardinal Seredi – Furst Primas of Hungary. Mr. Bayerlein and I were the only German officers who were provided quarters from 18 March 1944 to 4 May 1944 in the [princely] Palace at Estergom. Many conversations took place in my presence between Seredi (who was killed by the SS in 1945) and Bayerlein, which above all concerned the persecuted Jews in the area of the neighboring 16th SS Division.[2] The subsequent measures taken by Bayerlein led to a sharp disagreement with the commander of this division.[3] After transfer of the Panzer Lehr Division to France, Herr Bayerlein received a personal communication from Cardinal Seredi in which he thanked Bayerlein for his humanitarian disposition, and gave him the blessing of the church for a long life.

3. After taking command of the 3rd Panzer Division (winter of 1943/44) in Russia, Bayerlein ensured, through particularly strict orders, the humane treatment of the civilian population and especially the Russian wounded.

4. His deliberate rejection of the NS war leadership was particularly documented in his attitude toward the events of 20 July 1944. At this point in time, his troops [Panzer Lehr Division] were committed in the area of St. Lô. As the former Chief of Staff of the German-Italian Panzer Army under Field Marshal Rommel, Bayerlein stood in constant touch with Rommel as Commander of Army Group D. At these discussions, Bayerlein was informed of the preparations for the 20th of July. In particular Bayerlein, in my presence, expressed to Rommel his complete agreement with the principles of this 20th of July group. Bayerlein sent me – not his adjutant, or a General Staff officer – as his personal orderly to further discussions with Field Marshal Rommel about the issues (at that time I held the rank of Captain). This and his frankness about the Nazi war leadership incurred extreme mistrust, and in this way he ran the danger of being liquidated in the terror being spread ever wider by the N.S. leadership staff. Through the repeated consultation with Field Marshal Rommel – specifically on the 25th of June 1944 and on 5 July 1944 in the area of La Roch Gion/Sein, which I had to conduct on Bayerlein's behalf, I received for Bayerlein Rommel's direct personal instruction with regard to further behavior during the coming political events and the expected changes in the direction of the war that would come of them. I had a similar conversation with General Speidel and Bayerlein previously, in Paris with General Stulpnagel (who at that time was in overall command of France). The planned collaboration between Rommel and Bayerlein never came to pass only because Rommel, after our last conference, was wounded in an attack by a fighter [aircraft] near Liseux.

I gave a report about this entire series of events to the U.S. intelligence service in Normandy and eventually to the Secret Service at Camp 7, England.

For submission to a German Authority (De-Nazification Tribunal).

With reference to my Statutory Declaration of 25 November 1946 about the personality of the former Generalleutnant of Panzer Troops

Fritz Bayerlein

I have the following points to add, which especially show the humanity and empathy of Bayerlein for his troops – and among the following points in particular, undoubtedly Bayerlein's most impressive achievement: protecting the lives of thousands of soldiers – saving them from senseless destruction.

1.) On 4 November 1942, when the El Alamein position was already lost, the German Afrikakorps was defending in the area of Tel el Mappara against heavily superior enemy forces. In the afternoon hours this position had already been breeched by the enemy in two locations, with the Italian Corps on the right flank mostly wiped out. The D.A.K. commander, General von Thoma, had been captured, although he had in fact sought death in battle since he could not bear the senseless Führer command to "defend every foot of ground", or that "not a single step backwards" be taken (I was with him constantly, right up until just before his capture). In this critical situation Rommel gave over command of the DAK to the then Colonel Bayerlein, and with this also the decision of whether or not he wanted to carry out the Führer Befehl. Rommel withdrew to his rearward command post at Fuka (60 kilometers from Tel el Mampara) as soon as the assignment order was given. Bayerlein immediately decided not to carry out the Führer Befehl – and to withdraw instead, to the heights east of Fuka – by this action fully accepting any consequences for not carrying out the Führer's command. Bayerlein then personally lead the Afrikakorps back to Fuka during the nights of 4 and 5 November 1942. Bayerlein saved many German soldiers from death by this decision, as dangerous as it was for him personally, for if he had held at Tel el Mampara and defended there till the last man in accordance with the Führer's command, the Corps would have been encircled and utterly smashed by the murderous artillery fire and destructive airpower of the many times superior enemy forces. Thousands of German soldiers would have forfeited their lives. By this daring – and for him, personally dangerous – decision to evade, and for his disregard of the Führer's order, Bayerlein earned himself great respect with his soldiers that was well recognized by the troops under him – which I myself could discern and which I heard mentioned during my imprisonment in the Anti-Nazi camp in America.

2.) Also characteristic of Bayerlein is the view that he displayed even long before the lost El Alamein battle – quite publicly – that this senseless war had to be broken off, since otherwise the "festering sore that is Germany" would once and for all be totally cut out of Europe.

[Signature]
Alexander Hartdegen

• • •

D8 Held
Karl Held
Würzburg, January 3, 1947
Radio Technician
52/I Friedrich-Spee St.

AFFIDAVIT

I hereby swear to the accuracy of my statement below on the person of Mr. Fritz Bayerlein:

Between 1921 and 1945 I served three times under the command of former General Bayerlein. I also know him and his family very well in civilian life and therefore I can state the following:

1. From 1922 to 1925 I was a private in the company of then *Leutnant* Bayerlein (3rd Comp. J.R. 21). Even then, Mr. Bayerlein proved to be a comradely and particularly compassionate officer, who did everything for his soldiers. His democratic attitude and his social aptitude were well-known. Bayerlein was extremely well-liked and admired by all.

The following incident is typical:

On November 9, 1923 Bayerlein's company was sent to Munich to put down the Hitler putsch because his company was considered particularly reliable and loyal to the government and the Weimar constitution and because it never participated in the secret training of Black *Reichswehr* groups or Nazi organizations. When the company arrived, the putsch had been quelled for the large part, but during the clean-up action in and around Munich the company and particularly *Leutnant* Bayerlein were insulted, taunted and even spit on by the Nazi-loving population of Munich and other *Reichswehr* troops who supported Hitler.

The mere fact that this company was chosen for such a task shows that Bayerlein was democratically minded and loyal to the Weimar Republic. At this point, I would also like to mention that before his promotion to *Leutnant*, Bayerlein had been chosen to represent his company several times.

2. In the years 1935-1936, I worked under then *Hauptmann (Captain)* Bayerlein as a civilian employee in the staff of the 15th Division in Würzburg. Here once again, Mr. Bayerlein proved to be a kind and compassionate officer and therefore enjoyed the great approval and respect of his soldiers.

3. In his private life as well, Bayerlein showed the same decency and integrity of spirit. In particular, I must mention that he fulfilled his religious duties as well and did not miss Sunday services in a time when such things were no longer considered necessary or even desirable.

I can confirm here that his way of thinking and his actions were thoroughly democratic and socially minded. Bayerlein stood in stark contrast to the Ia-Officer *Oberstleutnant* Dostler, who adhered completely to party lines and constantly moved in the social circles of the *Gauleiter*, mayor, and other party big shots and was even on a first name basis with many of them, addressing many per *du*. I know that Mr. Bayerlein completely rejected this and he was detached and reserved in manner with the party members he had to work with. As a result, Dostler, who was his superior, mistrusted him greatly and pressured and humiliated Bayerlein whenever and however he could. While Bayerlein was known to his staff and troop for being completely democratic, Dostler was known as being the type of Nazi officer who would be recognized by the *Gauleiter* and indeed he was awarded a pistol of honor.

4. My third service encounter with then *Generalmajor* Bayerlein occurred in September of 1944 when I was transferred as a non-commissioned officer to the Panzer intelligence service of the Panzer Lehr Division where Bayerlein was commander. From the point of view of the troops that served under him, I can describe Mr. Bayerlein's character exactly. Mr. Bayerlein was known and very well-liked by every last one of the men of the division. Even as division commander, he lived with the troops and the manner and conditions in which he lived barely differed from those of his troops. He provided for his troop as best he could and spared them in action as much as he possibly could. Conversely, he put himself in the way of all kinds of danger and could be found most of the time on the front line of

the battle with his soldiers. I know that Bayerlein's way of carefully deploying his troops to avoid unnecessary losses was sharply criticized by his superior officers and that, in the end, he had to relinquish the command of his division unexpectedly in January 1945 when he saved a battle group of his division from a futile and deadly mission during the Ardennes offensive.

Bayerlein's rejection of brutal Nazi methods for warfare and deployment as well as for the treatment of local populations and prisoners of war was well-known and admired. Any member of the division could testify to this as I do.

His way of thinking and handling is best depicted by his actions of April 15, 1946 when General Bayerlein surrendered at the head of his entire corps in the Ruhrgebiet in a time when battle was still ongoing and such an action was still very dangerous. Through his decision, Mr. Bayerlein saved the lives of many soldiers and saved many German towns from senseless destruction. I know from my own experience there and from the comments of my comrades in the prisoner of war camps that this action of *General* Bayerlein met with great admiration and approval.

(signed) Karl Held

• • •

D9
Adam Hetzel
d.o.b.: August 1, 1917
salaried employee
Pferdemarkt 123 1/2
Deggendorf/ Ndb.

<u>AFFIDAVIT</u>
In full recognition of the importance of my statement, I depose the following affidavit.

Mr. Fritz BAYERLEIN was my company chief from the time I was called up on November 3, 1937 to November 1938 in the 2nd Comp. M.G. Battalion 6 in Coburg; at that time I was a private.

In his role as company leader, Mr. Bayerlein was extremely well-liked and admired by all of the company members for his compassionate attitude and for the great care he showed in protecting his troop. He was a man who had an open ear and a helping hand for all of his subordinates' troubles, both military and private, to a degree far above the norm in the armed forces. He used all of his professional authority as well as his private means to ensure the welfare of the men entrusted to him. That is why his troop loved him like a father. He took the fear out of the horrible time of recruitment for us soldiers because under his leadership the usual methods employed by the trainers who mostly still came from the hundred thousand man army were impossible. I know that his orders, which stressed the fair and careful treatment of his men, were resisted and sharply criticized by the older non-commissioned officers.

In my opinion, Mr. Bayerlein was an officer who in no way held to the beliefs of Prussian militarism which has had such a harmful effect on our people. His religious attitude was exemplary in every way. Under his leadership, every soldier was able to practice his religion freely and openly. I am not aware that Bayerlein ever spread any type of Nazi propaganda in his training; he trained his men strictly in military matters. His life style was simple for a man of his station and he was always ready and willing to use his own private means to alleviate the worries and troubles of his men.

In his capacity as commander and with his own private means, he made it possible for me to visit my seriously ill mother several times before her death and thanks to his very compassionate nature I was able to arrive at my mother's death bed just one hour before she passed away. He showed this exceedingly noble-minded generosity not only to me but to many other soldiers. For Mr. Bayerlein, a person's standing was not the important thing, and when it came to personal troubles, he had an open heart for everyone, even the humblest soldier.

In my entire military and private life I have never met another superior who possessed a more humane and magnanimous character than Mr. Bayerlein.

Deggendorf, January 26, 1947   (signed) <u>Adam Hetzel</u>

The validity of the signature of … (Adam Hetzel) … is hereby witnessed.
(stamped) The City of Deggendorf, January 27, 1947
Fee of 0.60 RM paid, No. 2053
D 9b: Hetzel

D9 b – Copy
Excerpt from a letter from Adam Hetzel, salaried employee in Deggendorf.
Deggendorf, January 26, 1947

Dear Mr. Bayerlein,
It was with great joy that I received your letter of the 13th of this month. Your request that I make a statement about your commission with the M.G.6 I can grant with great pleasure; I only hope that I can repay even in some small part the great good you did for me and all of my fellow soldiers. I am sure that anyone who served in a troop that you led could only report the best about your conduct. I hope that you can convince the Denazification Tribunal of your truly noble-minded and humane conduct with the help of this collection of statements. It would be a great injustice if a person like you who in his actions only wanted the best for the men he led and who helped to relieve so many hardships would now be made to atone for it. Your career … (letter provided ends)

Signed Adam Hetzel

• • •

D10
February 11, 1947
Hanna Huber
Massage Therapist
4 Kameterbichl, Neuhaus-Schliersee

AFFIDAVIT

I have known Mr. Fritz Bayerlein for over 15 years and have socialized frequently with the Dittmar and Bayerlein families. Therefore, I can swear to the following statement:

1. I was present during the incident of September 1941 when in front of a crowd of more than 100 people Mr. Bayerlein took action against German guards who were abusing Russian prisoners of war at the train station in Würzburg; he stopped the abuse and thereby subjected himself both to the crass insults of the crowd and to the formal charges brought by *Gauamtsleiter* Languth to the Gestapo.

2. On many occasions, I personally witnessed Mr. Bayerlein listening to foreign broadcasts in the company of his family and others including myself when he came home to Würzburg on short furloughs during the war.

3. I can confirm based on many incidents that Mr. Bayerlein never used the greeting *Heil Hitler* instead he pointedly used the greeting *Grüß Gott*.

I have been placed in the group of exonerated persons per a verdict of the Denazification Tribunal.

(signed) Hanna Huber
The validity of the signature above is witnessed by Mayor (illegible signature)
Schliersee, May 14, 1947

• • •

D11
Heinz Hiltmann
40 Ludwig Street
Hof-Sale
February 5, 1947

AFFIDAVIT

I have known former General Fritz BAYERLEIN since the African campaign of 1945. In the last few months of that campaign I worked closely with him. Because of our continual daily contact both within the scope of our duties and outside of our duties, I have been able to form an accurate and reliable picture of him as a man and a soldier and particularly about his relationship to the troops he commanded and his relationship to all other direct subordinates, i.e., personnel, teams and officers.

General Bayerlein who led the German Africa Corps during the more than six month-long difficult retreat and who in the end commanded all of the troops of the former Rommel army was exceedingly well-loved by the troop. He was considered to be an extremely capable military leader who was both humane and responsible, who never risked his men's lives unnecessarily, and who in particular never ordered actions that were militarily questionable or could result in a high number of casualties because of personal ambition or a thirst for glory. If at all possible, he was at the head of his fighting troops on a daily basis and without any thought to his own person and, especially in the difficult months of the retreat, he was ceaselessly concerned with trying to deploy the troops in the best and least dangerous way and to provide for them as best he could. The troops knew this and they placed the highest trust in General Bayerlein's leadership. He always paid great attention to the provisioning of the troops, the so-called troop support, which was the area I was responsible for.

The general had an especially warm and comradely personal relationship with his officers and staff teams from whom he demanded nothing that he was not willing to do himself.

His own way of life was very simple and unpretentious. For example, he refused again and again to make use of one of the many opportunities that presented themselves to take positions away from the front lines in the city of Tunis.

Very early on, General Bayerlein expressed his concerns about the further conduct of the war both in general and in particular in the African theater and in the last phase especially he personally suffered much in the knowledge that he could not align his orders to his deep conviction that to continue fighting was hopeless. Thanks in great part to his pure and fundamentally decent attitude, German warfare in Africa was in all respects, for example in the treatment of prisoners of war, fair and humane up to the very end, a fact that is even recognized repeatedly by those questioned on the Allied side.

Although for a long time he was barely healthy enough to remain in action, General Bayerlein continued his daily drives to the front lines until his increasingly debilitating arthritis rendered him fully incapable of moving and forced him to spend months in the base hospital.

In my honest opinion, not only was General Bayerlein not a true Nazi much less an active Nazi but he was not a militarist either in the sense of the Law for Liberation from National Socialism and Militarism.

I hereby depose this affidavit and swear to its accuracy.

(signed) Heinz Hiltmann

First State Prosecutor
Former Captain of the Res.
The validity of the signature above is certified by the city council of Hof represented by (illegible signature), Hof, February 8, 1947.

• • •

D12
Hegener-Hachmann
Hanxleden
January 15, 1947

The undersigned has given the following Statutory Declaration:
Several days before the entry of American troops on April 9, 1945 General Fritz Bayerlein was quartered on my property. I got to know General Bayerlein as a genial, friendly person. In his mild manner he displayed a great simplicity, despite his high rank. His personality, as I came to know it, brought him great respect and high regard from his subordinates. General Bayerlein often described the futile continuation of the war as

insanity. He strove to protect German property – something I must personally stress most strongly. When, on April 8th, a German heavy artillery piece was positioned directly on my property, I sought out General Bayerlein with a request to step in, since I was housing 24 children as well as many adults in my cellar. Indignant, he immediately ordered the guns repositioned to a distance of 300 meters from the farmstead.

As a former artilleryman in the World War of 1914-18, I well knew what serious consequences would ensue, were the gun to go into action [*on the farmstead*]. I thus owe a great debt of thanks to General Bayerlein, since his attitude saved not only the farmhouse, but also certainly contributed to the fact that here in Hanxleden, neither civilian nor soldier was killed.

Johannes Hegener Hachmann
The above signature was given
in my presence
Henneborn, January 15, 1947
Mayor

• • •

D13
Hartwig Huebner
Boeblingen
Stuttgarter Str. 72

Statutory Declaration

1.) On the basis of the suspension decision of the De-Nazification Tribunal of Mergentheim of Nov. 4, 1946, File number 33-1-2170, the De-Nazification trial against me was suspended in accordance with the 1st sub-paragraph of the Amnesty-Decree of 8/8/46.

2.) As a former subordinate of General Bayerlein, I confirm the following under oath:

From the 1st to the 4th of April 1945 Bayerlein's corps was deployed in the area around Winterberg. Winterberg itself was an area with many field hospitals, and quarters for bombed out civilians. I was aware of the Army Group order to protect/defend Winterberg, an important hub, to the last man. As leader of the Panzer Lehr's reconnaissance battalion, which was situated directly in front of Winterberg, I can therefore confirm the following: as the Americans attacked Winterberg on 2 April, General Bayerlein gave the order to NOT defend the civilian population. During the night of 2 to 3 April, Winterberg was left to the Americans without a fight by parts of my battalion. The troops, [incidentally] my battalion, took up positions north of the city. General Bayerlein ordered that the Americans in the city should not be fired on – nor should any round be fired into the town for that matter – this order was also carried out; and so it came about that neither the Americans, nor the Germans fired into the town during the entire combat action. The city was completely spared due to this. General Bayerlein, with whom I stood in constant contact during this time, reported to Army Group Model that the city had been taken by the enemy. The army group ordered the re-taking of this important road junction. General Bayerlein declined to carry out this order. My battalion stood to the north of Winterberg until 4 April without doing anything, and was then withdrawn further northward. By his choice of action General Bayerlein had saved from destruction the lives of many Germans and a lot of German property. That General Bayerlein acted this way despite the great personal danger that he exposed himself to by not following the Fuhrer order [*Führer Befehl*] for the holding of traffic intersections, says a great deal for him.

3.) I was with General Bayerlein constantly from January of 1944 onward and can confirm that he was humane in his combat operations, in his treatment of POWs and the civilian population of occupied areas. He gave the strictest orders for conducting the war in such a manner, and these were carried out to the letter by the troops.

Hartwig Huebner
Boblingen, the 7th of April 1947
The accuracy of the signature given above
is hereby confirmed
(SIGNATURE)

• • •

D15
Kauffmann, Kurt
Böblingen, April 5, 1947
72 Stuttgarter Street
Böblingen/Würt.

AFFIDAVIT
On
Mr.Fritz Bayerlein
A.) Preface:

I belonged neither to the Nazi party nor any of its organizations. To the contrary, I was punished by the *Reichsführer SS* for subversive and defeatist statements.

I served under Mr. Fritz Bayerlein as a close co-worker twice:

1.) From January 1940 to October 1940 as *Oberleutnant* and ordnance officer on the staff of the XIX Panzer Corps, whose 1st general staff officer Mr. Bayerlein was at that time,

2.) From January 1944 to January 1945, as *Oberstleutnant* and first general staff officer of the Panzer Lehr Division, whose commander Mr. Bayerlein was at that time.
B.) To the point:
I. General Remarks:

Mr. Bayerlein is one of the former officers who by force of their personalities and sympathetic natures soon won over the affections of their subordinates and comrades. He expressed his opinions quite strongly to his superiors. He possessed what we called in the army "civil courage". He did not allow himself to be blinded by slogans, or whitewash,

Major i.G. Bernd Werncke, Ib, Logistics Officer and Hauptmann Kurt Kauffmann, Ia of Panzer Lehr Division. Mr. Werncke remembered that he, Bayerlein and Kauffmann would secretly criticize Hitler, a court-martial offense. (Private Collector Photograph.)

Another dependable and collaborative witness for Bayerlein: Oberstleutnant i.G. Kurt Kauffmann, Ia. First General Staff Officer, Panzer Lehr Division. Kauffmann, long considered an anti-Nazi, was one of Bayerlein's favorite staff officers and confidants. He was transferred to Panzer Lehr Division on January 16th, 1944.

or by the advantages he could secure in his position, instead he considered each situation soberly and from a thoroughly ethical perspective.

Personally, he placed little value on the formalities that went with his position. He visited the troops dressed inconspicuously in his simple field uniform. Even in times of quiet or while the troops were being built up, he did not deviate from his modest habits. He himself made do with the crudest conditions, while at the same time demanding and striving for the greatest degree of support and comfort for the troop.

In the field, Mr. Bayerlein could be found in the most critical spots so that he could assess the situation from the viewpoint of the troops and make an appropriate report to his superiors.

He never ordered the impossible, just to be able to report to his superiors that "something was happening." He prepared missions in a way that ensured the safety of the troop as much as possible. If his demands could not be met to a minimum or even if bad orders were given by the High Command of the Armed Forces, he would only carry them out as far as they were in keeping with his responsibility to his men. In certain situations he even led on his own authority, against express orders.

It is only natural then that the troops with which he shared all dangers on a daily and even hourly basis (for example, I know that he was shot in his car by fighter bombers four times) soon came to know the fundamental character of their commander, which I have briefly outlined here, and stood by him with a degree of trust that is rarely seen.

His soldierly bearing, combined with his complete disregard for Nazi and militaristic views, the many proofs of his humane and comradely attitude towards civilians and soldiers, his disregard of danger, his disregard of his own personal safety and comfort, and his compassion for his troops made him appear to my eyes as simply one of the ideal types of military leader.

II.) Details to underline the characteristics mentioned above.
1. Careful and thoughtful deployment of the troops.
a.) Rescue of the Panzer Lehr Division from the Argentes-Falaise pocket.

Once the Americans had broken through the Normandy front, it was clear to every insightful officer that only a fast retreat to the Seine could prevent the complete destruction of the division. In spite of this, the High Command of the Armed Forces, completely misjudging the facts, gave the order to mount a counterattack. After considering our own options, the vastly superior numbers and, above all, provisions and equipment on the Allied side, Mr. Bayerlein sized up the situation quite correctly and maneuvered his division out of the pocket in a well-planned manner and against orders in about fourteen days of fighting – more against his superior officers than against the enemy itself. General von Funk of the Panzer troops wanted Bayerlein brought before a court martial because of his actions, but this was never done because von Funk was replaced and the turbulent development of the situation proved Bayerlein to be completely in the right.

Mr. Bayerlein's clear-sighted leadership saved many people from death and injury because in that pocket they would have been battered by the murderous artillery fire and the deadly action of the enemy air force. This way of leading troops with the aim of sparing life and limb was, it seems, being noticed by the higher-ups; (I know this) because one day when reporting to Field Marshal Model, he remarked to me: "Well, you guys just do what you think is right." But this also shows at the same time what a risk Mr. Bayerlein was running by taking these kinds of measures on his own.

b.) Fight in the Saar Territory.

In November 1944, the division was given the "historic" mission of saving the fate of Alsace by mounting a counterattack after the Allies had broken through the *Zaberner Senke.*

This mission, requiring about 2 army corps but given to only one division to execute, was so impossible that Mr. Bayerlein only carried out the "gist" of the order. By mounting the attacks with a narrowly defined objective and eventual cessation of attack, he kept the division from being surrounded and destroyed by enemy fire.

The result was that Mr. Bayerlein was sharply reprimanded by the 1st Army and later by the XII Corps, which "wanted to initiate a change in division leadership."

c.) Ardennes Offensive December 1944.

The fuel supply available for the preparation of this offensive was so short that it was impossible to mount a deep attack; even more so, since all Rhine bridges had been destroyed and it was impossible to replenish supplies sufficiently by truck in winter when the Eifel and the Ardennes region were covered with ice.

Fully aware of the situation, Mr. Bayerlein led his division in such a way that it was not destroyed by blindly following the motto of the day: "straight over the Meuse, without looking to the right or the left." While parts of the neighboring 2nd Panzer Division, which had unwisely pressed ahead, were destroyed, our division kept safe held in the hands of its commander and spared from senseless losses.

Once again, this leadership with a plan brought Mr. Bayerlein only harsh rebukes from the combat command general and the commander in chief.

One of his regiment commanders, *Oberstleutnant* (lieutenant colonel) von Poschinger, who on his (Bayerlein's) command avoided a push forward over Dasburg, was not granted an already pending promotion as punishment. Mr. Bayerlein, however, managed to arrange things so that this officer was not penalized.

d.) Unauthorized retrieval of the Poschinger combat group from the area around southern Hoscheid.

This combat group serving under another section was ordered to hold a hopeless position. Even though he was no longer in charge of the group, Mr. Bayerlein led this combat group out of an impossible situation in which it was ordered to hold to the last man, thus saving them from certain destruction.

This action resulted in a court martial for assumption of authority and defying the *Führer*'s orders "to hold positions to the last man."

The events described in a) – d) finally resulted in Mr. Bayerlein's sudden removal from his division on January 23, 1945 and transfer to a subordinate post on the staff of the army group.

2.) Protection of the Civilian Population

a. March into Hungary in March 1944

In a command meeting before the march into Hungary, Mr. Bayerlein announced his guidelines for the treatment of civilians, in particular the Jews. He forbade any type of purchase or requisition, not to mention plundering. He did not want, as he put it then, to dirty his hands or sully the honor of the division through dishonorable behavior. He threatened the harshest punishments for those who did not follow these guidelines. That is why there were no such excesses in his division like there were on a regular basis and in the worst form in the neighboring SS division, which in particular persecuted and harassed Jews.

b.) Extended stay with Cardinal Serédi, Primate of Hungary.

Throughout his time of action in Hungary Mr. Bayerlein stayed of his own accord in Esztergom with Cardinal Serédi, who though friendly with the Germans was also an opponent of the Nazis. His stay and social contact with the cardinal was politically very dangerous for Mr. Bayerlein It was an open demonstration of his own religious views and a rejection of the Nazi race theory since the Jews of Hungary were under the cardinal's protection.

3.) Work with officers who opposed the Nazis.

On the staff of the Panzer Lehr Division there were several officers who were not "clean" in the Nazi sense of that word. Despite his duty as division commander to remove these officers, he kept them on his staff and supported them substantially:

a. Mr. v. Heyden, *Leutnant* and ordnance officer, presently resident of Helmstorf/ Holstein, was employed on the staff by Mr. Bayerlein although a damaging evaluation stated that "he has a negative attitude toward the state and the war."

In order to avoid any negative consequences for Mr. v. Heyden, Mr. Bayerlein wrote him a new evaluation leaving out that comment and tried to counterbalance the harm done to Mr. v. Heyden's promotion outlook.

b. (I..)The undersigned was kept on staff despite the fact that the Gestapo was bringing a case against him for defeatist and subversive remarks. This did nothing to help Mr. Bayerlein's image in the eyes of the Nazis. He offered his continued support even if the case should end in an arrest.

c. Mr. Hartdegen, *Oberleutnant* and ordnance officer, presently resident of 17 Baumschulallee, Bann/Rhein, was especially critical of the party because of the many years he lived abroad. In spite of this, Mr. Bayerlein kept him on as his personal ordnance officer from 1942 up to his capture in July 1944. Mr. Hartdegen was later a co-founder of an anti-Nazi camp while he was an American prisoner of war.

4.) Listening to enemy broadcasts.

In order to get a clear picture of the worldwide situation undistorted by Nazi propaganda, Mr. Bayerlein regularly listened to enemy broadcasts in the company of his colleagues and assessed the information collected in this way in meetings with his subordinate commanders.

5.) Use of the *NSFO.* Mr. Bayerlein did not let the *NSFO* (National Socialist Leadership Officer) pose a real threat in any way. He prevented him from personally affecting the troop, ridiculed the NSFO's "work" in meetings with his commanders and saw to it that the little tracts from the NSFO were dealt with "as they deserved to be." At one such commander meeting he commented that now he had someone looking over his shoulder and he asked his commanders to be careful so as not to provoke even more Nazi interference.

6.) Personal devotion to duty.

Mr. Bayerlein was one of those commanders who lead from the front, that is, at the head of the troop. He was always where the danger was greatest, where decisions needed to be made. This he did in a fully unselfish manner, motivated by the thought of his responsibility to his soldiers, to give them the best support of the division's weapons. He risked his life in tireless visits to the troops, in attacks literally right behind the first armored tank, in defensive action at the center of the battle. That is why his troops' successes were excellent even though they had few casualties.

7.) Fundamental attitude.

I had the opportunity to speak with Mr. Bayerlein, alone or with like-minded people, about the situation in general and the German leadership, and to observe his actions on a daily basis. Mr. Bayerlein's clear-sighted view and his rejection of the Nazi system were obvious. Sycophantic behavior and obedience at any price were completely alien to him. He only did what he found acceptable to his own humane fundamental beliefs. I hope that the preceding account will aid in finding a fair course of action and in assuring him the freedom he deserves.

(signed) Kurt Kauffmann
The signature above has been certified by:
The Office of the Mayor
Böblingen, April 7, 1941
(illegible signature)

• • •

D16
Ludwig Maul
Automotive Parts & Supplies
Representative Würzburg
Mainleitenweg

AFFIDAVIT

I have known Mr. Fritz Bayerlein of Würzburg for approximately 20 years. Particularly during the war we got together very often when his work brought him here or when he was on leave. I was a sergeant in the vehicle park and whenever Mr. Bayerlein had a problem with his car, he came to me because of our long acquaintance. Since he belonged to the Armored Tank forces, Mr. Bayerlein had a great deal of technical understanding and interest. He talked to every mechanic in the workshop and socialized as a comrade with members of the armed forces. He often asked the soldiers about their families and their work in my presence. I never noticed any kind of military or militaristic attitude.

Mr. Bayerlein's overall conduct in my presence was without any militaristic element.

When I was invited to his home, we listened to foreign radio broadcasts with his family (sometimes his driver was also present) so loudly that I myself turned down the volume. I started to speak one day about the Africa Corps with a member of the armed forces, if my memory serves me well – a sergeant, and I asked after then *Oberst* Bayerlein. From my memory, I can attest to the following in Mr. Bayerlein's behalf: "The soldier explained to me that Mr. Bayerlein saved him from a court martial simply by (*throwing out*) the file. I can't remember any further details about this incident but one thing I can swear to was that the soldier said to me then that it was only thanks to Mr. Bayerlein that he had been let off so lightly. Like other Africa Corps fighters, this soldier also told me that Mr. Bayerlein was always right by his soldiers at the front.

He (Bayerlein) railed against Hitler and his staff to me. He called Keitel names like Reich's jackass and the others he called Santa Clauses. He was always angry about the continuation of the senseless war.

I am aware of the consequences of making a false statement and I hereby depose this affidavit.

Würzburg, May 18, 1947   (signed) Ludwig Maul
The validity of this signature has been duly witnessed.
Würzburg, May 19, 1947
City Council
(signed and typed) Amling
Clerk

• • •

D17
Anton Reitter
Ennetach/Mengen, May 5, 1947
Railway Worker
Kreis Saulgau

AFFIDAVIT

I was employed as driver and car maintenance man by former *Oberst* and/or *Generalmajor* Fritz Bayerlein from the spring of 1942 to my imprisonment on July 27, 1944. I participated with him in all the battles in Africa, Russia, and on the invasion front and accompanied him on almost all drives to and through the frontlines and, in general, lived with him throughout this time.

General Bayerlein took care of his soldiers like almost no one else and showed a high degree of human compassion in his dealings with the civilian population and prisoners. He himself never spread Nazi propaganda nor influenced his people in this sense, nor did he tolerate such propaganda in his area of command. I can say with a clear conscience that he did not hold Nazi views and that he considered the war to be a great evil. Already in 1942 at the Battle of El Alamein, he expressed his opinion that the war was lost not only to me but to others as well. He often told me that he considered it his task and duty to keep the troops he commanded out of harm's way and out of the senseless war as much as this was possible.

I can give numerous examples that underscore my views of the matter as described here:

1.) When the enemy broke through the Alamein front on November 4, 1942, *Oberst* Bayerlein led the Africa Corps back out of a hopeless situation, acting against orders to hold the position to the last man. We were condemned to death, in a manner of speaking, and we saw *Oberst* Bayerlein's decision to break out of the impending pincer movement as our salvation. I believe that many lives were saved by his decisive measure.

2.) On the retreat after the Battle of Alamein in November/December of 1942, *Oberst* Bayerlein prevented the troops, who had very few provisions left, from taking and butchering the small herds of sheep that belonged to the Arabs who lived in the desert. I can still remember exactly the incident just north of El Mechili when Bayerlein personally, by his very presence, protected the herds and kept them safe for their owners.

3.) During the decisive battle in Tunisia, *Generalmajor* Bayerlein sent soldiers home, in many cases just in time, away from the hopeless fighting in order to save them. In particular, only sons or only surviving sons.

4.) In Tunisia in April 1943, *Generalmajor* Bayerlein became very ill, so ill in fact, that he could barely move. In spite of this he stayed at his post and continued to drive to the front and put himself in the greatest danger because he felt bound by duty to prevent his troop from being led into ruin on the senseless orders of the 1st Italian Army whose command we were then under.

5.) *Oberst* Bayerlein (and *General* Bayerlein) never wore any decorations or insignia on his uniform in North Africa. He did not like big presentations but was always simple and modest. He never at any time wore general's insignia on his uniform collar or pants (not even in Russia or Normandy). That is because he was always to be found right on the front and never, except for periods of quiet, safe in the rear.

6.) When *General* Bayerlein came to Russia after his convalescence, he was appalled by the conditions he found there in regards to the treatment of the local population. Bayerlein quickly straightened things up in the division and made sure that the civilians were treated decently. We had just come from Africa, a theater of the war where, in this regard as well, everything had been conducted in a decent manner – a fact that was also acknowledged by the Americans – as I often heard during my time as a POW. For this reason, we found these methods of treating civilians and prisoners disagreeable.

Point 6 continued:

For example, a few days after the division had taken over the town of Litvinets (Ukraine), where the staff was located, *General* Bayerlein did not allow the population to be evacuated and he helped the people hide themselves in their cellars from the German units to avoid being displaced. He even kept the livestock from being removed so that the people could feed themselves.

In Konstantinovka near Tscherkassy, which was full of refugees, he had the starving population fed from the field kitchens. General Bayerlein and the members of his close staff almost always quartered in the houses of the local population with the civilians living there and never evacuated them. I can still remember that the house in Popovka near Smela was so full of refugees that Bayerlein made do with just one room for himself and his ordnance officers and clerk.

7.) After successfully breaking out of an encircled Kirovograd in the Ukraine on January 8, 1944, an action which went against orders and led to a great success without losses, *General* Bayerlein enjoyed the boundless trust of his soldiers and the troop felt safe and secure under his command, convinced that they would not be senselessly slaughtered.

8.) During the march into Hungary in March of 1944, *General* Bayerlein protected the Jewish population of Esztergom, Párkány, and other towns, did not allow them to be evacuated and prevented expropriation and plundering. Many Jews thanked him for this as the division withdrew from Hungary. *General* Bayerlein stayed with Cardinal Serédi in Esztergom and let himself be seen with the cardinal in public. He attended church services in the cathedral and participated in the troop camp services as well.

9.) On the battlefields of Normandy in June 1944 *General* Bayerlein was shot at by enemy fighter bombers four times; his cars went up in flames. Miraculously, he himself was not injured in any of these attacks. He went on with his drives to the front even when this was most dangerous because for him it was a matter of course to come to his troop, which was in the middle of the heaviest defense combat.

10.) *General* Bayerlein did not spare his own staff either – this can be seen by the fact that he positioned the division staff in the front line of defense between Soulles and Pont Brocard when the Americans broke through at St. Lô. This position was later attacked by about 30 U.S. tanks which rolled right over the staff; some of the staff members were taken prisoner, including me. In the night, Bayerlein fought his way through to the rest of his division, not to leave them in the lurch.

11.) During my imprisonment in the USA I heard only the highest opinion of *General* Bayerlein from the German POWs in the camps. His surrender with all of his troops in the Ruhr territory on April 16, 1945 met with great approval. Even several American newspapers that we got to read in the POW camp reported only the best about *General* Bayerlein, although they usually had nothing good to say about Germans and German generals. This shows how highly the American public regarded General Bayerlein.

12.) I will always remember *General* Bayerlein as the most irreproachable officer and person I have ever met, and even during my imprisonment I was sure that nothing would happen to him after the end of the war.

I myself was never a member of the Nazi party nor any of its organizations.

(signed and typed) Anton Reitter
The signature of Anton Reitter was sworn to and subscribed before me.
Ennetach, May 12, 1947   (illegible signature)
Stamped: Town of Ennetach, Kreis (district) Saulgau

• • •

D18
Dr. Rudolf Smets
Würzburg, April 6, 1947
Parish Priest   21 Schießhaus Street

AFFIDAVIT

I first met then *Major* of the General Staff and later *Generalleutnant* Fritz Bayerlein in the year 1939 during the Polish campaign, when he was the first officer of the 10th Panzer Division general staff and I was the division's Catholic chaplain. We were together on the staff of the 10th Panzer Division until February 1940 when Mr. Bayerlein was transferred to the General Guderian's staff. In the years that followed when Mr. Bayerlein was home on furlough we met repeatedly in Würzburg where I had moved after I was discharged from the armed forces.

Mr. Bayerlein enjoyed the highest esteem of the officers as well as the soldiers of the 10th division. The regard in which he was held by the division commander, General Schaal, was expressed on many occasions but in particular at the farewell celebration that was prepared for him on the occasion of his transfer to General Guderian.

Mr. Bayerlein distinguished himself through his military prowess, tireless diligence, personal courage and constant preparedness for duty. He shared the dangers and the deprivations of war with the fighting men; he was a noble-minded comrade to the officers, a conscientious and solicitous superior to the soldiers, and a scrupulous and judicious advisor to his division commander. He prepared the deployment of the troops carefully and considerately in order to avoid unnecessary losses. In the division, the wounded were provided with all available means; this was true for both our own wounded men as well as wounded enemy prisoners. The civilian population in the combat zone was treated properly and unnecessary burdens were avoided.

Mr. Bayerlein was a true soldier and refused to spout Nazi phrases as so many others on the division staff unfortunately did. As the Catholic chaplain of the division I received invaluable support from him in my work. This support was appreciated even more because of the fact that there was often a marked bias against the army chaplaincy among the division staff. Under these conditions, the personal backing of Mr. Bayerlein for the concerns of the field chaplaincy was of particular importance and is thankfully acknowledged to this day.

I was the Catholic chaplain of the 10th Panzer Division from September 1, 1939 to June 6, 1940 when I had to leave the service because of a serious leg injury I received in Amiens. I was never a party member; because of my refusal to stop covering the Old Testament in school religion classes I was fired from my position as adjunct religion teacher from two secondary schools and I was forbidden from teaching religious education in the primary schools of my parish Nidda/Oberhessen by the *Reichsstatthalter* in Hesse.

(signed) Dr. Smets

• • •

D19
Dr. Peter Straub
Mühlbach, May 10, 1947
Post Karlstadt am Main

AFFIDAVIT

In full recognition of the importance of my statement and cognizant furthermore of the consequences of making a false affidavit, I depose the following affidavit.

I. Regarding my person: Peter STRAUB, born on February 14, 1909 in Freiburg i. Br., Doctor of Law, resident of Mühlbach bei Karlstadt/Main.

II. Regarding the case: Mr. Fritz BAYERLEIN well known to me personally from the time of his function as Rommel's chief of staff in Africa and subsequently as commander of the German troops with the 1st Italian Army on the Tunisian southern front.

I myself was at that time, i.e. since October 25, 1942, employed as the interpreter for the German liaison officer with the XX Italian army corps; on January 16, 1943 after the loss of my chief, I myself became the personal liaison officer of Rommel and his chief of staff, Bayerlein; after Rommel was relieved of command and the German *Afrikakorps* was placed under the 1st Italian Army (March 1943) and Bayerlein was simultaneously appointed commander of the German troops with the 1st Italian army, I was confirmed as the liaison officer with the XX Italian Army Corps. I held this post until the surrender of the German army group in Africa on May 13, 1943. After that, I was transported as a POW to the USA by the Americans.

In the aforementioned positions I got to know Mr. Bayerlein both on a professional as well as a non-professional basis through almost daily discussions of the situation and in close quarters. Therefore, over the course of these many months, I was not only able to see for myself exactly what kind of relationship Bayerlein had with the troops but also what his personal attitude was in regards to how the Nazis were conducting the war and leading the country.

1. In my opinion, Mr. Bayerlein is a personality who has his heart in the right place, a healthy dose of common sense and good instincts, and who displays a truly refreshing decency and sincerity towards both superiors and subordinates. Furthermore, he has a gift, which is quite rare in the military, the gift of being able to not only listen to other opinions with an open mind, but also to be able to accept them and if need be to adopt them without prejudice.

I observed these characteristics of Mr. Bayerlein again and again in our personal interaction on the long and nerve-racking retreat from El Alamein to Tunis. As a die-hard reservist I was very touchy and critical when it came to active officers; for me "active" and "Prussian" in connection with the military meant the pure blind stubbornness of doing things "on principle" which has come to cost Germany so much. Bayerlein was the exact opposite: for him the individual was what mattered and then it was a person's performance, not his prestige, rank or status that counted. For instance, once he had to make a decision about a complaint lodged by an active *Oberstleutnant* (Lt. Colonel) about a *Leutnant* (2nd Lieutenant) of the reserves; Bayerlein had given the *Leutnant* the same official position that the higher-ranked *Oberstleutnant* held in another unit. Bayerlein dismissed the complaint as unfounded; the *Oberstleutnant* never forgave Bayerlein for not backing him at all costs against the little *Leutnant*.

2. Of course, Bayerlein could also be hard and forceful with the troop – but only when the circumstances and the well understood interests of the troop itself demanded it. His concern for his soldiers always guided his actions; and he did everything within his power to help his men bear their difficult lot. I will never forget the beaming faces of the "*Afrikaner*", or members of the Africa Corps, when they spoke of their *General* Bayerlein. Very often when I wanted to visit Bayerlein at his command post, I was told that he was at the front; that is how I saw him return from the front one day in a dirty, ripped uniform after having just crept forward along a mountain ridge, which could be seen by the enemy, to his men on the very front-most lines despite heavy enemy fire. He explained modestly: "What I can endure, my men have to endure; but what my men endure, I really have to be able to endure all the more." These weren't words to be fed to the PK (Propagandakompanien) correspondents, but just the answer given in response to the timid remonstrances of worried comrades. Bayerlein was a man in the heart of his people and that is why they had blind trust in him.

3. For Mr. Bayerlein, his military side was only an outer form that was unavoidable in times of war but never rubbed off on his intrinsic nature. His very character described above is the best proof that Mr. Bayerlein cannot be considered a militarist in the sense of the Law for Liberation. Everyone has a feeling for whether his superior sees and exercises the power given to him as a privilege or a duty but the front soldier is particularly sensitive in all regards; the judgment of the "old Afrikaner", that is the long-term members of the Africa Corps, is all the more reliable and can be taken at face value because, in the big family of the German *Afrikakorps,* the virtues and vices of the higher officers were known to all. Bayerlein did not try to align the life of the German people to a policy of military power but rather and much more he tried to free them from it; politics, like militarism and brute force were just as alien to him as they were abhorrent to him.

4. It was neither in his nature to spread Nazi propaganda nor to even defend it. Like Rommel, Bayerlein too realized that the African campaign was bound to fail already in El Alamein. Neither of them ever made a secret of this realization – not in the Führer's Headquarters nor to the commander in chief in the south, Kesselring, nor to their own comrades in arms nor to their Italian allies. They stayed with their troops to save what could still be saved. Thanks to Rommel and Bayerlein the enemy never succeeded in breaking through the southern front; a break in that line would have cost thousands upon thousands of German soldiers their lives. In this way and through superior strategy and tactics they

spared them practically any larger bloody battle and instead transported on their own authority countless numbers of soldiers back home. Bayerlein could not demonstrate his rejection of Nazi war conduct any more clearly and effectively than this.

I also remember several meetings with Mr. Bayerlein in Tunisia during which he scathingly criticized the deployment of groups of the "Hermann Göring" division on the Tunisian western front, the commanders responsible for them, as well as their protection through the NS (National Socialists) in Berlin: the "H.G." got all the munitions and didn't even know how to shoot, their officers even received the Knight's Cross medal for the reckless "hero's deaths" of their men and then they were called back home, while we, on the southern front, instead of being given ammunition, were given the responsibility for those amateurs' botched conduct of this war, whose victims each one of is in reality.

5. I learned just how far Bayerlein's example influenced the soldiers when on my way back home from my imprisonment as a POW, I stopped in a transit camp in northern France in March of 1946: an infantryman who was asked when he had taken the insignia off his uniform replied: "right away, when I found out that General Bayerlein had set that good example." I'd like to comment that taking off the insignia was the external sign among all the German POWs that a door to the past was being shut once and for all and it was a hotly debated issue.

From this little incident I realized that Bayerlein, even after the collapse, must have stayed the same person he was before – a man who was able to find a way out of any situation – a way into the future, and who was able to go on ahead of others to lead the way.

(signed) Peter Straub

The signature above of Dr. Peter Straub is duly witnessed.
Mühlbach, May 10, 1947.
Mayor: (signed and typed) Krückel
(stamped: Town of Mühlbach b. Karlstadt a. M.)

• • •

D20 *(translated by Gary Wilkins)*
Hans Speidel
Freudenstadt, May 8, 1947
Hartranfstr. 48
Generalleutnant (retired)

Statutory Declaration

I have known General of Panzer Troops Fritz Bayerlein for many years. As a tank leader, he put himself out to an extraordinary degree for the well-being of his troops, who went through fire for him. He was the image of a model soldier, and one who rejected any and all militaristic reasoning.

When General Bayerlein sought me out on 1/16/1944 at my combat headquarters in Novo Ukrainka (I was Chief of the General Staff of 8th Army), I spoke with him for

Generalleutnant Doctor Hans Speidel, (Professor h.c. Dr. Phil.) also helped Bayerlein by providing written testimony to the Spruchkammer Tribunal. Speidel was implicated in the July 20th Bomb Plot to kill Hitler and kept the Gestapo at bay and from torturing by him using his logic and intellect. He attained the rank of General in the post-war Bundeswehr and remained on friendly terms with Bayerlein. (Photo courtesy of Herr Peter vom Brocke)

the first time about the need for finding an immediate end to the war. General Bayerlein showed himself right then to be a decisive opponent of National Socialist rule and its criminal leadership.

As Field Marshal Rommel made preparations in early 1944 to independently end the war in the West and in consequence to remove the National Socialist regime from power, the Panzer Lehr Division under *Generalleutnant* Bayerlein was also transferred to the Western Front. On May 5th, Bayerlein reported to a warm welcome by GFM Rommel, who knew Bayerlein well from the African campaign, where they had become quite close. Rommel informed him in broad strokes about our preparations and intentions. As a follow up to this I had a discussion with Bayerlein about the impossibility of any invasion defense in view of the current balance of power relationship [*between German and Allied forces – Transl.*], in particular with regard to air power – and about the necessity of drawing conclusions from this. General Bayerlein put himself unconditionally at our disposal for cooperation and any needed action. Because of this, we also foresaw a particular purpose for him if our plans were successful.

During operations, close contact was maintained with Mr. Bayerlein through his ordnance officer, Captain Hartdegen, through whom I announced an intended visit to Bayerlein at headquarters on July 10th. I wanted to inform Bayerlein of the details of our preparations. The attempt at a visit failed on the battlefield of Caen however, due to a British attack; events were then drastically precipitated due to GFM Rommel's ultimatum to Hitler on July 7th and his subsequent serious injury on July 17, which dashed the realization of our plans.

On August 18th I saw General Bayerlein for the last time at the command post of La Roche-Guyon, when Hitler removed GFM von Kluge from his post and replaced him with GFM Model. We discussed the absurdity of the *Führer Befehls* for the counterattack on Avranches, in place of a useful political and operative decision that could bring salvation. We also discussed what possibilities still remained to us, after the failure of July 20th.

General Bayerlein resisted to the absolute best of his abilities the National Socialist rule by force and in so doing, accepted all the dangers associated with this attitude.

Dr. Hans Speidel
Generalleutnant (retired)
Last Chief of the General Staff of Field Marshal Rommel,
Political Prisoner from 9/4/44
Until release by the 1st French Army on 4/29/45

GFM = *General Feldmarschall* (Field Marshal)
This was the common written abbreviation for the highest attainable rank in the German Army, Luftwaffe (Air Force), or Navy (the Navy rank title being "Gross Admiral"). In all, there were a total of twenty-six individuals in the German Armed Forces during World War II that held the rank of General Feldmarschall in the German Army or Air Force, or Großadmiral in the Navy. (Gary Wilkins' note)
Führer Befehl = *Führer* Command/Order: These were the usually 'futile" orders issued by Hitler himself, often oblivious of the damaging consequences, or likely ineffectiveness of the action; they were issued more often than not simply from a desire to make a point; often in complete disregard of the situation's military logic and almost always with no apparent thought or care about the frivolous and irreplaceable loss of German soldier's lives that would clearly result from such an order. Some senior commanders chose to disregard such orders – but this choice was made at considerable risk. (Gary Wilkins' note)

• • •

D21
Elise Schmidt
Höchberg, April 25, 1947

<u>AFFIDAVIT</u>
From 1936 to 1939 I was employed by then *Hauptmann* Fritz Bayerlein who after the death of his mother lived with his nephew; I ran their household in Frankfurt am Main, Coburg and Jena until the start of the war. Since I was with Mr. Bayerlein and his nephew on a daily basis and we also ate all meals together, I knew everything that was going on in the household. Therefore, I am able to give an exact description and fair judgment of Mr. Bayerlein like almost no other person in that time period.

Mr. Bayerlein is a very decent and good-natured person who quickly won the respect and the trust of everyone he had anything to do with. He lived very modestly and quietly and he never made a big deal of his military rank and position. To the contrary, when he was off duty, he always wore civilian clothes and did not like to show himself in uniform in public.

He had no love for the Nazis and avoided associating with anyone from the party or the SA or any of those sorts of people. In the three cities mentioned above he never had contact with any party members. In his own family circle, he often expressed his rejection of the Nazi party and its doctrines, in particular the persecution of the Jews. In fact, he showed his own religious beliefs openly and even urged his company to attend religious services regularly every Sunday either on duty or off duty. He was a good role model and attended church regularly. No pictures of Hitler or Nazi bigwigs hung on the walls of our apartment as they did in the homes of almost every family after 1939. Mr. Bayerlein and the rest of us never used the greeting *"Heil Hitler"*, not at home nor with the other people who lived in our building and not ever in public either, even though a high SA leader lived in the next building and once complained about this.

Mr. Bayerlein never spent a lot of money on himself but he often spent money on needy members of his company or their families and helped many in this way.

In his company Mr. Bayerlein enjoyed great respect, admiration, and trust. I know that his people, many of whom I knew personally, raved about their commander and would walk through fire for him. I heard this myself from numerous company members since I attended all company events. The company was very sad when Mr. Bayerlein had to leave them because of a transfer to Jena. Mr. Bayerlein lived only for his company and did everything for it. Any former company member could tell you the same and could tell you this better than I can.

If Mr. Bayerlein is now going to be punished for all his good deeds, his work, worries and trouble that he had as a soldier, then I think that this would be the greatest injustice that could befall a person.

I myself was never a member of the Nazi party or any of its organizations and am not incriminated by the liberation law.

(signed and typed) Elise Schmidt, née Hupp)

This document was signed before me on
May 9, 1947, Höchberg,
Town Council
(illegible signature) 1st Mayor

• • •

D22
Erhard SCHWARZ
Köblerhof/Bei Kördorf
Farmer Post DIEZ/Land
French Zone

AFFIDAVIT

I, Erhard SCHWARZ served during the war in North Africa, Russia, and Normandy from November 1941 on. The last rank I held was *Obergefreiter*. From the spring of 1942 on, I was a command post clerk under former *General* Bayerlein. In December of 1944 I was transferred from the front to manage a Panzer Lehr Division clothing depot. (This happened because I was my parents' only son.) There I was taken prisoner by the Americans at the beginning of April and I have only now returned home from my imprisonment in the USA. During the African, Russian and invasion campaigns I was a very trusted aid to *General* Bayerlein to whom I am not related by birth or marriage. In this capacity I had insight into many things including secret matters.

I am not affected by the liberation law.

As I have been asked to give an account on *General* Bayerlein, I would like to say that it is not necessary for me to make a general statement. That *General* Bayerlein was different from the great majority of other officers and generals, that he hated and fought National Socialism, that he advocated more for his men than for their leaders, that he took care of his soldiers and deployed the troop he commanded with care and consideration and that he only fought decently – all of this is too widely and well known for me to need to bring further examples. All of that has been known for a long time not only by the people who were with him and who served under him but also by the Germans and Americans (especially in the newspaper reports) in the POW camps in the USA.

Therefore I only want to single out and highlight certain points, I want to describe what I know about the active resistance that General Bayerlein put up against National Socialism and what he did after the failed assassination attempt on Hitler of July 20th when such resistance could only be carried out through the most careful measures.

1. After the surrender of Tunisia and even earlier than this, it was clear to us old *Afrikakorps* members that the war was lost and we would have to come to an acceptable peace. On May 14th, a fairly large group of us at the Köblerhof heard a foreign radio broadcast from Radio Calais that confirmed our views. Among other things the announcer said (and this has remained word for word in my memory): "And now, something that we all know but no one wants to say, friends, the war is lost, Hitler's crew bit off more than they can chew." Apart from *General* Bayerlein, seven other people heard this broadcast, including my parents, the Dittmar family, and our cook.

2. Around the 8th of May, *General* Bayerlein was just leaving Rommel's staff quarters in Nogent-le-Rotrou (France) with *Hauptmann* Hartdegen when he said the following, more or less, to me in confidence: The English and American invasion will be successful. The Atlantic Wall will not hold the Allies back. What happened to us in North Africa will happen to us again in France. We'll be cut off from Germany by enemy air forces, we won't get any more supplies, and in the end we'll be destroyed. In this European scenario, the Rhein will take the place of the Mediterranean (in the North African theater). Nothing will make it over the river to us. Any continuation of the war is useless. If the higher-ups don't understand that, then there needs to be a change in leadership to one that brings us an acceptable peace, like Rommel wanted already back in 1942 after El Alamein.

3. In the invasion battle in Normandy the division got a new NSFO (National Socialist Leadership Officer), in the person of an SA *Brigadeführer* named Blieschis. There must have been a reason why such a staunch and reliable party man was being assigned to us as "political commissar" and watchdog. At that time, many thought it must be because Bayerlein was so close to Rommel. In the troop as well, people believed that there must have been a reason for this appointment. *General* Bayerlein treated this NSFO very diplomatically, however, so that the NSFO was formally recognized but could not have

any real effect. Bayerlein did not let him loose among the troop, which was fine with Mr. Blieschis since he didn't like to do that anyway because there was a lot of shooting. However, Mr. Bleischis' weekly letter to the troops was allowed to be circulated among the troop where it was not taken seriously but instead was seen as a joke or used as toilet paper.

4. Before the Ardennes offensive on December 12th *General* Bayerlein was on his drive back from Ziegenberg, where there had been a big meeting, to the division staff quarters in Müden a.d.Mosel by way of the Köbler Hof, where I happened to be. *General* Bayerlein said to me then (my mother also heard some of what he said) that something would begin in the West, but that this thing was so senseless that he would not plunge his division into ruin. The attack was hopeless and simply amounted to murder for the troops. He would not let himself be encircled and would see to it that his men would not be slaughtered. The division was only 1/3 in tact; everything was in short supply, especially fuel. The whole thing was the botched and foolish plan of amateurs, so that you had to take things into your own hands. I know that *General* Bayerlein's first thought was for keeping his troops safe as much as he could and that he was committed to saving as many people and as much German property as he could in this hopeless fight, which after July 20th no one could stop anymore until the Allies forced us to stop. Even then, Bayerlein was the only commander on the German Western Front to surrender with his troops, as we heard then on the U.S. radio broadcasts when we were in the prisoner of war camp in Cherbourg waiting to be transported to the USA.

(signed) Erhard Schwarz

The signature above has been duly witnessed.
Kördorf, May 22, 1947
Mayor (illegible signature)
Stamped: Town of Kördorf

· · ·

D23
Margarethe Dietrich
Würzburg, April 29, 1947
translated by Gary Wilkins

Statutory Affidavit

Swearing to the accuracy of my statements I declare the following about the person of Mr. Fritz Bayerlein:

I have known the Bayerlein family and in particular, Mr. Fritz Bayerlein and his mother Luise Bayerlein (with whom he lived), since 1911. I worked in their household from 1930 onward. It is sad that I now have to give a character attestation about Mr. Bayerlein/ that I am now called on to attest to Mr. Bayerlein's character – however, I can in fact give him the best possible testimonial. Mr. Bayerlein is a very good-natured and noble-minded person who has done much good for many people, myself and sons-in-law included. Herr

Bayerlein lovingly cared for his elderly mother, who finally grew very ill and passed away due to extreme agitation over the results of the Nuremberg Racial Laws of 1936.

Herr Bayerlein lived quite simply and in a reserved manner and saved every penny so that he would be able to build his own home at some point.

From 1937 on, he was transferred to Frankfurt, Coburg, and Jena from 1937, but he often returned home to Würzburg in order to visit his sister – at which time I was always together with him. He never passed up the chance to visit his mother's grave or to attend the regular church services, as he had done since childhood. I feel this aspect should be stressed in particular, since no one wanted to know about God and religion anymore during the time of Hitler.

Herr Bayerlein often expressed his anti-Nazi views to both my sons-in-law and me.

Both of my sons-in-law served as soldiers under *Leutnant*, then *Hauptmann*, Bayerlein, and they are full of praise and respect for this just, humane, and sympathetic superior. I have heard the same from many other people. It would be a crying shame and the greatest injustice if, because of the denazification process, anything were done that harmed Herr Bayerlein after all his good deeds and his personal decency, when he merely did his duty as a soldier and a human being.

I am just a poor woman myself, and was never with the Hitler Party [*NSDAP – transl.*] or the *Frauenschaft**, but rather I hated Hitler, the Nazi Party and its bigwigs – and never hesitated to express my opinion about this, even in public.

[Signature]
Margarethe Dietrich

The signature on the preceding statement made by Mrs. Margarete Dietrich, née Strenzel, widow and resident of 52 Friedrich-Spee Street in Würzburg is hereby duly witnessed and certified. Mrs. Dietrich presented a valid piece of identification.
Würzburg, May 6, 1947
Justizrat: (signed) Engert
Notary

* National Socialist women's organization for women.

• • •

D24
Wilhelm Funke
Hof, June 2, 1947
Presently at 1 Schiller Street

AFFIDAVIT
As the former company commander of former *Generalleutnant* Fritz Bayerlein, presently in Oberursel, 101 Hohenmark Street, I depose the following affidavit regarding his personality and attitude toward National Socialism and militiarism:

1. Mr. Bayerlein was my company officer from 1922 to 1927. He was absolutely reliable, a solid and dignified man with a clear eye for the possibilities at hand and a pronounced sense of justice and decency. He has always been, even in his time as *Leutnant*, an enemy of boastfulness and has never been a so-called "fake." In my opinion, two things were important to him: training our soldiers to be healthy, strong and decent people and keeping <u>any</u> political influence far away from them.

2. The 3rd Company of the *Reichswehr* Infantry Regiment 21 at that time had nothing to do with the "Black *Reichswehr*" or with the training of Nazi groups. In addition, it also rejected any connection to such groups (unlike other companies of the battalion). For this reason it was one of the very few northern Bavarian units true to the constitution and reliable enough to be sent to Munich-Großhadern on November 9, 1923 to put down the so-called Hitler or "beer hall" putsch. The troop was too late to intervene but the individual company members had to fend off a lot of abuse (insults, jostling, spitting) from the Hitler supporters in the streets.

3. Bayerlein was neither a militarist nor a warmonger. He never applied for positions on the general staff; it was always his ambition to do his duty unobtrusively in all situations. His rise to high military positions in later years was solely thanks to his personal qualities and his well-maintained composure in all situations which I know even his enemies in the African theater of combat would acknowledge.

I myself am not related to Mr. Bayerlein by blood or marriage, was not a party member, and am not incriminated by the law of March 5, 1946.

(signed/typed) Wilhelm Funke

The signature above is hereby duly certified:
Hof, June 2, 1947
Administrative District Office Hof/Saale
(signed/typed) Alfred Seibicke,
Head of the Economy Office

• • •

D27 Hitler Youth
Hitler – Youth
District *(Bann)* **309**
Würzburg, March 11, 1942

Your son Friedrich has still not registered with the Hitler Youth despite the summons made by the Supreme Bürgermeister on January 24, 1942. In order to avoid the penalties defined in §12 par. 2 of the Youth Service Decree, I request that you make a late registration on March 16, 1942.

Leader of the District Würzburg-City 309
(signed and sealed)
Oberstammführer

The authenticity of the signature above has been duly certified by:
Würzburg-Heidingsfeld, May 27, 1947
Würzburg City Council
District Administrative Office Heidingsfeld
(illegible signature)

Chapter 5 Endnotes

1. This sentence was partially cut off and was reconstructed by the translator working from the context of the text.

2. Knight's Cross.

3. Resident of Würzburg (male).

4. Nazi law that made it a crime to criticize the government.

5. *Oberkommando der Wehrmacht*: Armed Forces High Command

6. Orders from Hitler himself

7. In German, a closer relationship between people is denoted by the use of the familiar form of the second person pronoun you, or *du*. Use of this pronoun shows a pronounced familiarity between speakers.

8. *Hunderttausend-Mann-Heer*: According to the Treaty of Versailles, the German army was to be a non-political army limited to one hundred thousand professional soldiers.

9. *Heil Hitler* or Hail Hitler was a Nazi greeting, as opposed to *Grüß Gott*, an old-fashioned religious greeting used in southern Germany (Bavaria) and Austria.

10. *Reichsführer-SS*: Himmler's title as national head of the Schutzstaffel.

11. *National Sozialistischer Führungs-Offiziere*. NSFOs were sent to the troops to motivate them and turn them into fervent Nazis.

12. *Translator's note*: this word was illegible in my work copy of the original document. Working from the context and the letters I could read, I believe this is a good guess. *Nicole Insanally*.

13. Officials appointed by the Nazis to oversee and control the governments of the federal states of Germany. It was their job to ensure that Nazi guidelines were followed.

14. During the war, the Nazi propaganda companies made pictures and films of the German troops.

15. This clandestine radio station was actually a British "black" propaganda broadcast designed to demoralize the German soldiers. It broadcast news, music, and even Hitler speeches to hide its true intent of spreading discouraging information.

16. NSFOs were Nazi staff members sent to the soldiers to turn them into fervent Nazis.

6

General Bayerlein's Verdict

"I started this war with the most wonderful army in Europe: today I've got a muckheap. I have no leaders any more, my generals are incompetent, the officers are no commanders, the troops are wretched." — Frederick the Great

Fines, Imprisonment, or Exoneration?

Obertaunus *Spruchkammer* Problems

The Military Government of Hesse had to deal with problems with the Obertaunus *Spruchkammer*. Mainly timeliness was cited and the Military Government's Denazification Division Field Inspection report reflected a dismal forecast of another three years to complete the Hesse current backlog of trials. They were "limping behind" and the report recommended improvement in the *Spruchkammer's* organization and enlargement of their work-output to decrease their backlog, but no real suggestion was offered on how this tasking was supposed to be accomplished. Suggestions offered were organizational improvement, increase in work-output of individual employees, and increased endeavors. With the trials projected to be winding down, the three-year time frame wasn't an option. The report also mentioned that investigations were "extraordinarily weak and about 5,000 cases existed in which no investigation had been started."[1] The inspector acknowledged that investigators had a transportation problem; vehicles were in short supply and gasoline available to the German public almost non-existent.

The Hesse Obertaunus *Spruchkammer* Tribunal contained two panels which could sit simultaneously, eight public prosecutors, six chairmen and fifty-seven assessors. The field report addressed the failings of the German public prosecutors. The prosecutor in Bayerlein's tribunal, Gustav Freyeisen, was praised for his efficiency, but suspended from office for alleged *Fragebogen* falsification. The senior field advisor for the Military Government evaluated the other seven prosecutors. He stated in his summary that they were in general satisfactory, but some were judged as slow, weak when presenting cases, too new in the office to evaluate, and in one instance the incumbent removed for "abuse of position as a public prosecutor."[2] The efficiency of the six Obertaunus chairmen was also addressed. Chairman Johann Jellinek of the Christian Democratic Union party, was on Bayerlein's tribunal the month before and had only been on the panel for two months. The field inspector considered Jellinek satisfactory, he opined that the standard for all six chairmen varied considerably, and one in particular, Friedrich Kalk, was "by far the best, and the rest compare unfavorably to him."[3]

Protokoll

Translator's note: This information was filled into a pre-printed form. Sections of the form that were not filled out because they did not apply were not translated. Nicole Insanally)

Open Court Session of the Denazification Tribunal Obertaunus
File No. Ot: 3366
Record of Proceedings of the open court session of *September 15, 1947*

Present at the hearing in the case against auto mechanic and former Generalleutnant Fritz Hermann BAYERLEIN, born on January 1, 1899 in Würzburg and resident in Hohemark, Oberursel/Taunus, were:

1. Johann Jellinek , Chairman
2. Jean Dinges and Johann Krimmel, Members
3. Gustav Freyeisen, Public Prosecutor
4. Margot Plebuch, Court Recorder

Summoned and appearing in person before the court in this matter were: the party concerned as well as his legal counsel, Attorney Ernst Wahl of 9 Henricus Street, Oberursel/Taunus. Witnesses were not summoned.

Under examination, the party concerned stated that: he is the auto mechanic and former *Generalleutnant* Fritz Hermann BAYERLEIN, born on January 1, 1899 in Würzburg and resident in Hohemark, Oberursel/Taunus, and unmarried.

The charges were then presented by the public prosecutor –
The party concerned was asked if he had anything to say to refute the charges. He stated that:

He came from a family of very modest means and was able to attend Gymnasium with the help of a scholarship stipend. His father was an old Social Democrat and was well read in the subject of politics which he tried to introduce his son to. From the age of eighteen in the year 1917 until the end of the war, the party concerned took part in the serious action in the West; the hardship of that time and the terrible toll it took on his fellow sufferers are indelibly etched in his memory. At that time he served as a simple infantry soldier, declining from the outset to become a candidate in the officers' corps whose elitist nature was repellent to him. After his discharge from the army, he wrote several articles published in the newspaper, the *Fränkischer Volksfreund*, in which he spoke out against the National Socialists' reactionary tendencies in the *Freikorps*. He was, at the time, the company leader of the 3rd company of the 21st regiment of the *Reichswehr*. This company was neither involved in the *Black Reichswehr* nor in the training of NS groups. In fact, unlike other companies, it rejected any connection with such groups. During the so-called "Hitler (or Beer Hall) Putsch" on November 11, 1923, this company was one of the few companies in northern Bavaria considered to be loyal to the constitution of the Weimar Republic and reliable enough to be sent to Munich-Grosshadern to put down the putsch. Company members were jostled and verbally abused by Hitler's supporters during this incident.

He himself had always been an ardent Social Democrat and opponent of National Socialist views. For him the *Reichswehr* was solely a military instrument, and as such, was subordinate to the state and existed to serve the state, rejecting "tradition" and establishing itself on the basis of the Weimar constitution. For this reason, he had no connections with the *Black Reichswehr* and refused to train its members.

In response to the chairman's question as to whether it had been possible for him as company leader to refuse to train the *Black Reichswehr*, he responded: "This training was a voluntary thing(") and that is why he could just refuse to do it. He had other views and wanted nothing to do with Hitler officers. Even after the Nazi takeover, none of these basic conditions had changed for him. He rejected any connection to the ideology of the Third Reich and avoided party members in any way he could. He never belonged to the NSDAP or any of its organizations. Moreover, he was a devout Catholic and always attended service. Against all National Socialist rules, while he served in Hungary in 1944, he stayed with Cardinal SEREDI who was later killed by the Gestapo. While he was there, he appeared with the Cardinal in public and also attended his church services. He even urged his troops to attend camp services and gave the camp clergymen his full support. Nazi sentiments were not tolerated under his command. He retained opponents to the Nazis on his staff, for example HARDEGEN, KAUFMANN, and VON HEYDEN, who had all been noted as untrustworthy in their files. He did many things and always opposed the policies of the Hitler supporters.

In 1941 he was in Würzburg on furlough, recovering from an injury. He was out for a walk with his sister and nephew and dressed in civilian clothes when he reprimanded some camp guards at the Würzburg train station because they were mistreating a few of the Russian POWs they were accompanying; as an officer, he ordered the guards to carry a sick prisoner into the camp despite the protests from the crowd of onlookers. His intervention and rebuke of the guards resulted in a court martial for him and the loss of his sister's store that was forced to close its doors after this incident. At his court martial, he found out that mistreatment of prisoners was promoted by Himmler. He was accused of sympathizing with the prisoners.

Furthermore, he issued strict orders on the treatment of prisoners of war on the front, prevented the evacuation of the local population in Russia, and in addition saved POW Camp HEMER (25,000 men) by sending over an American major who was a POW at the camp to the American units that were mistakenly firing on the camp. He had also provided this camp with food from his supplies and later handed it over to the Americans.

He refused to support Nazism in any way and also refused to enrich himself through Nazism. When he was awarded the Oak Leaves to the *Ritterkreuz*, he turned down a further offer of land, explaining that he did not want to secure advantages through this system and did not want to be counted among the landowning military "gentry". (*Author's note*: Bayerlein accepted an apartment from Heidingsfeld city property. It was not a Jewish confiscated property).

His rank as a general enabled him to do everything to bring an end to the war. He did not carry out the *Führerbefehle* (Hitler's own orders) and tried again and again to lead his troops out of the war. Against Hitler's orders, he tried repeatedly to save what could still be saved. "Fight to the last man" was a motto he neither recognized, nor followed.

As Rommel's Chief of Staff in 1942, he deliberated with Rommel on how to bring about a speedy end to the war, renouncing a final victory for Germany. Rommel went into the *Führer's* Headquarters where he put forward his suggestions. All of Rommel's suggested plans were brutally and forcibly rejected. The party concerned was at that time deployed to Russia and Rommel lost his post as commander on the invasion front. Later Rommel was sent to the western front by Stülpnagel, who was involved in the plot of July 20, 1944; there, Rommel informed the party concerned in a private meeting about the state of the resistance movement on the Western Front and the plot to get rid of Hitler. He stayed in further contact with Rommel. All of the plans made with Rommel failed. In a state of delirium, Stülpnagel, who had injured himself seriously after the failed assassination attempt, disclosed Rommel's involvement in the plot. After a car accident, Rommel was forced to commit suicide in front of Hitler's adjutants because of all of his links to the assassination plot. After Rommel and he had decided to try to put an end to the war, the party concerned tried again and again to put up resistance in strategic and/or tactical areas and made it possible, as far as it lay within the reach of his command, to lead his troops out of the war and keep them from certain destruction. When he and his division, along with 2 other German divisions, were surrounded in the Ukraine near Kirovograd where they were ordered by Hitler himself to stay and defend to the last man, he disobeyed this order and acting on his own initiative, he escaped with his division, and apart from two wounded men, he brought them out unharmed and saved them all from certain destruction.

In August, 1944 he did not carry out the order to lead the Panzer Lehr Division out of the pocket of Argentan-Falaise to mount an attack on Avranches and once again, in disregard of Hitler's order, he brought his division out of the pocket and into safety. This resulted in another court martial and a harsh rebuke from the V. Panzer Army.

Furthermore, he did not follow Hitler's orders to mount a counterattack in November of 1944 in the Saar Territory for which he was threatened to be removed from the troop. He surrendered the city of Winterberg against strict orders to hold it. Because of this, the city was handed over to the Americans undamaged.

On April 16, 1945 he handed himself and his 30,000 men over to the Americans at Iserlohn/Ruhrgebiet and surrendered. This was the first and only capitulation by a higher commander in the West. Through his surrender, he not only saved the lives of many German and American soldiers but also kept a lot of German property in the war zone around Iserlohn from being destroyed and completely demolished. He evacuated the city of Dortmund without a fight and against orders and surrendered the city of Winterberg to the Americans against Hitler's strictest order and without a fight. He always lived modestly and shared both joy and sorrow with his soldiers on the front line. He stayed in dugouts and temporary command posts just like his soldiers and only wore his medals, decorations and badges of rank in rare cases and on special occasions.

For this reason, he remained in close contact with his soldiers up till the day of his surrender and even later, earning their great esteem as a commander and a man. After the war when he was released from American custody, he began to work as an auto mechanic in order to start a new life and help his German fatherland rebuild.

After each witness____expert____ was examined and each document was read, the party concerned was asked if he had anything more to state…

The Public Prosecutor and the party concerned as well as his legal counsel – received the judgment on their statements.

The Public Prosecutor requested that *the party concerned be placed in the category of exonerated persons according to article 13 of the law of March 5, 1946.*

The party's legal counsel *stated that the law did not apply to the party concerned and therefore the party concerned has to be considered cleared of all incrimination.*
The party concerned was given the opportunity to have the final word.
He had nothing more to say.
After closed deliberation by the tribunal, the chairman pronounced the following verdict by reading the sentence,
giving the grounds for the sentence and explaining the rights of appeal.

Verdict:
The party concerned is not incriminated according to the law. The proceedings against him are dropped.
    The costs of the proceedings will be assumed by the state.

The Members   The Chairman
(signed)Krimmel, Jean Dinges, Jellinek

Begründung
The militarist verdict narrative – *Begründung* of the Hesse *Obertaunus Spruchkammer* slightly repeats the verdict above, but is provided again as part of the translation of the trial file:

Bayerlein
The subject of this investigation is considered to be exonerated despite the formal charge against him on the grounds that he falls into the category "militarist" according to the law. Since the party in question is not incriminated in any way according to Art. 8, the Tribunal finds that this law does not apply to his case. The costs of this case will be assumed by the state.
Grounds for decision:
The party in question was able to clear himself of all and any incrimination; already in his childhood, through his upbringing in his parents' home, he developed a pronounced sense of justice and decency in his social attitude. In the war of 1914-1918, in which he took part as a common soldier, he rejected a career path as an officer out of his conviction that he would only offer his services as a soldier to a democratic state. After the war he spent a few more years working in the demilitarization process, which was then taking place. When the Republic demanded a safeguard for its state structure, the party in question signed up for 25 years of military service, guided by his socialist ideals. Because of his exemplary leadership of his troops and the trust he had earned among his subordinates, he was often chosen as the representative of the troops he led. In further illustration: Bayerlein's company, which

was considered to be particularly true to the constitution (of the new Weimar Republic), was the one given the order to suppress the Putsch of November 9, 1923 in Munich. After 1933, the defendant was promoted to higher military ranks because of his exemplary conduct and abilities. He participated in the Poland campaign in 1939 and the fight against France in 1940 as a staff officer of the 10th Panzer Division. It was in this group, that the hopelessness of this war due to the vast superiority of the Allied forces was first recognized and discussed in detail by Rommel and his colleagues. After his unsuccessful attempts to end the war in a respectable manner, General Field Marshal Rommel took Bayerlein into his confidence, discussed and initiated the preliminary preparations of an indirect resistance. On the Africa front, the defendant failed to carry out a "*Führersbefehl*" (or strict order given by Hitler himself) for the first time when he withdrew the troops serving under him near the town of Fuka, although Hitler had commanded that no troops retreat. This saved the lives of many soldiers. Another episode which took place in Würzburg, when Bayerlein was home recuperating from a wound, clearly shows the defendant's character: At a train station in Würzburg, Russian POWs, who were being transported, were beaten with ox whips by the escort soldiers. The defendant, dressed in civilian clothes at the time, saw this and took action – giving the soldiers the order to put a POW, who had collapsed, on a stretcher and have him carried. The angry crowd of onlookers spoke out vehemently against the intervention by the defendant and his sister – (one of them) going so far as to file a lawsuit which eventually led to the closing of the subject's sister's clothing shop. In his later actions on the Russian front, the party concerned once again displays his social-minded attitude toward the less fortunate as well as his troops. As he did in Africa, he tried once again in Russia to protect the property of the local population. On the front at Kirovograd, Bayerlein refuses to carry out a *Führerbefehl* for the second time. Of particular note, is his conduct in Hungary where he stayed with Archbishop Seredi, Furst Primas of Hungary at his Palace in Esztergom, where he supported the Archbishop in his efforts to protect the local Jewish population. Seredi later became a victim of the SS. When he is called to the Atlantic front by Rommel, who places great trust in him, the subject once again offers his services to the resistance movement building within the military. Rommel, Stülpnagel, Speidel work together on these plans. After the failed undertaking of July 20, 1944, Stülpnagel attempts suicide but only succeeds in wounding himself. In his delirium, he discloses Rommel's involvement. Rommel, who must also depart from this life shortly after, and the party concerned agree that each will play his own part in trying to bring an end to the war with the aim of saving many lives. On the retreat, Bayerlein finds several opportunities to avoid engaging the enemy until he finally surrenders without the permission of his superiors in April 1945. On the entire length of the march from France back to the Ruhr, he makes sure that the orders for the destruction of factories and utilities are not carried out. By involving an American congressman, the subject saved a POW camp in his sector that held 25,000 Allied soldiers. Thanks to him, the cities of Winterberg and Iserlohn remained undamaged because he refused to defend them in flagrant disregard of a direct order.

All of this is clear evidence that the party concerned put up resistance far beyond his powers by sheer force of personal courage. There is absolutely no incrimination and the Tribunal was able to pronounce the aforementioned verdict.

. . .

Abschrift

Hessian State Ministry   **Bad Homburg v.d.H. , September 15, 1947**

The Minister for Political Liberation

Denazification Tribunal Obertaunus

Certified Copy

File No. Ot. 3366 Je/Pl

In compliance with the Law for Liberation from National Socialism and Militarism of March 5, 1946, the Denazification Tribunal Obertaunus pronounces in the case against the auto mechanic and former *Generalleutnant* Fritz Hermann Bayerlein, born on January 14, 1899 in Würzburg, and resident in Hohemark, Oberursel/Taunus on the basis of the hearing the following

Verdict:

The party concerned is not incriminated by this law.

The case is dismissed.

The costs for the proceedings will be assumed by the state.

The Members:

The Chairman:

(original document signed by) Dinges

(original document signed by) Jellinek

(original document signed by) Krimmel

This copy has been duly certified by

(signed illegibly)

Court Clerk

After his release from captivity on April 2, 1947, Bayerlein faced another challenge to his freedom – the Spruchkammer Tribunal. After he was exonerated, Bayerlein began working at the 7707th European Command Intelligence Center (ECIC) in October 1947. Here Bayerlein comments to a Main Post newspaper reporter about an article that stated he'd received the Diamonds to the Ritterkreuz. Bayerlein stated he received the Swords to the Ritterkreuz and wanted the newspaper to correct the error. Note the condition of the two men – widespread food rationing and shortages reflect hunger and malnutrition of millions of people in Europe. (Newspaper clipping courtesy of the Dittmar-Bayerlein Family Collection, credit to the Main Post, Würzburg, Germany, date of publication unknown.)

Uncle Fritz and his nephew and namesake, Fritz, enjoy a nap on the trip from Italy to Würzburg in March 1942. Bayerlein cradles the youth's head on his shoulder during the long train ride. (Photograph courtesy of the Dittmar-Bayerlein Family Collection.)

A Main Post newspaper article published on the 40th anniversary of General Bayerlein's surrender in the Ruhr. (Newspaper clipping courtesy of the Dittmar-Bayerlein Family Collection, credit Westfalenpost, April 1985.)

Oberst Bayerlein about March 1943, prior to his promotion to Generalmajor. Bayerlein provided testimony that in Africa he stopped German and Italian troops from taking lambs and kids from Arab shepherds to supplement their canned ration diets. Bayerlein was given a young goat as a gift. (Photograph courtesy of the Dittmar-Bayerlein Family Collection.)

Oberleutnant Bayerlein during a field visit in Africa. Part of the Denazification Trial proceedings involved investigation into field activities and checking the types of uniforms the men wore. Bayerlein was not a member of the Waffen-SS and never wore its uniform. (Photograph courtesy of Herr Stefan Ommert.)

The brothers-in-law, Fritz Bayerlein and Matthäus Dittmar, young Fritz's father, enjoy a sunny day away from the war as they relax in Würzburg. (Photograph courtesy of the Dittmar-Bayerlein Family Collection.)

First portrait of Generalmajor Bayerlein. His new position was German Chief of Staff of the 1st Italian Army. (Deutsche Chef des General Stabes bei 1. ital. Armee), worked under his commander, General Meese. "It was dreadful," he wrote to Field Marshal Rommel, "... I was able to struggle through to May 5th ... when the end stood tangibly near." (Photograph courtesy of the Dittmar-Bayerlein Family Collection.)

Left: Würzburg photographer J. Stumpf's portrait of Generalleutnant Bayerlein wearing his Oakleaves to the Knight's Cross (Eichenlaub zum Ritterkreuz.) (Herr Peter vom Brocke Collection) Right: Matching J. Stumpf's portrait of Bayerlein without his Schirmmütze visor or Dienstmütze service cap. Regardless of the occasion Bayerlein preferred his more casual field cap, the M43 Einheitsfeldmütze and wore it from Africa to his formal surrender in the Ruhr Pocket. (Herr Peter vom Brocke Collection, uniform analysis per Gary Wilkins)

"A tired old battle horse," a Panzer Lehr Division officer aptly described Bayerlein. By March 1944 Bayerlein had experienced five years of war and was physically exhausted, and as seen in this photograph, very saddened by events in Hungary. (Bundesarchiv Koblenz Bild 78/33/2)

Left: Rested from the battles from D-Day to the rush across the Rhine River, Bayerlein recovers at home on sick leave from a shrapnel wound and sprained ankle on August 23rd. During September 1944 he recovered at home. Bayerlein took time to have the local photographer record his latest decoration, the Swords to the Ritterkreuz (Eichenlaub mit Schwertern zum Ritterkreuz). Adolf Hitler signed the message for the award at 0900 hours the morning of July 20th, 1944. (Photograph courtesy of the Dittmar-Bayerlein Family Collection.) Right: Matching portrait from quarter profile. Bayerlein needed the recovery at home before facing the next action, Wacht am Rhein (Watch on the Rhine) – the last ditch Ardennes Offensive.

Chapter 6 Endnotes

    1. A high school with a challenging curriculum aimed at preparing students for higher studies and culminating in a university entrance examination.

    2. Illegal paramilitary groups whose formation after World War I went against the Treaty of Versailles terms.

    3. A boycott of Ellen's boutique forced her to close.

    4. Added by translator for clarification.

    5. Added by translator for clarification.

    6. Attempted assassination of Hitler.

7
The Chains of Command
the Consequences & the Judgments

"One asked oneself how it was possible to continue without becoming a murderer ... one thought that it might be best to put a bullet through one's brain." — Generaloberst Heinz Guderian.

To Win or to Lose?

"Intellectually and emotionally there was a long way to go from the opinion: "Germany will win," to "Germany will have to win", to "Germany will be defeated," to finally: "Germany should not win" or "better being defeated than a winner under Hitler," Mr. Manfred Rommel recalled that these were the sentiments of many German people during the course of the war. "Among the women and men of resistance were many who walked this intellectual path."[1] Mr. Rommel continues, "… Hitler was able to pursue his strategy which destroyed Germany and wrecked havoc on other nations as well. So the words proved to be true which Johann Wolfgang von Goethe mentioned in his remarks on demonic personalities in history: *"emo contra deum nisi deus ipse"* – simply: 'Only the gods can destroy the gods.' The majority of Germans, many of them feeling that they were in the same boat with Hitler, whether they liked it or not (especially in the Eastern part of Germany) fought until the bitter end. No further attempt was made to get rid of Hitler and to end the war by way of a German rebellion against his disastrous leadership."[2]

The Nuremberg Tribunals

Captured major war criminals found themselves facing the Allied tribunal after the war's end. Many escaped capture and trial by committing suicide by hanging, taking poison or by shooting themselves. As the Allies continued the relentless search for the guilty, many attempted to hide in the mass of German prisoners, work on farms, blend in with factory workers, or attempt name and identify changes. Victims pointed out their tormentors – the officers and guards, and those who had aided them. The United Nations War Crimes Commission had a total of 36,800 names of potential witnesses and those who would be charged with war crimes. The United States courts in Nuremberg began the trials for the party *Bonzen* (bigwigs) during a two-year period from July 1945 through 1947. The International Military Tribunal in Nuremberg placed the twenty-four top-ranking Nazis in the forefront for this highly publicized trial. For "crimes against humanity" and "waging an aggressive war," the excuse of "only following orders" or serving as the "head of state" was no longer considered an immunity from indictment and trial.[3] The trials continued on into late 1949, bringing justice and reprisal to the field marshals and generals who served outside of the Berlin circle.

Original caption reads: Scene of the International Military Tribunal at Nuremberg Germany. Air view shows the Nuremberg Palace of Justice (large building in center) and at the right the courthouse in which the trials of Hitler's ex-chiefs are being conducted. In rear of the Palace and surrounded by a wall can be seen the prison area and buildings which have housed the war crime defendants for the past seven months. Nuremberg, Germany, 11/20/45. There was a series of trials held at the Palace, the first being the NSDAP Parti Bozen (party bigwigs) who were the twenty-four top-ranking Nazis. Other trials were conducted for officers and guards held accountable for murdering prisoners of war, Jews, and gypsies. Area commanders were also held accountable for the actions of SD and SS units under their control and in their geographical areas. (Photo credit: U.S. Army Military History Institute, Carlisle Barracks, Pa. World War II Collection, Signal Corps Photo ETC: HQ-45-63468; Photographer: Tec 5 Raymond D-Addario from 3264 Signal Photo. Svc. Co.)

Lunch at Nuremberg. Conditions for the witnesses were only slightly better than for those standing trial. Original caption reads: Witnesses held in the Nuremberg jail awaiting their turn to testify line up at the noon meal. Extreme left (back to camera) is Adm. Nicholas Horthy, former Hungarian Regent, speaking with Field Marshal Erich von Manstein; right front is Field Marshal Albert Kesselring, Italian Theatre Commander; right rear (with hand to ear) is Generaloberst Heinz Guderian. (NARA, U.S. Army Signal Corps, SC 218560, dated 24 November 1945)

Original caption reads: Nazi defendants in the Nuremberg War Crimes trials stare intently at a chart of the party organization introduced in the third day of the trial. Hermann Goering, left, listens to testimony via earphones. Rudolph Hess, who usually sits between Goering and Ribbentrop, is missing in this photo. He had been complaining previously of severe stomach cramps and was given medical treatment outside the courtroom. Other defendants shown left to right in front row: Keitel, Rosenber. Back row: Donitz, Raeder, Schirach, Sauchkel, and Jodl. 11/22/45. Signal Corps Photo #ETC-HQ-45-64379 (Capt J. H. Herod) from 3264 Sig photo Sv Co., SC 215210-S (Photo credit: U.S. Army Military History Institute)

In tribunal proceedings, businessmen, members of the SS, SD, and Gestapo, extermination squads, camp guards, general officers, and slave labor bosses were to be tried under Control Council Law 10 which covered crimes such as "committing aggressive warfare" and for the first time in history "crimes against peace and crimes against humanity."[4] It was not only the defendants who had to worry about the trials. In many instances witnesses for the prosecution didn't have entirely "clean hands of events" and surely had been "more than onlookers to an incident."[5]

The Generals: Blind Yes-Men or Reluctant Servants?

General Siegfried Westphal, former Chief of Staff to Rommel, wrote an account of his experiences as a German staff officer after the war. His purpose was to recount the facts as he recalled them, and objectively explain how the German Army, as well as the German people themselves, were drawn progressively deeper into National Socialism over a twelve-year period under the dictatorship of Adolf Hitler.[6] General Westphal provided his own insight into the workings of the *Wehrmacht* under Hitler's orders during the war. His rationale was that if the Army commanders, "took everything without resistance, then… Hitler would have no reason to mistrust them, to show them his animosity, to watch over them and cut their ration of authority to the minimum. The commanders with a sense of responsibility – and these were in the majority – did not simply give up the struggle. They stood up for their convictions whenever the situation allowed it. Their fight was one of life or death. Of course, they believed that a limit was set to their resistance of Hitler by their duty of military obedience…According to law all officers, including the generals, were liable to service. They could no more refuse service than could the ordinary soldier or conscripted reservist… It was their fate that they were delivered over, like the whole nation, into the hands of a man who was a master in exploiting the loyalty, faith, and political inexperience of the people."[7]

General Westphal noted that of the eighteen field marshals in the *Wehrmacht*, "nine were, one after another, dismissed from their posts; three were killed in the war (von Reichenau, von Bock, Model: three more paid the death penalty after July 20, 1944 (von Witzleben, von Kluge, Rommel; one was taken prisoner (Paulus): and only two – Keitel and Schoerner – remained in service to the end. The *Generaloberst* situation was similar. Two of them were executed (Hoepner, Fromm); two were dismissed in dishonor, five died in the field (von Schobert, Hasse, Hube, Dietl, Dollmann), and only a few remained in service to the end without being called to book."[8]

Another weapon in the Führer's armory of terror to exercise control over his recalcitrant officers was the infamous *Sippenhaftung* Law. Enacted shortly after the July 20, 1944 bomb plot to assassinate Hitler, the law essentially held a commander's family responsible for his conduct in the field. If he surrendered his troops and himself, his family was held hostage and accountable for the man's actions. The wife would be separated from her children and sent to a concentration camp; their young children would be farmed out to other German families. The threat of family reprisals kept the commanders in line with carrying out Hitler's orders – the men loved their families, and their safety was a constant worry. Even the enlisted men, if they were of a mind to desert or surrender themselves, lived under this threatening cloud of discovery by Nazi elements. If the SS caught a field commander in the act of surrendering his forces, the commander and his soldiers faced a court martial as a traitor under Hitler's traveling court, which conveniently brought along an execution squad.

Bayerlein as Prisoner of War

"If Hitler had been killed by the bomb [July 20th], the war would have ended last July," General Bayerlein said in a post-war interview while a prisoner of war. Providing insight to the question of why they continued to fight, Bayerlein stated: "I and the generals I knew were sorry that the bombing attempt failed to kill Hitler. Though we knew Germany could never win, we kept on fighting because of fear. For many months there had been no point in fighting, but the Army was so full of *Spitzeln* (stool pigeons) that to stop was impossible. No compromise was possible because as the war went on, it became a political war. We were scared as hell all the time."[9]

One of his subordinate officers, former *Oberleutnant* Hellmuth Henke, stated that he'd heard a rumor of Hitler's order condemning General Bayerlein's surrender in the Ruhr pocket on April 16, 1945. Serving as an aide and translator on the General's Panzer Lehr Division headquarters staff, Herr Henke recalled that Bayerlein, as commander of the LIII *Armee Korps* who had surrendered, was to be stripped of his decorations and reduced in rank to a private. If he was captured, he was to be arrested, court-martialed and executed.[10] As with many others who saw the continuation of the war as "useless bloodshed"[11] and wished to bring it to an end, Bayerlein was considered a *Landesverräter* [traitor] to his Hitler oath of allegiance.

Bayerlein's actions while a prisoner of war at Oberursel lend credence to this rumored Hitler order. *General* Walter Botsch, among other German generals, called Bayerlein to account for his collaboration with the Americans while a prisoner of war at the Military Intelligence Service Center at Oberursel. The day of his surrender in the Ruhr one of Bayerlein's statements to Colonel B.A. Dickson, the First U.S. Army's Assistant Chief of Staff, was that he and *General* von Waldenburg, "are expected to be condemned to death in absentia and degraded in the *Wehrmachtbericht*."[12] Some of his fellow prisoners had a long memory of Bayerlein's surrender; in their belief it was a traitorous act, as was his open association with the Americans in the prisoner of war camp.

In the spring of 1946, when a U.S. Army directive ordered that all German general officers were to be consolidated at Camp Allendorf #20, Bayerlein protested the transfer, typing out a letter of appeal to his American Historical Division officer, Major Hudson. Taking the other generals' threat against Bayerlein seriously, Hudson notified his chain of command, and within hours Bayerlein was sent to the German hospital at Bad Neuheim for a medical check up, then to a conference in his home town of Würzburg for a few days to keep him out of immediate danger from his former colleagues. *General* Botsch, Bayerlein stated, had threatened him with the statement that his former comrades at Camp Allendorf were "waiting for you." They had a score to settle with him; he would be "shut out and put on trial, and this is the end for me at this camp."[13] With the intervention of the staff of the U.S. Army Historical Division and the Military Intelligence Service Center #4, the decision was made to keep Bayerlein housed at Oberursel – and safe from the vengeful hands of his former commanders and associates. He continued writing his battle accounts for the U.S. Army's Historical Division and began working in the Camp King motor pool as a mechanic, changing truck tires. Bayerlein was released from captivity on April 2, 1947.

Oberstleutnant F.W. von Mellenthin, Generalleutnant Ludwig Crüwell, Oberstleutnant Fritz Bayerlein and staff officer link arms and smile for the photographer. Photo taken in November 1941. After the war and internment as prisoners of war, von Mellenthin relocated to South Africa to run a family business; Crüwell was appointed to the Bundeswehr; and Bayerlein worked at the Military Intelligence Service Center, Oberursel. All of the men worked on writing German battle histories for the U.S. Army's Historical Division as prisoners-of-war. (Credit: NARA, College Park, World War II Collection.)

The "Butchers' Dogs?" – the German General Staff

An *Afrikaner* associate of Bayerlein's was *General* F.W. von Mellenthin, who had served as Field Marshal Rommel's Ic (Intelligence Officer), from June 1, 1941 through September 15, 1942. In a post-war interview at his home in Johannesburg, South Africa, *General* von Mellenthin provided some background and his viewpoint of the German General Staff Officer cadre.[14] First of all a candidate for General Staff training was required to take a week-long extensive examination. *General* von Mellenthin recalled that out of 1,000 officers who assembled to take the exam, "only 150 or so were admitted to the *Kriegsakademie* [war academy]."[15] *General* Ludwig Beck developed the curriculum, shortening it from three to two years. Beck's goal was to fill positions as quickly as possible for Hitler's expanding army. Von Mellenthin recalled, "The only break in desk work was the weekly field exercise with maps, but without troops or equipment."[16] After the lectures and staff exercises the candidates were sent on cross-training assignments with other arms branches to complete the familiarization of the entire army. The cross-training usually lasted three months. The second year of General Staff training was more of the same – only "more grueling, as marginal candidates were harshly weeded out."[17]

    General von Mellenthin recalled his service in Africa under Rommel, stating about his former superior, "he was the toughest task master I've ever known. He spared no one, least of all himself." Rommel could be, "scathingly rude to his principal staff officers, but never rude to his soldiers or his prisoners of war." Von Mellenthin openly admired his superior although their worlds were miles apart as von Mellenthin was a member of the noble "von" class, and Rommel, and men such as his Chief of Staff, *Oberstleutnant* Fritz

Bayerlein, were raised in middle-class families. "Rommel insisted his officers eat troop rations, even though they were permitted to mess separately. This often amounted to only stale, wormy bread, washed down with a cup of brackish water," von Mellenthin recalled. (There might have been no water at all if Rommel, with his Schwabian shrewdness, had not brought along dowsing experts from Germany to search for water holes.)[18] In the field Rommel distrusted his General Staff officers as they "reported to him publicly, and *on* him privately to the chief of the General Staff in Berlin." Von Mellenthin stated, "As a fighting soldier, he viewed us with distrust; he though we might attempt to supervise – even take over."[19]

Von Mellenthin had high praises for another famous commander, *Generaloberst* Heinz Guderian, who ranked second in his opinion, under Field Marshal Erich von Manstein.[20] "Guderian was brave, brash, bold – and difficult; he locked me up!" von Mellenthin remembered. It was late in 1944 in the West, and von Mellenthin served as chief of staff of Army Group G under *General* Herman Balck from December 1942 until late 1944 in fighting on the Russian and French fronts. Evidently Guderian took a dim view of von Mellenthin's reported insubordination to one of Guderian's subordinate officers. Von Mellenthin laughed in remembrance and stated that after Guderian "gave me a proper dressing down," then he "clapped me under house arrest for a week, then sacked me."[21] His respect for Guderian never wavered as he stated, "I mean no disrespect to J.F.C. Fuller or Liddell Hart or Charles de Gaulle as great theorists of armored warfare, but it was Guderian; he was the doer. He took the theory and made it practice."[22]

Von Mellenthin stated that Hitler would have been better served to follow the basics of General Staff strategy rather than following his usual "inspired hunches."[23] Von Mellenthin recalled that he:

> "... could never envision that Hitler would totally reverse Clausewitz, turning the relationship between the politicians and the military upside down. The politician would order war; the military would counsel restraint. He would order attack; they would counsel delay. When General Staff officers tried to explain to Hitler the difficulties inherent in winter operations in Russia, the Führer reviled their timidity. His generals 'should be like butchers' dogs that would attack anything in sight,' Hitler ranted in one of his temperamental fits. Instead, they were mainly courteous, courtly men who acted more like cautious corporate directors. Hitler took to calling the General Staff officers cowards, stating their 'minds were fossilized in obsolete habits of thought.'"[24]

Two reasons that *General* von Mellenthin gave as reasons not to defy Hitler's rise to power were: Paragraph 36 of the "Defense Law, which stated 'Soldiers may not engage in political activity'; and the "30 June 1924 General Staff decree which specifically forbade involvement in politics ... mandating 'the officer does not become a politician, he remains a soldier.'" "One of my *Kriegschule* classmates tried to kill him," recalled von Mellenthin to Lieutenant Colonel Carlson:

> On March 21, 1943 *General* Rudolf *Freiherr* von Gersdorff made an attempt during an exhibition of captured Soviet weapons in Berlin. He placed two bombs in a Soviet overcoat he was demonstrating, each with a delayed fuse set to explode in 20

Generaloberst Heinz Guderian at the Festung Brest-Litowsk on September 22, 1939 preparing to meet Soviet officers to celebrate the dividing of Poland. Oberst Walter Nehring, Guderian's XIX Army Corps Chief of Staff, is standing to Guderian's left; and Major Bayerlein, Ia, First General Staff Officer (Operations), stands respectfully at attention near the doorway. After the war all the Allies wanted a shot at Guderian for "waging aggressive warfare." (Bundesarchiv Koblenz Bild 146/80/4/30)

Generaloberst Guderian, commander of Panzergruppe Guderian and his "modern army" on the Soviet front. (Bundesarchiv Koblenz Bild 183/B 10093, Propaganda Kompanie: Kriegsberichter: Huschke)

The Guderian Card Game. Original caption reads: Former Nazi Generals sweat out their turn at Nuremberg Trials. Held as witnesses for Nuremberg War Crimes trials, a foursome of ex-generals while away the time conversing and playing cards in the Nuremberg City Jail. Left to Right: Field Marshal Sperrle, Air Force chief; Generaloberst Heinz Guderian, Inspector of Panzer Troops; Generaloberst Hans-Jürgen Stumpff, Air Force chief; Field Marshall Erhard Milch, General Inspector for the Air Force. (NARA, U.S. Army Signal Corps, SC 218575, dated 24 November 1945.)

minutes. His plan was to place himself in such close proximity to the Führer that they would both be destroyed by the blast. Unexplainably, Hitler left the exhibition after only three minutes. He probably had a sixth sense. The assassination attempt, held at the *Zeughaus* on *Unter den Linden*, nearly ended in solo disaster for von Gersdorff, who had to flush the fully activated fuses down the toilet after Hitler left.[25]

Von Mellenthin opined about Hitler's philosophical autobiography *"Mein Kampf"*: "None of us had taken it seriously. Thousands of copies were available, but most General Staff officers considered it so much twaddle… convoluted Bohemian *Plattdeutsch* [low German]."[26]

"I must lose my tan.": Guderian – on the Denazification Process

While interred as a prisoner of war, former *Generalinspektor der Panzertruppen* Heinz Guderian talked at length to the Seventh Army's interrogation officers; they were curious about him as an individual, his view of his superiors, and his role in the war. The report states:[27]

It would appear that only after a long inner struggle did Guderian decide to express his opinion about Hitler and his staff from a critical standpoint. . . Guderian claims his position toward National Socialism to have been a completely neutral one, and that he never paid much attention to the movement. He further states that he had seen Hitler for the first time on the occasion of the opening of an exhibition in Berlin ... Guderian admits that he had been impressed favorably by the successes of the Government and the Party, which had commanded the confidence of the people. To this were added the achievements in the social field, the providing of employment, which greatly impressed him and his colleagues. At any rate the Party methods had never received their sanction, but they had hoped that the moral decay (*Sittenverohung*), which they considered a "childhood disease" and a hangover from the "political upheaval period" would wear off as time went on. "Unfortunately the opposite took place," he stated. Guderian thinks that the persecution of Jews must be rejected because of its disastrous effect. Without doubt, the immigration of undesirable Jewish elements from Central and Eastern Europe to Germany brought with it unpleasant developments which led to an antipathy on the part of a great number of Germans toward the Jews. In their solution to this problem National Socialists are termed by Guderian as being "a great catastrophe for which there could be no excuse". He claimed to have been aware of the existence of concentration camps and had realized that "they weren't convalescent homes". "BUT WE KNEW NOTHING OF THE HORRIBLE THINGS WHICH HAVE NOW BEEN DISCOVERED."

Austria's *Anschluss* and the incorporation of the Sudentenland into the Reich were, in Guderian's opinion, actions which were still undertaken as part of the effort for peaceful solutions of international problems, all the more so since they enjoyed the sanction of both England and France. "With the German march into Bohemia and Moravia the policy of common sense and a peaceful solution of problems was tossed aside. I realized that this new trend in Central Europe could not endure. The conflict with Poland was provoked nonchalantly and without much effort. The possibilities for a peaceful settlement were not fully exploited.

Concerning the plans for the campaign in the East, Guderian claims not to have been informed. Nevertheless, Guderian states that, several months prior to the advance into Russia, he realized what was going on since he took notice of the various troop movements. "I could never grasp or understand the war in the East. From the beginning I considered the issue as hopeless. The war in the West was still in progress, and it bordered on insanity to attack in the East while we still had England on our neck. Thus we had the dagger in our back before we ever got started. It is nonsense to maintain that the Western Powers stabbed us in the back while we were fighting Bolshevism, for we were already at war with them."

Concerning Hitler Guderian made the following comment: "He undoubtedly possessed the characteristics of a genius – but genius and insanity are often closely allied. As, in December '41 (the date of Guderian's first discharge), I looked into Hitler's eyes, I got the impression that all was not well with him. I cannot define it more clearly. At any rate, one got the impression that one was dealing with a man whose thoughts were no longer in this world."

During all of these years, Guderian states, he had never believed in the possibility of a German victory. To him it had only been a question of keeping the war as far away as possible from German soil or, at least, protecting the Eastern border from a Russian breakthrough. Wherever he had found it possible, he had pointed out the futility of continuing the struggle and had also attempted to influence the foreign policy in that direction. He relates that he discussed these problems with Goebbels and Himmler very seriously in 1943 but met with complete lack of understanding. He also stood in close contact with Dr. Speer, who in an earlier memorandum to the *Führer* had made it quite plain that "the war was lost". But even Speer's influence was not sufficient to bring the *Führer* and his associates to their senses. Although he, as a general, was expressly, and under threat of punishment, forbidden to discuss official matters with the Foreign Minister, (as it was similarly forbidden to discuss intended operations with other generals) he went to see Ribbentrop early this year in order to present to him the hard facts concerning the situation in the East and to demand that he do everything in his power to initiate negotiations. This, Ribbentrop refused. Guderian said that attempted negotiations later via Sweden "began in such a pitiful manner that they could not possibly be taken seriously by the enemy, and thus failed."

...Early in March another discussion with Admiral Doenitz and Himmler took place; they both considered any negotiation attempt senseless. Doenitz stated, "We must fight on to the bitten end." This conversation was to have been kept secret, but in spite of this Hitler learned about it and, several days later, in one of the daily discussions of the situation called Guderian a "*Landesverräter*" (traitor). On March 25th Guderian was sent on sick leave.

Guderian attempts to explain this dilemma by giving the picture of a German general holding a responsible position who was aware of the fact that he was fighting for a lost cause, and simultaneously found himself under order to a leadership consisting of incompetant or insane individuals. "It was no longer permitted to apply for a discharge. One had to stick it out. One asked oneself how it was possible to continue without becoming a murderer. It is impossible to picture this atmosphere for an outsider. Often one thought that it might be best to put a bullet through one's brain.

But that would not have helped the German people any. During those years I spent many a sleepless night, and I breathed a genuine sigh of relief when offered sick leave. Things had become unbearable for me."

Guderian considered Hitler to be primarily responsible for the war, the military developments and all the crimes committed in Germany's name. But he states that the guilt was also shared by the men around Hitler, who lacked the courage to speak the truth. "Aside from that there are criminals who ought to be punished. We would prefer to do the job ourselves. Of the generals none enriched himself materially or committed atrocities, in fact they even saw to it that atrocities ordered from higher-ups were not carried out. In Orel we received the order to let the population starve, although sufficient quantities of food were on hand. This order, however, was not carried out. In fact, we posted notices throughout the city to the effect that the subsistence (food supplies) for the population was guaranteed."

Guderian states that he spent four weeks of 1932 and the same period of time in 1933 in Russia, and was deeply impressed by the few things he got to see. He says that in a comparatively short time enormous things were accomplished in the industrial as well as the economic fields. "The tractor works in Kharkov were so huge that they would make the Krupp works appear like a tiny blacksmith's shop."

Guderian admits a great portion of the German people fell for the "Pied Piper" (as he termed Hitler in his conversations with his wife). He claims that the German people had realized long ago how mistaken they had been and had paid dearly for their errors. "99% of the German people need no education to become kind. The German people are not cruel. Not even the few bestial individuals among them can alter that fact. What the German people need is the re-establishment of justice. They need just treatment and directions. Justice and sensible political measures – that is the crux of reeducation."

After the war, Guderian wrote in a letter to a query from Gault MacGowan, a reporter with the North American Newspaper Alliance, that "I don't intend to seek excuses for real crimes. I protest against your statement that the things were reproached for my comrades 'are orthodox teachings of the Prussian military school.' I am myself a Prussian, and I shall remain proud of this fact to the end of my life. The orthodox Prussian school was that of justice and order; and if Hitler and his ministers of justice would have followed the orthodox Prussian school we would have had no war criminal trials at all. Unfortunately they were not Prussians."[28]

In a form letter dated September 12th, 1947 the Headquarters of the EUCOM's 7708 War Crimes Group requested clearance for Guderian's extradiction to Poland from the Headquarters of the 970th CIC Detachment. Guderian was held at OCC, Nuremberg. The reason cited was "in connection with war crimes," and the letter further stated, "subject is responsible for leveling of the city of Warsaw."[29] Chief Counsel for War Crimes, Brigadier General Tedford Taylor, concurred with the extradition. Ultimately, Guderian was cleared of war crime involvement and was not extradited to Poland, to his great relief. He was released from captivity in June 1948.[30]

Field Marshal Maximilian von Weichs, Commander-in-Chief, Army Group "B" on the eastern front and Supreme Commander Southeast during the occupation of Greece, Yugoslavia and Albania. (Shown here as a general.) (Photo courtesy of Herr Peter vom Brocke Collection)

Generalleutnant Bayerlein greeting chief Field Marshal von Weichs visiting in Budapest, Hungary, April 1944. (Photo courtesy of Dittmar-Bayerlein Family Collection)

Von Weichs and Bayerlein in Budapest, Hungary, April 1944. Von Weichs would be placed on trial for war crimes and extradited to Yugoslavia while Bayerlein faced lesser charges as judged by the Denazification Tribunal. (Bundesarchiv Koblenz Bild 146/87/138/32A)

Original Caption reads: Former Field Marshal Maximilian von Weichs, one of the officers on trial before the International Military Tribunal at the Palace of Justice, Nuremberg Germany for his role as Commander-in-Chief, Army Group "B" on the eastern front and Supreme Commander Southeast during the occupation of Greece, Yugoslavia and Albania. Von Weichs had visited Bayerlein and Catholic priests at Esztergom in Budapest, April 1944. (NARA-US Army Signal Corps Photo EUCOM 47-00940, 26 June 47)

Generalfeldmarschall Freiherr Maximilian von Weichs

As commander of the troops in Hungary, Field Marshal Maximilian von Weichs[31] visited the commander of the Panzer Lehr Division, whose training and operational area encompassed Esztergom, located north of Budapest. The Field Marshal visited Bayerlein and met with the priests of the Esztergom Cathedral. Von Weichs, like Bayerlein, was Catholic although Bayerlein changed from Protestant to Catholic to suit the situation.[32] His Excellency, Hungarian Archbishop Serédi Jusztinián, had befriended *General* Bayerlein, to the extent that Bayerlein even moved his headquarters into the Cathedral. The Archbishop was outspoken about the mistreatment of the Jews, and in his Mass condemned the Nazi anti-Semitic policies and brutality. Hungarian Regent Miklos Horthy[33] spoke with Bayerlein in his headquarters at the Archbishop's palace and implored him to try to stop the abuse of the people and the deportation of the Jews. In his Panzer Lehr Division's operating sector Bayerlein successfully stopped the SD and SS harassment of the Jews to the Archbishop and Regent's satisfaction.[34] Unfortunately, the reprieve was short lived, as the Panzer Lehr Division began its transfer back to France on May 4th, 1944. Hitler ordered stronger SD action in Hungary, including aggressively deporting the Jews, and the squelching of resistance. Archbishop Serédi was executed in October 1944 for his continued protests against the deportation of the Jews. Since he had contacted the West regarding a change in sides, Regent Horthy abdicated the same month and was taken to Germany and imprisoned. Evidently what Bayerlein was able to accomplish on a temporary basis, von Weichs was either not willing or able to do for the entire region.

In his affidavit to the Office of the U.S. Chief of Counsel, the former Field Marshal von Weichs stated:

STATEMENT
1. From 15 July 1942 until the beginning of February 1943 I was commander-in-chief of Army Group B in the East. From July 1943 until the end of March 1945 I was commander-in-chief of Army Group F and commander-in-chief in the Southeast.
2. During my tour of duty as commander-in-chief of Army Group B pursuant to orders I had combat groups of the SD under me. These combat groups were furnished to me by the OKH for the alleged purpose of taking over the responsibility for counter-intelligence in operational areas. When I heard that the SD [*Sicherheitsdienst*] was straying from its proper mission of counter-intelligence, I immediately called in the leaders of the combat commandos and ordered them to halt such measures immediately. In addition, I ordered my Ic/AO [Intelligence officer] to supervise the activity of the SD in the future. I had taken upon myself the right of disciplining the leaders of the combat groups when necessary. I believed that the personal qualifications of my Ic/AO could give me the assurance that his supervision would be conscientiously carried out. This was all the more important because in my opinion such measures resulted merely in arousing the otherwise peaceable populace against the troops. Furthermore, I had Hungarian, Romanian and Italian troops under my command, and every effort had to be made not to give them a bad impression of German techniques. Since the highest political and military authorities had the intention of placating the normally pro-German regions of the Ukraine and Don in the quickest military way

possible, I believed it illogical to employ SD methods. According to reports which were received from the *Reichkommissariate* by the SD and myself, such methods had very damaging results. I was always of the opinion that the missions and methods of the SD constituted danger for the troops.

(signed) Baron v. Weichs

In a series of special interrogation reports conducted by the Headquarters, 7th Army and the Interrogation Center, von Weichs provided his insight and opinion on Hitler and the war guilt. He arrived at the Seventh Army Interrogation Center on May 2nd 1945. In the Prisoner of War Bulletin (PWB) report on May 30th 1945, von Weichs interview was as follows:[35]

>   Concerning Hitler and the Regime he claims to assume the same attitude as the majority of his colleagues. In the beginning, he states, certain hopes for Germany's *"Wiederaufrichtung"* (re-establishment) were pinned on the National Socialist movement. Everything which occurred in the latter years, in particular the persecution of Jews, was unworthy of cultured people. "Through this war, the National Socialists have plunged us into exorbitant misery, and were I to judge them, I would not hesitate in shooting all of them."
>
>   He found it *fürchterlich* (dreadful) having to play a leading military role under Hitler's command. He would have handed in his resignation long ago had this became impossible under a Hitler order which came out in 1943. The removal and appointment of generals Hitler reserved as his personal choice. He had an "infallibility" complex and believed of himself, as he stated in a conference, that he was the only person who could solve Germany's problems, and for that reason must solve them all throughout his life.
>
>   From the very beginning, he claims, he did not believe in a "total victory" as envisaged by the National Socialist propaganda. After the fall of Stalingrad he considered the situation as completely hopeless.
>
>   Question of War Guilt. Upon the question regarding his judgment in the issue of war guilt, von Weichs replies, somewhat hesitantly, "It seems rather clear now who started the fight in Poland, and one should not have started it."

By October 1945 the tone of the interrogators toward von Weichs appear to change. The "Final Interrogation Report" by the Seventh Army Interrogation Center during October 1945 is flatly critical of von Weichs and his seemingly unrepentant attitude. The interrogation reads this, "report reflects the personality of its author – a man who possesses most of the undesirable characteristics of a German professional soldier. Von Weichs claims to have disapproved of Hitler's policies; but the *Feldmarschall* "could do nothing about it." Although he admits his share of responsibility during the conflict, he denies authorization of unfair combat methods." The report continues its warning, "It is suggested that readers of this report bear in mind at all times the position of its source. Von Weichs is defeated but far from beaten into submission and does not respect the United Nations policies. He still tries to use the Nazi method of "divide and conquer" with Russia as his favorite scapegoat.

He cannot suppress disappointment at Germany's defeat. There is no trace of an admission that Germany wronged the whole civilized world by embarking on her attempt to conquer the rest of the world":

<u>Hitler regrets an Oversight:</u> "It is common knowledge that the *Führer* personally directed operations during the war and that he was even less receptive to suggestions during the conflict than ever before. His distrust of leading military commanders grew constantly. His attitude toward the General Staff is expressed by the statement, which according to good authority, he made: 'Our General Staff is the last remaining 'fraternity' which I unfortunately neglected to dissolve.' Actually Hitler could not afford to do without the General Staff since he needed its services too much. But he did everything in his power to suppress us.

Von Weichs continued, "There was no basis for the idea that our General Staff constituted a dangerous secret organization. No German General Staff officer ever had any ambitions other than to be a dependable and conscientious leader, subordinated to his commander-in-chief. I cannot deny that such officers were prone to criticize and freely express differences of opinion. But that was exactly for what they had been trained! Hence it should not be surprising that some of its young members, particularly those belonging to OKH Operations Sections who were in a good position to see the fateful errors of leadership, would give vent to their sharp criticism. Nor can it be denied that a number of GS officers were connected with the events of 20 July 44, a fact which precipitated a ruthless weeding-out among their group.

<u>Shortcomings of a Political General</u>: "The events of 20 July 44 served as a stepping stone in Himmler's rise to power. At that time he succeeded in becoming a full-fledged member of our army high command, by assuming control of our *Ersatztruppen* (Reserve units). Our newly organized *Volksgrenadier* divisions were also placed under his command.

"It is my opinion that Himmler's brains were no match for his unlimited ambitions. Through personal contact with this man I discovered that his ideas on matters of military leadership and training were downright childish. He believed, for example, that racial consciousness and political regimentation were more important to military success than thorough training and good soldiership. This person surely would have been a political as well as a military menace to any army under his command. And this person admitted openly that his ultimate aim was to become commander-in-chief of the army!"

<u>Himmler give up his Army Command</u>: "In order to gather more military laurels, Himmler assumed command successively over an army group at the southern part of the Western Front, and another at the northern end of the Eastern front. It may be that he realized his own inability to command troops, or maybe he lost his appetite to become a generalissimo. Himmler's endeavors showed, however, that in Germany's greatest hour of need, our High Command had degenerated to a point where experienced military leaders could be displaced by incompetent politicians.

<u>Wehrmacht Officers and Domestic Policies:</u> "German generals have been reproached for failing to bring about improvements in Germany's domestic policies, for failing to stop Nazi atrocities. But how can one expect an officer to exert influence

in matters beyond his official jurisdiction if he cannot even do as he pleases within his own realm!"

The Futility of Resignations: "It had been suggested that our senior generals should jointly indicate their opposition and, if necessary, threaten with resignation. Anyone who knew Hitler closely, however, who knew of his willfulness, his dislike of resistance, and of his violent temperament, realized that such a demonstration would be in vain, and might lead to dire consequences. Furthermore such resignation need not be accepted because the law provides for lifetime military service of commissioned officers.[36] A later decree even explained the ruling that all attempts of resignation other than those induced by illness were to be considered as sabotage, and would lead to severe punishment."

After completing his interrogations, the Seventh Army transferred von Weichs to the USFET Military Intelligence Service Center in Oberursel on October 12, 1945. Serving as Commander of Army Group F in the Balkans, Field Marshal von Weichs controlled both the operational and occupational forces. These forces included SS units, and the responsibility for their actions fell on his head in his war crimes trial. His troops had operated from Hungary and Austria against allied forces in Yugoslavia. Von Weichs was charged, as Commander-in-Chief of the Southeast area and Yugoslavia, as "responsible for the commission of murder and other crimes in Belgrade."[37] The USFET War Crimes Branch, Deputy Theater Judge Advocate, approved Von Weich's extradition to Yugoslavia on March 31, 1948.

General der Panzer Truppen Wilhelm Ritter von Thoma, shown here earlier in his military career. (Bundesarchiv Militärarchiv Freiburg, Personalakte)

Bayerlein and von Thoma in Africa. The two men evidently had a close friendship – both were Bavarian – Bayerlein from Würzburg and von Thoma from Munich. (Credit: Bundesarchiv Koblenz)

Above: Bayerlein and von Thoma listen to a captured British prisoner. Time frame is just before the El Alamein battle, November 1942. (Credit: Bundesarchiv Koblenz) Bottom left: An interpreter intercedes as Bayerlein's attempts to communicate in English with the British prisoner fail. Both sides treated prisoners humanely. (Credit: Bundesarchiv Koblenz) Bottom right: The interrogation of a captured British soldier continues. Both British and Germans treated their prisoners in accordance with the Geneva Convention. The British soldier has been given a cigarette. After the war Bayerlein and Lucie Rommel edited the Field Marshal's papers and published them under the title "Krieg ohne Hass" literally "War without Hatred." This appears to be the case between the British and the Germans. After the Americans fought the Germans in Tunisia at Kasserine they developed a visceral hatred for the Germans. (Credit: Bundesarchiv Koblenz)

The Prisoners of War in America – The *Afrikakorps* Generals

The post war treatment of German generals and the General Staff taken prisoner in the European theater would be drastically different from those taken captive by the British and Americans in Africa. High-ranking officers and generals, such as *Generalleutnant* Ludwig Crüwell, *Generaloberst* Hans Jürgen von Arnim, *General* Kurt *Freiherr* von Liebenstein, *General* Theodor Graf von Sponeck, *General der Panzertruppen* Gustav von Vaerst, *Generalmajor* August von Quast, and *Generalleutnant* Karl Bulowius were initially sent to Britain, then later transported to the USA for the duration of the war.

One general left behind in Britain was *General der Panzertruppen* Wilhelm Ritter von Thoma. He appears to have died from complications following the amputation of his leg in 1945 by British surgeons at the Wilton Park officer's cage. He is listed as a prisoner of the British from November 4th, 1942 to 1946. One presumes that he was then handed over to the Americans, who had taken over the SS complex at Dachau and were using part of it as a POW establishment.[38]

The generals received the royal treatment from the Brits; their "Blair House"[39] in Great Britain was an opulent standard used to measure the more primitive camps in the USA. The *Afrikakorps* generals experienced a rather rude awakening upon their transfer to POW Camp Clinton in Mississippi. However, the novelty of having generals in their camps, and the question of what treatment should be afforded them caused a great deal of quandary to the Prisoner of War Division and the Provost Marshal General's Office. Guidelines required that the generals should be treated in deference to their rank. This was also done in order to garner a favorable impression of democracy and of America to take back to post-war Germany. Rapidly taking advantage of the uncertainty of the Americans on the care and feeding of German generals above and beyond the treatment of the minions of enlisted and subordinate officers, von Arnim wasted no time in protesting a multitude of perceived ills and shortcomings of the American camp.

Beginning his tirade, General von Arnim prepared a list of what were described by the Provost Marshal's Office as "petty grievances and unrealistic demands." These deficiencies were also given to the Swiss representatives, who concurred with von Arnim's demands. Nothing was too good to be demanded – a swimming pool, or access to one, a tennis court, a library, films – either 16mm or 35mm would suffice, lectures, educational projects, a canteen, personal aide-de-camps, photographs and belongings, paintings to be sent home to Germany; the list grew. In the meantime the former Afrikakorps enlisted men at Camp Clinton sweated under the hot Mississippi sun and worked with picks and shovels on construction of a Mississippi Valley River model project.[40] Two of the more reasonable concerns were the generals' uniforms – wearing only the Afrikakorps issue in the wintertime in Mississippi the men were cold and needed warm clothing and underwear – and the floors in their compound needed insulation.

The German generals were also concerned that the enlisted men serving as aides would be reporting any differences in treatment back to their comrades in the soldiers' compound. Under the command of Field Marshal Rommel in Africa both officers and men received the same rations and lived under the same field conditions. However, von Arnim saw things in a vastly different light. In Africa the men had grown accustomed to seeing their officers share their fate in the fighting at the front. However, out of view of the austere Rommel, von Arnim demanded special treatment and the other generals were obliged to go along and support their superior officer. With the lavish treatment, afforded the generals by the British to the bare-bone facilities of the POW camps in the USA, von Arnim was in for an eventual harsh dose of reality.

Using the opportunity to size up the generals for reorientation or psychological warfare purposes, the Provost Marshal General's Office sent Captain Walter Rapp to speak with the generals under the pretense of addressing their concerns. It was explained to the prisoners that a translator would just bog things down with a third person, so a captain fluent in German was assigned to take care of their desires and requests. General von Arnim was the senior general and spokesman, believed that it was high time the Americans made an effort to correct deficiencies. Hence he was not suspicious of ulterior intelligence or exploitation motives. However, according to Captain Rapp, his purpose was effectively masked by "making a special effort to take care of all their various petty requests and complaints. Every effort was made to keep any possible suspicion on the part of the United States personnel as well as prisoners of war at an absolute operational minimum."[41]

Captain Rapp provided his impressions of the senior *Afrikakorps* generals and European generals captured after D-Day. His task was to sort out potential "cooperative anti-Nazi" generals form the hopelessly pro-Nazi contingent. In two monthly reports covering November and December 1944, he evaluated his subjects. Highlights on a few of the men from Captain Rapp's report follow:

"General von Arnim: This general is probably one of the least appreciable officers for our interests, and impresses me as being very much pro-Nazi. He exercises a very severe command over the rest of the officers, not only by the virtue of his rank, but also by the fact that he constantly is threatening them with retaliation of court martial in post war Germany. While General von Arnim is superficially very courteous and correct, it can be assumed that underneath such a camouflage he has a rather genuine dislike for everything the United States stands for. I do not consider him very intelligent or well educated, and how this man has reached such a position as he did is almost unbelievable, were it not be for the fact that he is a good Nazi and took only command after everything was lost in Tunisia. It is recommended that this officer be left alone to stew in his own juice and no further effort be made from any side to approach this general. As a matter of fact, General von Arnim stated that too many United States officers within the last three or four months had been much too nosey in trying to find out who he was and what his political beliefs are. He stated further that he is quite aware that we are making an attempt to proselyte them and try to obtain the cooperation of German general officers, and warns us that any one of such actions on our part will only run into his stiffest opposition. Some time ago there was an officer at this post, for a duty of about three days, who came from the Captured Enemy and Material Branch of War Department G-2 (Colonel Sweet). It seems that this officer did not use much good judgment in dealing with the Germans and has aggravated some prisoner officers in a rather strong way, such that at present peculiar things are about to happen again.

"Lt. General Crüwell: This general is a former G-4 of Field Marshal Rommel. He has been in captivity since June 1942, and this confinement has had a definite effect on his mental attitude since he is a person certainly suffering from "Barbed Wire

Disease." he speaks good English, which he learned during his years of confinement in Great Britain, and has only been five months in this country. He is very well read and is very interested in English and American literature and has expressed the desire to get books that will help him in further studies. He makes the impression of being a cautious and careful man, who at no time during conversation would commit himself about his political outlook. He has, however, made various remarks which made me wonder and I might say at this time that he is certainly worth watching.

"von Liebenstein: This general was a former German military attaché in Paris and Stockholm. He is very polite and suave and gives the impression of being completely at ease while discussing military and political problems. He was captured at the end of the Tunisian Campaign and was transferred to us only several months ago from a British Prisoner of War Camp. He could be classified as being moderately Anti-Nazi without having said so directly, but implied it by statements when questioned about his political views. Having had a diplomatic career, he is a very cautious man who, during only one conversation with him, does not care to commit himself as yet. He speaks various foreign languages, is very cultured and takes great interest in art, painting, as well as music. He certainly will be further contacted by this officer, since I consider him in the long run reasonable and am sure that with time and patience, he can be given to understand what we are driving at."

In April of 1945, based upon Captain Rapp's input, Major Paul Neuland of the Field Service Branch made the final selections in their opinion of the anti-Nazi generals to transfer to POW Camp Dermott, Arkansas. An American general made the trip to escort the top five German generals who seemed like prospects "for some special and undisclosed purpose." The five generals selected were: Gustav von Vaerst, Theodor von Sponeck, Kurt *Freiherr* von Liebenstein, Behto Elster and Ludwig Bieringer.

Captain Rapp brought some additional insight into the beliefs of the different groups of general officers and the dates and theaters of their capture:[42]

There is at present definite proof of an existing friction amongst the population of the generals' compound. This condition was explained to me as follows: We hold two groups of general officers, one group which was captured prior to June, 1943 and those who were captured after that date on the European continent. The generals made prisoners prior to June 1943 are called by their own comrades *"Afrikaner"*, which means Africans because there were at one time or another members of Marshal Rommel's Africa Corps fighting between Egypt and Tunisia. The other group of generals is called by their comrades *"Franzosen"* or Frenchmen, because these individuals were captured during the invasion of France. The element of time is the only interesting angle in this discussion. Those generals who were captured during the North African campaign are by now approximately eighteen (18) months in captivity and are living in a so-called dream world. They have never been witness to an assault from the air on Germany, nor did they feel the success of the Russian offensive. They only received their information from our newspapers and radios or from such other general officers who have been captured recently. They only believe what they want to believe and discard the rest as propaganda. To them, the appearance of so-called

Secret Weapons and new men of the caliber of Marshal Rommel, is still in the realm of possibility. Letters they received from home say little or nothing about the hardships their own families have to go through. Taking the above facts into consideration, one must realize that these individuals are least susceptible to our ways of life and thought. They still believe in Hitler and his ability to win this war; however, the group who was captured in France or in Germany herself is of an entirely different kind. Some of these men have been in Germany in the last four or five months. They have personally felt the shortage of food, the rule of the Gestapo and the destruction through air power. Many of these individuals have lost their own homes and families, and such horrible experience has made a lasting and profound impression upon them as far as the ultimate outcome of this war is concerned. If these officers dare to report some of the conditions prevailing at present in the Fatherland to their colleagues who were captured a year and a half ago, they are called pessimists, defeatist or even traitors. Thus we come to the conclusion that there exists a remarkable rift between the "*Afrikaners*" and the "*Franzosen*". By the way, such a condition exists, of course, also among the enlisted men. At present those generals captured in France who foster anti-Nazi sympathy are still in the minority. It is recommended that all generals be segregated according to their date of capture as soon as an opportune moment presents itself. This, it is believed, is the best way possible to avoid putting the stigma of Nazi or anti-Nazi on individual generals. It is probably the most innocuous way to perform the task of segregation."

Rommel (right) shared the experiences – and the rations – of his troops at the front, as did his subordinate commanders. Here Rommel meets with Generalleutnant Walter Nehring (3rd from right) as Bayerlein, Chief of Staff, (2nd right) listens. Time frame of photo is June/July 1942 in Tobruk. (Bundesarchiv Bild 101/785/299/4A)

Generaloberst Hans-Jürgen von Arnim surrendered his African forces to the British near Tunis on May 12th, 1943. He was imprisoned by the British in the "Blair House" (a luxurious chateau) then was sent to the U.S. in 1944 and interred at Camp Clinton, Mississippi. Von Arnim, unlike Rommel, insisted on preferential treatment while his soldiers labored in farm fields. (Photo Credit: Imperial War Museum)

Rommel, shown here with German and Italian officers. His Chief of Staff, Bayerlein, looks on as Rommel uses his maps. Bayerlein acknowledged after the war that he and Rommel knew the war was lost when they faced air superiority in Africa. When the British received American aid in the form of tanks, trucks, aircraft and ordnance, Rommel knew they were facing a bitter struggle. (Bundesarchiv Koblenz Bild 101/786/327/19.)

The tired and resigned Field Marshal goes through the motions of planning and fighting in the last few months of the desert war. Bayerlein (r) listens to the other officers' situation brief – showing the well-known expression of sticking out his lower lip. In the Normandy fighting one of his Panzer Lehr Officers, Lt. Hellmuth Henke, described this characteristic as Bayerlein's "razz" that he wasn't liking or buying a story line – that something was amiss.

Well published photograph of Generalleutnant Ludwig Crüwell with his Afrikakorps Chief of Staff, Oberstleutnant Fritz Bayerlein. Photo taken in January 1942. Crüwell, captured by the British when his surveillance aircraft was shot down and its pilot killed, was confused with Rommel. He was eventually sent to a compound, a chateau in London called "The Blair House." As with other African theater general officers, he was later transferred to Camp Clinton, Mississippi. (Bundesarchiv Koblenz Bild 146/84/28/15A)

Original caption reads: General Crüwell passes through Cairo on his way to internment. (Imperial War Museum, British Photographers credited: Lt. Murray; Sgts G. Morris, Travis and Berman, 1 June 1942; Pictures from the Libyan Battle.)

Generalmajor Kurt Freiherr von Liebenstein, former Chief of Staff to Guderian in Panzergruppe 2 in Russia – Bayerlein was the Operations Officer. Shown here as Commander of the 164th Light Division in Africa. He surrendered under von Arnim on May 12, 1943. (Photograph courtesy private collector.)

Gefreiter Eugen Grätz of Würzburg Germany (center) with two Afrikakorps comrades at POW Camp Ellis, Illinois. The men worked at the Rockfield Canning Company in Granville. While the enlisted men worked, General von Arnim annoyed his captors with dreams of swimming pools, furniture for his luxury personal accommodations and tennis courts. Gone were the Rommel days of a general sharing the same quarters, fare and fate as his men. (Photograph courtesy of Herr Eugen Grätz.)

Generalleutnant Theodor Graf von Sponeck, commander of the 90th Light Division in Africa. Bayerlein, von Sponeck and von Liebenstein worked closely together in the final month of fighting and retreating. Von Sponeck was caught up in the surrender, as was von Liebenstein – Bayerlein was transferred to Italy on a medical flight, saving him from captivity. Von Sponeck was sent to Britain, then to Camp Clinton, Mississippi. He was later transferred to Camp Dermott, Arkansas. He also worked for the U.S. Army Historical Division in writing unit and battle history for the Americans. (Photo courtesy of the Dittmar-Bayerlein Family Collection. Photo taken by Bayerlein.)

Rommel is flanked by his Chief of Staff, Bayerlein, as von Liebenstein, Commander of the 90th Light Division, stands smiling behind Bayerlein. In Russia, with Bayerlein as Operations Officer, and von Liebenstein as Chief of Staff of Panzergruppe 2, the men broke the bad news to Generaloberst Heinz Guderian on Hitler's plans for invading Russia.

The Generals in Prisoner of War Camps in Post-War Germany

The Afrikaners in POW camps in America were in for a rude awakening upon their transfers back to the Old Country shortly after the end of the war. The USFET Historian, Colonel S.L.A. Marshall directed one of his historians, Major Kenneth Hechler, to find German generals for a project he envisioned in documenting the other side of the war from the Germans' perspective. An enlisted man, Sergeant Beck, was sent on missions to attempt to locate these men. Compared to the pampering of the British, and the ridiculous demands by General von Armin while held a prisoner in Camp Clinton, Mississippi, Sergeant Beck noted the treatment and "shocking conditions" in his report to Major Hechler:

> The Camp Commandant at Neustadt recognized that conditions were bad ... "that 10% of them (generals) were sleeping on the floor, and three generals had been shot, for reaching through the wire fence to gather weeds they might smoke as tobacco. None of these men had been issued a tobacco ration for the last five months, or had been permitted to write home for the same period of time. (At Hersfeld they told me that they were buying such things as toothbrushes and soap from the guards. At the same time, the pay due them had not been distributed.) He assured me, and I in turn passed on to the generals his assurance that conditions at Hersfeld would be better. However, at Hersfeld I found that the Camp Commandant was actively promoting the discomfort of his prisoners. I saw that twenty to thirty PWs were quartered in one room in triple-decker buds, with enough room between the beds for a man to go through sideways, but no chairs or tables. The generals complain of bed insects, and the food, I am told, is insufficient. On 19 October a doctor from the 7th Infantry visited the camp after ten generals had been removed to the hospital, and, I am told by the camp personnel, said that most of them are in the preliminary stages of malnutrition. Even more striking is the camp order that every PW must run – not double time – to the latrine at night and the instructions to the guards to shoot freely 'to give them a hard time.'"

The Theater Chief Historian, Colonel Marshall, stated that Sergeant Beck's report, "was about as helpful as a club to secure better treatment for the prisoners." Colonel Marshall stated, "When I received this report, I incorporated it into a report that I made orally at one of Lee's[43] staff meetings."

Hitler's Determination and Disposal of his Generals

Hitler could be both generous with his field marshals and generals and murderously vengeful. On one hand, he was exceedingly generous when awarding his commanders the various decorations, such as the *Ritterkreuz*. Often the award was accompanied by property, homes, farms and even vast estates and cash. *General* Hasso von Manteuffel reportedly turned down 200,000 *Reichsmarks* upon his decoration with the Diamonds to the *Ritterkreuz*.[44] Rommel reportedly turned down a private estate.[45] Upon the award of the Swords to the *Ritterkreuz* in July 1944, Bayerlein received a four-tenant apartment building in Heidingsfeld, a village across the Main River from his hometown of Würzburg. The property was originally a city tenement housing project, built in 1931.[46] Bayerlein, always a tight-fisted man, was delighted with the income prospect.[47]

Hitler's other hand was usually closed in the form of an iron fist – he ordered the court martial and execution of those officers that displeased him or disobeyed his orders. The death of Rommel and many others implicated in the July 20th bomb plot shed blood on *Der Führer's* hands as well as his lackey, Field Marshal Keitel. Guderian was sacked and fell into disfavor, as did Field Marshal Gerd von Rundstedt. The men were fired and recalled as the occasion fitted Hitler's uses.

In summary, about 300 General Staff officers were killed in the war, including many murdered upon Hitler's orders. The toll of the war on the general officers had also been a heavy one. Air attack and suicide were the highest causes of deaths of general officer commanders.[48] *General* Franz Halder, who was the former Chief of the General Staff, sat in a concentration camp awaiting his fate, as did *Generalleutnant* Dr. Hans Speidel, Rommel's Chief of Staff in Normandy. Many other field marshals were dismissed when they displeased Hitler.[49]

According to *General* Warlimont, Hitler, "was at his best in conjuring up day dreams for both himself and other people."[50] Warlimont recounted Hitler's philosophy by direct quotation:

> "Not long ago I was reading a volume of Frederick the Great's letters. In one of these letters he wrote: 'I started this war with the most wonderful army in Europe: today I've got a muckheap. I have no leaders any more, my generals are incompetent, the officers are no commanders, the troops are wretched.' It was a devastating estimate. But nevertheless that man got through the war ... Military qualities don't show themselves in an exercise on a sand model. In the last analysis they show themselves in the capacity to hold on, in perseverance and determination. That's the decisive factor in any victory. Genius is a will-o'-the wisp unless it is founded on perseverance and fanatical determination. That is the most important thing in human existence. People who have brainwaves, ideas, etc., will get nowhere in the end unless they also possess strength of character, perseverance, and determination. Otherwise they merely ride their luck. If all goes well they are up in the air; if things go badly, they're down in the depths and give up everything straight away. One can't make world history that way. World history can only be made if, in addition to high intelligence, in addition to thorough knowledge, in addition to continual alertness, a man has fanatical determination and the courage of his convictions, which will make him master of himself . . . no one can last forever. We can't, the other side can't. It's merely a question who can stand it longer. The one who must hold out the longer is the one who's got everything at stake. We've got everything at stake. If the other side says one day: 'we've had enough of it', nothing happens to him. If America says, 'we're off. Period. We've got no more men for Europe'; nothing happens; New York will still be New York, Chicago will still be Chicago, Detroit would still be Detroit, San Francisco would still be San Francisco. It doesn't change a thing. But if we were to say today, 'we've had enough', we should cease to exist. Germany would cease to exist'."[51]

Post-war Reckoning: The High Command Trials and Verdict

The International Military Tribunal is known for its first and most publicized trial, the Major War Criminals Trial – otherwise referred to as "The Nuremburg Trial". However, in all there were about 64 in total, covering the post war period from November 1946 until late 1948, with others following into the 1960s.[52] Case Number 12, or "The High Command Trial," took place from December 30th, 1947 through October 28th, 1948 and included 14 officers, counting anti-Nazi *General* Johannes Blaskowitz, who committed suicide under suspicious circumstances on February 5th, 1948.[53] This trial also included *General* Walter Warlimont, formerly the Deputy Chief of Wehrmacht Operations Staff at Hitler's headquarters. In his trial during October 1948 Warlimont received a life imprisonment sentence, which was later commuted on appeal to eighteen years in prison. In 1957 Warlimont was released on an amnesty plea.[54]

Field Marshal Albert Kesselring, who commanded the Luftwaffe in the desert campaign, was tried from February 17th through May 6th, 1947.[55] Since he commanded troops in Italy, he was charged with war crimes. The bill of indictment constituted two counts: Count 1 of "being party to the murder of 355 Italians"; Count 2 that he "incited troops under his command to murder civilians for reprisals" and in "violation of the laws and customs of land warfare."[56] With the verdict of "guilty on two counts," and punishment by "death by shooting" Kesselring found himself consoling his own attorneys who were sure of his exoneration and shocked by his sentence.[57] Later, with his death sentence commuted to life in prison, Kesselring was incarcerated in October 1947 in Werl prison. He was put to work gumming paper bags. "My performance, for a sixty-five-year-old Field Marshal, was recognized as quite respectable ... When after some months I was asked how I liked the work, I replied, 'Well enough. In my wildest dreams I never imagined I should become a paper-bag gummer.'"[58] Shortly afterward, Kesselring was transferred to the Historical Division to aid in writing the German side of the war. In July 1952 he underwent surgery, and three months later, he was granted clemency and released.[59]

The *Herren Klub* and *Die Bruderschaft*

The *Herren Klub* – with Guderian as a member – consisted of informal secretive post-war meetings of high-ranking German officers. Another group, or *Bund*, Guderian favored was called "*Die Bruderschaft*."[60] Both were considered "alleged neo-fascist organizations" by U.S. Army military intelligence. These groups were kept under close surveillance, continuing into the early-1950s, with field agent reports by the 66th Counter Intelligence Corps Detachment tracking their subjects and sending in periodic updates.[61] Although Guderian was no longer of interest in war crime proceedings, his comings and goings were still of interest to the Army intelligence community. The agent reported that it was difficult to obtain information about Guderian's present political and military beliefs because he lived in a rural area near Schwangau, and his neighbors willingly kept him informed about the presence of strangers. The agent noted, "Guderian received an unknown number of German government representatives and foreign military experts."[62]

Paying the Fiddler – Accountability

Much controversy was generated about the field marshals, the generals and the general staff officers regarding what they knew, when they knew it, and why they did nothing to stop Hitler. This debate still rages sixty years after the end of the Second World War. There were many who acted – and died – for their valiant actions in an attempt to stop Hitler, his regime and his followers. The larger sacrifices are recognized, such as the July 20th bomb plot. But still the question arises. On a smaller scale, one man's decision and his faith and his belief in what is right, what is wrong and how a civilized society should treat its citizens plays into the large question of how to stop Hitler and bring an end to the war. Even division commanders debated silently in the privacy of their own thoughts, or among only their closest and loyal trusted associates. What one man can do is demonstrated in the case of Fritz Bayerlein, with his slowdown and surrender of his own forces when he recognized the outcome and what victory would represent for Hitler, versus the defeat for his own nation.

Who was a valiant commander? Who was ultimately a traitor? Can a soldier or an officer be considered a traitor to Hitler and the oath he ordered pledged to him, but a protector of his country and its people? One can argue the philosophy of destiny, and of fate, or just the inevitable outcome – all seem to weave a never-ending controversial path through history.

Chapter 7 Endnotes

1. Mr. Rommel to author, P. Spayd, copy of a speech given on July 27, 1994 to the German Embassy in London.

2. Ibid.

3. Bosch, William J., "*Judgment on Nuremberg, American Attitudes Toward the Major German War-Crime Trials*," The University of North Carolina Press, Chapel Hill, 1970, 4.

4. Davidson, Eugene, "*The Trial of the Germans, An account of the twenty-two defendants before the International Military Tribunal at Nuremberg*.", The Macmillan Company, New York, 1966, 29.

5. Ibid., 28-29.

6. Ibid., v.

7. Ibid., 63.

8. Ibid.

9. Army Talks, Vol. IV, 5 June 1945.

10. Herr Hellmuth Henke in visit with author, March 2003. Lt. Henke was wounded during the Ardennes Offensive and send to a hospital in his hometown of Hameln to recover. The U.S. Army captured him as he stood in town with his wife.

11. Bayerlein's surrender offer contained these words sent to the First US Army's Seventh Armored Division's Commander, General Robert W. Hasbrouck: "*LIII Korps ist bereit, die Waffen zu stricken, um weiteres nutzloses Blutvergiessen zu vermeiden. Bitte Feuer einzustellen. Erbitte weitere Weisungen.*" translated: "LIII Corps is prepared to capitulate to avoid further useless bloodshed. Please cease fire. Request further instructions. (signed) Bayerlein, Generalleutnant." NARA Microfilm, MS# B-836 (German).

12. General Robert W. Hasbrouck Papers, Carlisle Barracks; Report of Headquarters, First U.S. Army, Office of the A.C. of S., G-2, dated 17 April 1945.

13. NARA, POW file, Bayerlein, letter to Major Hudson dated June 6, 1946.

14. Military Review, interview of General F.W. von Mellenthin in an article, "*Portrait of a German General Staff Officer*," by Lieutenant Colonel Verner R. Carlson, U.S. Army Retired. pp. 69-81.

15. Ibid., 71.

16. Ibid., 72.

17. Ibid.

18. Ibid., 74, 75.

19. Ibid., 74.

20. Ibid., 79.

21. Ibid., 78.

22. Ibid., 79.

23. Ibid., 80.

24. [22] Ibid.

25. Ibid.

26. Ibid.

27. German Intelligence Section, Special Interrogation Series No. 9 (PWB/SAIC/9), dated May 31, 1945, in conjunction with the U.S. Seventh Army Interrogation Center. Heinz Guderian, former *Generalinspektor* of the German Armored Force, Chief of the General Staff from July 21 to March 28, 1945. NARA RG 319/270/84/18; Box 638.

28. NARA, IRR File XE 010802, Volume 2 of 5; US Army Counterintelligence Record, Heinz Guderian.

29. HQ, 7707 War Crimes Group, European Command, NARA RG 319/270/84/3/5, Guderian File, Box 71A, Volume 5, Folder 3/3.

30. Kenneth Macksey, "*Guderian, Creator of the Blitzkrieg*", Stein and Day, New York, 241.

31. According to US Army background information on file at the NARA; RG, 319/270/84/10/1, IRR Personal File, Box 245A, Declassification: NND 931141: "Generalfeldmarschall Freiherr Maximilian von Weichs was born on November 12, 1881 in Dessau, son of a Court official of the Grand Duchy of Anhalt. On the completion of his education at Munich High School in 1900, he entered the 2nd Bavarian Heavy Cavalry Regiment as an officer candidate. Two years later he was commissioned a second lieutenant, and after 9 more years, in 1911, he was promoted to 1st lieutenant. Immediately prior to mobilization in 1914 he was attached to the Bavarian General Staff with the rank of captain. During the First World War he served on the General Staff of a Bavarian cavalry division. After the war, during 1925 to 1927, he was an instructor at the Infantry School and then returned to the 18th Cavalry Regiment. In December 1933, he was appointed commander of the 3rd Cavalry Division and upon its conversion to the 1st Panzer Division 15 months later, he was confirmed to that command. In April 1935, he was promoted to Generalleutnant. At the beginning of World War II, during the Polish campaign in 1939, he served under General Blaskowitz in the 8th Army. In October 1939 he was given command of the newly formed 2nd Army in Western Germany. As a result of the campaigns in the West in 1940, he was promoted to Generaloberst and awarded the Ritterkreuz. In the Balkan campaign he commanded Army Group F to include the occupation troops in Hungary. He is a big boned man with a clean-shaven, studious looking face. He wears horn-rimmed spectacles, which give him the look of a university professor rather than a general."

32. Author's Note: Bayerlein's mother (Louise Denkmann) was raised Evangelical, and his father (Donat) was Catholic. The city of Würzburg where they lived is predominately Catholic. His mother moved from the town of Magdeburg, near Berlin, to Würzburg in 1890, on her 21st birthday. Louise was the illegitimate daughter of Emile Denkmann. Emile's father was the Magdeburg mill master. Fritz Bayerlein's unknown grandfather was rumored to be Jewish, a fact that Bayerlein confessed in his post-war interrogations, stating he was "of non-Aryan descent" and was to be discharged from the Army. Bayerlein would at times claim to be Catholic and at times Protestant; he was adept at practicing both religions.

33. Miklos Horthy served as Regent of Hungary from 1920-1944. A former Admiral, Horthy joined the Axis reluctantly, not wishing to fight with the USSR. Neither did he wish to alienate Britain and the USA. He provided troops in fighting in Yugoslavia and sent a division to the USSR, but in March 1944 he tried to recall his troops, which Hitler disapproved. As a result, Hitler ordered troops (Panzer Lehr Division included) to help aid Horthy's decision to stay with the Axis powers. Horthy attempted to stop the persecution of the Jews in his country by the Germans. In August 1944 Horthy began negotiating with the Allies and withdrew from the war in October 1944. Hitler sent in General Otto Skorzeny, who occupied the Citadel in Budapest. Horthy abdicated and was interred in Germany until May 1945. (John Keegan, Editor, *"Who's Who in World War II,"* Thomas Y. Crowell Publishers, New York, 114-115.

34. Zrinyi, Kiado, *"Seredi Jusztinian Hercegprimas Feljegyzesi 1941 – 1944,* [Seredi – The Archibishop's Notes] Budapest, 1990. 108. [translated from the Hungarian by Mr. & Mrs. Peter Novak]

35. HQ 7th Army, PWB, CPT, German Intelligence Section, Special Interrogation Series No. 5. Ref No. PWB/SAIC/5, 30 May 45. NARA, RG 319/270/04/10, IRR File Box 245A, von Weichs. Declassified: NND 931141.

36. In the Reichswehr, officers signed a term of service for 25 years, enlisted men were signed for 12 years of service. When Hitler instituted the draft in1934, every man was required to serve one year of service.

37. Deputy Theater Judge Advocate, War Crimes Branch, United States Forces, European Theater, to Central Registry, Counter-Intelligence Branch, G-2 Division, U.S. Forces, European Theater, form letter dated May 9 1946, request by the Yugoslavian government for extradition. Response for extradition approved on March 31, 1948. NARA; RG, 319/270/84/10/1, IRR Personal File, Box 245A, Declassification: NND 931141.

38. Information on General der Panzertruppen Wilhelm Ritter von Thoma is courtesy of Mr. Prosper Keating. Mr. Keating also noted, "Wilhelm Josef Ritter von Thoma was born in Dachau on September 11th, 1891 as Wilhem Josef Thoma and is listed as having died in Dachau on April 30th, 1948. The knighthood, which was non-hereditary, came with the award of the Knight's Cross of the Bavarian Military Order of Max Josef on July 5th, 1916 in the South-Western sector of the Russian Front, the highest award for bravery in the Bavarian Army."

39. Arnold Krammer, *"Nazi Prisoners of War in America,* " Stein and Day, New York, 1983 Second Printing. 35.

40. Office of the Provost Marshal General, POW Camps, NARA, RG 389/290/34/16/ Entry 459A, Box 1161, Declassified: NND 770123. Camp Clinton, Mississippi; Camp visit dated May 5 – 7, 1944.

41. Ibid., HQ Army Service Forces, Office of the Provost Marshal General, Branch Office, Subject: Weekly Progress Report No. 1, Prisoner of War Camp, Camp Clinton, Nov 20th – 27th, 1944 Inclusive. The purpose of the visit was to collect intelligence information from the Generals for the Director of Security and Intelligence, Army Services Forces. The Fourth Service Command, Atlanta Georgia was briefed regarding the visit to Camp Clinton.

42. Ibid., Segregation, HQ Army Service Forces, Office of the Provost Marshal General, Branch Office, Subject: Weekly Progress Report No. 2, Prisoner of War Camp, Camp Clinton, dated Dec 8, 1944, period covered: Nov 28th – Dec 7, 1944, page 3.

43. General John H.C. Lee, OVERLORD Logistics Commander & Deputy Commander of US Forces.

44. Barnett, *"Hitler's Generals,"* 433

45. Mr. Manfred Rommel in visit with author, P.A. Spayd.

46. *Stadtarchiv,* Würzburg Germany, *Adresse Buch 1931.* Author's Note: Property noted as owned by the City of Würzburg. Bayerlein remodeled the attic to suffice for his living quarters; none of the tenants left the building. The Morstein family lived there until the General's death in 1970. In 1973, the new owner of the building evicted Herr Heinrich Morstein and his wife because he didn't like the cooking aromas.

47. Spayd, "Bayerlein," 172.

48. MacLean, French L. *"Quiet Flows the Rhine, German General Officer Casualities in World War II,"* JJ. Fedorowicz Publishing, Canada, 1996. 50.

49. Carlson, *"Military Review",* 81.

50. Warlimont, Walter, *"Inside Hitler's Headquarters 1939- 45,"* Presidio, Novato, CA., 1964, Translated from the German by R.H. Barry. 495.

51. Ibid., 495-496.

52. Information from the Jewish Virtual Library; website: http://www.us.israel.org/jsource/Holocaust/WarCrimes. html, as of December 13th, 2003.

53. Ibid.

54. Barnett, *"Hitler's Generals,"*170-171.

55. Ibid.

56. Kesselring, "The Memoirs of Field Marshal Kesselring," Presidio Press, Novato, CA. 1989, 298.

57. Ibid., 305.

58. Ibid., 312.

59. Ibid., 313.

60. OPMG, POW Camps, NARA, RG 389, Camp Clinton, Volume 4 of 5. Report dated 28 April 1948.

61. Deputy Theater Judge Advocate, War Crimes Branch, United States Forces, NARA; RG 319/270/84/10/1, IRR Personal File, 970th Counter Intelligence Corps, Region XII, European Command (EUCOM), Agent Report, by Erling R. Jacobsen & George M. Terry; dated June 5, 1951. Report on Guderian; Declassified NND 856013.

62. Ibid.

8
Rumblings of Discontent

" They may not have cleaned their own houses thoroughly, but they at least removed the major dirt. "
— *General Lucius D. Clay, Deputy Military Governor, U.S. Zone*

German Pensions, Pay, and Food Parcels

The Allies finally realized the economic problems relating to the freezing of military and civil pensions and its hardship on families and the German economy. In early January 1947 the Law for Liberation was amended retroactive to May 1st, 1946. The 16th Implementation Regulation concerning the Payment of Pensions removed the restriction on the payment of both public and private pensions, annuities and benefits. However, a caveat was a 'hold' order on the payment extended to Group I (Major Offenders) and Group II (Offenders) convicted under the Denazification Tribunal. The new regulation included a provision that these pension, annuities and allowances could be classified as confiscatable property under the Law and the *Spruchkammer* could order their forfeiture.[1] However, general officers and General Staff Officers had a longer wait for their pensions to be paid; many waiting as long as 1949 for their restitution.

As prisoners of war writing for the U.S. Army Historical Division, the generals and their staff officers were well paid for their efforts. Although the initial Historical Division program omitted pay, the Military Government authorized salaries for the generals after a decree that they could be employed in a capacity "other than common labor." The "permanent staff" consisting of these reliable and cooperative officers received a flat rate of 400 to 700 Reichsmarks per month. After October 1947 this permanent party group was authorized "to live with their families in quarters assigned to them."[2] They were given a meal a day, in addition to their German ration cards, and also given sundries from the post exchange which were scarce on the German market – items such as soap, shaving supplies, toothpaste and tobacco. The "temporary consultants", those men whose presence and input to the program would be limited and brief, were paid a rate of 100 Reichsmarks per week. The salaries were paid beginning on September 1st, 1947. Funding for the program was arranged with the support of the Historical Division, Office of Military Government for Greater Hesse and the Director of Civilian Personnel of the Second Military District.[3]

For his writing for the Historical Division Fritz Bayerlein received a monthly base payment of 120 *Deutschmark* [DM][4] per month and supplemental food parcels which were urgently needed by him and his family. In December 1946 he received a generous Christmas bonus from the Division equal to one month's pay. After his discharge from prisoner of war status on April 2nd, 1947 Bayerlein and his family lived on the local economy and suffered shortages along with the rest of the populace. Bayerlein's weight and good health waned after his release as a prisoner of war working both as an *Automechaniker* in the Oberursel Motor Pool and writing for the Army's Historical Division. Bayerlein had been treated well by the Americans, and they honored his request to separate him from his fellow generals during his internment. He was fed better since he was considered a working laborer. Bayerlein, unlike many others, was a man not afraid to dirty his hands, he pointed out in an interview with a newspaper reporter just prior to his release. This point won him no friends among his former colleagues.

In addition to the prisoner payments, the Army gave out food parcels and sundries to the men after their release from the POW camps in 1947. At times food was in short supply; the Americans were having a difficult time with the German farmers selling their produce on the black market where they received higher prices and better barter. The Historical Division's food parcels were welcome additions to the sparse diets of the locals. During the winter months of 1948 and into late June of 1949 Bayerlein received two food parcels per month and about six dollars in sundries from the Post Exchange. When he was finally approved for employment after his *Spruchkammer* Trial, Bayerlein received his security clearance and began working for the European Command Intelligence Center.

Draw-down of the Denazification Program

In January 1948 U.S. Army intelligence reports noted the existence of a growing discontent among the Germans with the denazification program. In instances relatives were held in labor camps long after serving their sentences pronounced by the *Spruchkammer*. Subsequent rumors of recent amendments to the denazification procedures fell on welcome ears – both German and American. Rather than holding their own *Landtag* accountable for passing the Law for Liberation, the people looked to the Americans as responsible. The common answer for stripping the program further was: "At last the Americans are realizing the blunder they made and now wish to liquidate it. As they refuse to absolutely repeal this law, they permit amendments to change it from time to time which lessen the power of the original law. This last amendment means only those Nazis charged with misdeeds will be tried. Why didn't the Americans do this in the first place? This denazification has taken too long already."[5]

In the initial implementation of the denazification program those individuals who were described as "little or unimportant Nazis" were punished and fined heavily, as opposed to the ones lucky enough to fall further in line behind the initial onslaught of trials. This more lenient treatment was viewed as unfair to the ones who had earlier trials and suffered under a heavier penalty as opposed to those who managed to wrangle themselves a later trial. A proposal for an amnesty was suggested – provided that persons state that they regretted their former political acts and demonstrate that they would be willing to be good citizens of a democratic state. The objective was to win new friends in support of a democratic Germany and, at the same time, hold accountable the Nazis who committed "real misdeeds."[6]

The Office of Military Government for Hesse, chief of the Denazification Division noted in his April 1948 report that "Protestant and Catholic church officials are protesting that the Law for Liberation was too strict and incriminated far too many people, while on the other hand the *Spruchkammer* officials protested that the changes to the Law for

Liberation made it too lenient." The Military Government's policy and any change had its pendulum effect, and opinions would sway accordingly. The latest changes approved by the *Länderat* amendments to the Law were: "elimination of pre-trial employment sanctions for all persons except those in Category I; removal of military government supervision of trials handled by the tribunals; revocation of all Military Government post-trial employment sanctions; elimination of the delinquency and error report system; and finally, the removal of regulations which provided for Military Government concurrence in the charges to be placed against a respondent by the public prosecutors."[7]

Further protests against the *Spruchkammer* tribunals came from the church. A proclamation from a Protestant church minister who disagreed with the continued prosecutions under the *Spruchkammer* called instead for forgiveness and pardons for their citizens. In a Sunday sermon on February 1st, 1948 the minister read his protest against the denazification program and referred to the Army as a "so-called *Hirtenbrief*' [*trans.* pastoral letter]:[8]

> "The denazification brought tremendous difficulties into our country. Injustice and inefficiency in the execution of denazification planted deep hate among the population, so that further cooperation in the execution of the liberation law can no longer be brought into conjunction with the basic ideas of Christianity. It is therefore suggested to all Christian Germans to discontinue cooperation in the denazification program. Cooperation is considered to include the following positions: *Spruchkammer* president, public prosecutor, assessors, investigators, and witnesses for the prosecution."
>
> As long as such positions are occupied by Christians, the "*Hirtenbrief*' asks them to discontinue their cooperation in denazification.

A few days later news reached the Office of Military Government for Hesse that the clergymen of all Protestant churches in the Hesse and Nassau *Kreis* had taken matters into their own hands concerning denazification. The Military Government kept a watchful eye on the protests, always cognizant that communists and former Nazis, as well as the well-intentioned, blended with the self-serving to create a stew that could boil over. In the Church missal, the official viewpoint of the ministers was as follows:[9]

> The Lord's grace granted us a New Year and summons us as Christians to do our duty, for He has given us the office that preaches conciliation…The administration of the church has been observing with increasing apprehension that our people do not follow the way of conciliation, but that unkindness and hatred are spreading out. And again and again it comes to light that a great part of the actual and increasing bitterness is due to the handling of the so-called denazification.
>
> Right from the beginning, the Protestant Church has done whatever possible for the liberation of the people from the false doctrine of National Socialism; and yet from the moment the Law of Liberation was published, the church pointed out as a warning that this law might easily lead to impenitence, with a great part of the people being compelled to bring forth their own justification and so demonstrate their guiltlessness. The church has furthermore laid stress upon this law being easily made an instrument

of retaliation. But those fears have been far surpassed by events; the attempt has failed all along the line to extirpate National Socialism by means of the law. On the contrary, this way of denazification has brought about circumstances recalling at any moment the bygone years of terror.

Hundreds of thousands of men are living under a permanent pressure, yielding to the temptation to avail themselves of all kinds of lies and untruth in order to cleanse their cases. Tens of thousands lost their jobs and are either waiting for their sentence in concentration camps or, the sentence having been pronounced long ago, for release. The old system of punishing the kin has come back, and after [*the Spruchkammer*] has cleared out and decided one case, the majority of the cases are then quashed, thus no possibility is given to foresee when this [the trials] will come to an end.

The Protestant Church often laid stress upon its proposal to pass sentences exclusively in cases of demonstrable and demonstrated violation and crimes, but no one would ever listen to this. Now the entire catastrophe is evident. Our people have not been lead on the path of conciliation, but that of retaliation; and the seeds of new hatred have come up exuberantly…

We have therefore to forbid the chaplains of our congregations for the sake of the offices and that of our parish to partake in the responsibility for such an annoyance any more…

The aforesaid missive is to be proclaimed to all parishes at all divine services Sunday *Sexuagesimae* (1/2/48). Wiesbaden, at the beginning of Passion-Time 1948.

Protestant Church for Hesse and Nassau Administration.

It was the opinion of the Office of Military Government Hesse Headquarters that the Catholic Church would not take any steps to comment on the Protestant Church's missive. Further, it was believed by the U.S. Military Government that the missive was not election propaganda, but "a purely clerical matter." One political party representative disagreed and stated it was propaganda and an attempt to rally against the communists, who take a strong position in support of the *Spruchkammers*.[10] However, the protests were to no avail, the Catholic Church did not publicly follow in support of the Protestant church, and the *Spruchkammer* Trials continued.

"Just You Wait Until the Americans Leave!"

A Military Government intelligence report for Hesse cited pending problems for many of their German employees:

> Some of the Military Government employees are becoming worried about the time when denazification, public safety, and other Military Government functions are given back to the German government. It is a known fact that a good many indigenous German personnel will be laid off in the next several months. These people are presently looking around for other jobs, and it is expected that possibly there will not be enough trained personnel to see the Denazification Program and other Military Government functions through.
>
> Another aspect is the town's attitude towards those Military Government employees. It is reported that other agencies in the *Kreis* are coordinating and

allegedly resolving that they won't hire Military Government employees once the denazification program ends. Other reports indicate that the population is secretly elated at the plight of persons employed by the Military Government (MG) and are saying that, "now that the Americans are through with these collaborators, we will see what a tough time they'll have finding work." Almost every employee in this office has stated that at one time or another they have been warned that they would be in for a great deal of trouble once the Americans leave. Several employees state that they are now having their first difficulties in this phase. Some persons have put feelers out to see if they could obtain employment in June after many of the Military Government functions are turned back over to the German Government. The attitude of the people is that no one wants to hire an MG employee, and consequently they are obliged to seek employment in larger towns where they are not known.

Comment: It is definitely believed that persons who may have had difficulties with their denazification at one time or another and are now reinstated in their former positions will fight against hiring former Military Government employees who had anything whatsoever to do with Special Branch work. Much of the attitude toward the Military Government is typified by the actions of the German people themselves, who reportedly have warned people of severe consequences at a latter date for going to Military Government asking the assistance of MG employees in housing problems, refugee affairs, etc. It is reported almost daily to this office by persons working for the Military Government that they fear the day when the Americans move out. Many of the employees are getting scared in view of the coming reduction of personnel, the warnings they receive from the population, and the bad prospects with regard to further employment.

An interesting incident took place at a trial in Kronberg when a lawyer – in defense of his client, who had worked for the Gestapo – likened the Military Government to the Gestapo. He said, "that during the Nazi regime people were threatened by the Gestapo, and now they are threatened by the Military Government", and he asked rhetorically "who is worse?" Reportedly, the public in attendance at the trial applauded and left commenting, "that the day of revenge will come." The defendant was sentenced to three years in labor camp.[11]

Ultimately the Military Government drafted and the *Länderrat* approved the "Law Concerning Provisions for Future Employment of Denazification Personnel," thus recognizing the problem of the threats against their loyal German employees. In an amendment to the law on January 13th, 1948 the public prosecutors and all employees of the *Spruchkammer* were guaranteed their future employment or compensation. Essentially this was job security. The new law's provisions included offers of positions of corresponding status when their work with the denazification process had finished. The law also provided for benefit payments in instances when comparable work could not be found. These benefits would be paid up to 18 months. This action served as a big morale boost and "considerably eased the minds of the *Spruchkammer* employees,"[12] whose interest in their work and productivity increased. The Military Government also began an analysis of the areas where the workload was heaviest and behind schedule and which district's workload was almost completed. The public prosecutors and *Spruchkammer* employees were transferred to serve the areas that had the greatest need to eliminate the backlog.

The Historical Division's Generals

From the fourth quarter – October 1 through December 31, 1947 – the Denazification Division's historical report noted that a great deal of time and effort was expended to "dispose of a group of former German general staff officers who for two years were employed by the [U.S. Army's] Historical Division in writing a special history of the German participation in World War II."[13] A special tribunal was finally established by the direction of the Military Governor to dispose of cases of these high-ranking officers at their place of internment in Allendorf and Neustadt, near Marburg. With the cooperation of the OMGUS Denazification Division, Office of the Chief Historian,[14] and the reluctant Minister for Political Liberation of Land Hesse, details were worked out to conduct "priority trials" for the group of former German generals and General Staff officers employed by Historical Division. It was a blow to the morale for these men to see their uncooperative former colleagues released ahead of them, their trials completed. Most of these men had earnestly worked in the Army's best interest only to be rewarded with continued captivity, a continued backlog of writing, and growing demands for special projects. Their fate still rested in the hands of the *Spruchkammer* Tribunal. However, the Minister for Hesse made a point that it "was illegal to try the former German officers employed by the Historical Division anywhere but in a German camp." The Minister proposed instead to transfer the men to a German Civilian Internment Enclosure at Darmstadt when they had completed their work for the Army. No one was anxious to go there, preferring to remain at Neustadt. The Director of the Military Government for Hesse fired off a letter to the Minister of Hesse which stated that only those men who had arrest warrants filed by the Neustadt tribunal would be sent to civilian camp. Many of the generals were released to return to their homes, and others released from custody.[15]

Beginning in January 1948, denazification trials began for the 205 generals and officers remaining at the Historical Division. With the exception of 19 men, all were acquitted. Of the 19 officers: two were convicted as Group I, Major Offenders, and were sentenced to ten years in labor camp with the confiscation of all property; two were convicted as Group II, Offenders, to serve five years in labor camp and confiscation of all property; five men were convicted as Group III, Minor Offenders, and their punishment was two years probation, and limited to ordinary labor. Their fine was a forfeiture of forty percent of all their property with a minimum 500 *Reichsmarks*. Nine men were charged in Group IV, Followers, and fined 2,000 *Reichsmarks*. Only one man was exonerated, Group V: no punishment was levied.

Demise of the Denazification Program

Francis Case, of the House Select Committee on Foreign Aid, recommended that all denazification proceedings be closed on May 8, 1948 with full amnesty for lesser offenders and followers.[16] A Youth Amnesty and a Christmas amnesty had been granted in 1946 to relieve the enormous backlog of cases. A youth amnesty was granted with the rationale that young children were acclimated to the Nazi propaganda in schools and organizations, hence were unable to refuse the indoctrinations. A Christmas amnesty was granted for those people who were poor, sick, old and obviously not a threat and hadn't profited from National Socialism. Seeing their jobs float away with the dwindling current of cases, the Denazification Division noted public prosecutors and chairmen of the many tribunals were purposefully slowing down *Spruchkammer* operations. But General Clay, asked for his opinion by the Army, stated, "Each month of trials and releases leaves a constantly smaller backlog, which, however, contains increasingly the bad actors. A general amnesty would free these bad actors and would really discredit the entire program."[17]

The Final Numbers in the U.S. Zone

The tribunals in the U.S. Zone tried over 930,000 individuals.[18] By the end of December 1947 over 3 million *Meldebogen* were received and analyzed. Of this amount over 2.1 million people were not charged. The chargeable cases totaled about 880,000. The public prosecutor "quashed" over 260,000 for the Youth Amnesty, and 275,000 were discharged for the 1946 Christmas Amnesty. By the end of June 1948, out of 20,300 original charges under Group I, 'Major Offenders,' 1,284 were found guilty and 404 sentenced to between 5 to 10 years in prison. For Group II, 'Offenders, Activists and Militarists' about 318,000 were charged, 18,900 found guilty, and 7,900 and of this number sentenced to up to five years in a labor camp and fined a minimum of 1,000 *Reichsmarks*. Group III, 'Lesser Offenders,' totaled 180,000 who were charged and 97,200 convicted, of which 75,300 were fined less than 1,000 *Reichsmarks*. Group IV, 'Followers,' were the largest group, with 365,100 charged, and 445,100* found guilty (*Note*: This larger total includes those individuals who were downgraded from Groups I and II.) About 463,600 people were fined less than 1,000 *Reichsmarks*. The 'Exonerated' tally was 16,100, and the cases with 'Proceedings Dismissed' totaled 298,400.

The penalties for some Groups were mandatory, and the *Spruchkammer* could use its own discretion on the punishment for the other groups. The penalties ranged from imprisonment for up to ten years, property confiscation, special labor details, and employment right restrictions.[19]

Result of Denazification

In his conclusion over the results of the Denazification Program General Clay contended, "It takes courage to back a hard program which directly involves over twenty-five percent of the population. I am convinced that major Nazi leadership was driven from hiding by the law and excluded from leadership for years to come. Certainly there was restored to citizenship a large group who now have full rights, and yet on the record can be charged as having been Nazis. As to the degree of guilt of the individual and his contribution to the growth of the Nazi party, there will ever be differences of opinion. If the nominal Nazi had not been restored to citizenship and given the opportunity to lead a normal life, we can be sure that political unrest of a serious nature would have developed sooner or later. Moreover, the punitive and exclusion measures were administered by tribunals responsible to public bodies elected by the German people. They may not have cleaned their own houses thoroughly, but they at least removed the major dirt."[20]

The Cold War Begins

As Military Governor, General Lucius D. Clay, stated:

> "The 'Cold War' … absorbs much of the energies, talents for leadership, and resources of the majority of the peoples of the world. Man must devote his best thought to security, his sustenance to the maintenance of large fighting forces, and his inventive genius to the development of new and more terrible weapons of war.
>
> "Why has this come about? When may it end so that we may live in a stable world at peace with one another?"[21]

The war against Nazism ended – only to be replaced with the Cold War against Communism. Much can be said about the change from communism to terrorism.

Chapter 8 Endnotes

1. Office of Military Government for Greater Hesse, Subject: Payment of Pensions under the Law of 5 March 46, dated 29 Jan. 1947. NARA, Box 1115.

2. Detwiler (editor) *"German Military Studies,"* 76.

3. Donald S. Detwiler, Editor, *"World War II German Military Studies, A Collection of 213 special reports on the Second World War prepared by former officers of the Wehrmacht for the United States Army, Volume 1."* Garland Publishing, Inc., New York, 1979.69.

4. In a transition phrase after the war, the old *Reichsmark* (RM) currency was replaced with *Deutschmark* (DM).

5. Report No. 167, dated 26 January 1948, Denazification, Intelligence Reports, Jan. 1, 48 – Dec 31, 1948, by Major Charles F. Russe, NARA , RG 260/390/49/27/5-7/ Box 1125.

6. Ibid.

7. Office of Military Government for Hesse, Denazification Division, Wiesbaden Germany, 28 April 1948, NARA RG 260/390/49/27/5-7, OMGUS Records of the Denazification Branch, Box 1127.

8. NARA: Office of Military Government, Liaison & Security Office, Landkreis Maintaunus (Hesse) Information Report No. 27 (Sociological), Box 1125.

9. Ibid., Office of Military Government for Hesse, Information – Report, dated 3 February 1948.

10. Ibid.

11. Ibid.,OMGUS for Hesse, Kuausib & Security Office Frankfurt, dated 16 January 1948 Obertaunus, Field Advisory Reports, Box 1121.

12. OMGUS Records of the Denazification Branch, 28 April 1948, page 9; NARA RG 260/390/49/27/5-7, Box 1127.

13. OMGUS, Denazification Division report file, Box 1127, pg 21.

14. At the end of the war, the Historical Division was under United States Forces European Theater (USFET). In March 1946 it was redesignated as Office of the Chief Historian, European Command (EUCOM), and shortly afterward changed again to Historical Division, EUCOM. Source: Detwiler, (editor), *"German Military Studies"*, Chronology 223.

15. Detwiler, (editor), *German Military Studies*, 72-73.

16. Clay, *Decision*, 259.

17. Clay, *Decision*, 259.

18. Clay, *Decision*, 260.

19. NARA RG 260/390/49/27/5-7, OMGUS Records of the Denazification Branch, Box 1115, Office of Military Government for Hesse, Subject: Operation of the Law for Liberation from National Socialism and Militarism, dated 9 December 1946, signed by the Chief of the Denazification Division, Hubert I. Teitelbaum.

20. Clay, *Decision*, 262.

21. Lucius D. Clay, *"Germany and the Fight for Freedom."* Harvard University Press, Cambridge, Massachusetts. 1950.

9
The Difficult Past

A time to talk . . .
When a friend calls to me from the road
and slows his horse to a meaning walk,
I don't stand still and look around
On all the hills I haven't hoed.
And shout from where I am, What is it?
No, not as there is a time to talk.
I thrust my hoe in the mellow ground,
Blade end up and five feet tall!
And plod: I go up to the stone wall
For a friendly visit.
— Robert Frost

Working for the U.S. Army

In April 1947 after his release from prisoner of war camp, Bayerlein began working for the Military Intelligence Service Center (MISC). The organization changed names during June 1947 to the 7707th European Command Intelligence Center (ECIC). Bayerlein kept his employment with the new organization. Part of its mission now included gathering intelligence information from returning prisoners of war – usually from the Russian-held territory. As part of his employment Bayerlein was required to sign a Pledge to Secrecy. One of his tasks was interrogating German prisoners returning from the East and reading intelligence information from East Germany. He had two alias names – "Fritz Berger' and 'Fritz Schultz'. His first name was often changed from "Fritz" to "Fred."

The Landkreis Liaison and Security Office of the Office of Military Government in Greater Hesse sent a letter to the ECIC requiring the dismissal of Fritz Bayerlein, labeling him as "unemployable"[1] since Bayerlein's employment as a civilian fell under Law Number 104 for Liberation From National Socialism and Militarism.[2] The Law provisions stated that General Staff Officers and general officers were only to be employed as "ordinary labor." Work at ECIC was prohibited also; his work was not ordinary labor by any means. Colonel Philp, commander of the ECIC, wrote a letter in his behalf, citing Bayerlein's, "full cooperation, completely and willingly, on any project on which he was involved, always consistent with honor and truth." With this referral and one from EUCOM Theater historian, Colonel S.L.A. Marshall, Bayerlein was able to hang on to his job.

Shortly after he was exonerated by the verdict of the Obertaunus *Spruchkammer* in October of 1947, Bayerlein was finally hired as a foreign national U.S. Army civilian employee. Bayerlein's first duties were to interview returning German prisoners of war and escapees of U.S. Army interest on activities of the Soviets in the Eastern Sector. Bayerlein had been very persistent in perfecting his English. During the late-1930s he had taken an English course, so he had the basics. However, with his usual tenacity, he committed himself to learn more while interred as a POW.

According to former U.S. Army Technical Sergeant Fred Prejean, the 7707th ECIC was redesigned as the 513th Military Intelligence Service Group (MISG). He was in charge of the Message Center and Top Secret Control Section. "Lieutenant Colonel Howard H. Ruppart was the last commanding officer of the 7707th before it was designated the 513th. I was there during this time. He was replaced by a Colonel Frances E. Fellows." Mr. Prejean described the functions of the Intelligence Group: "Initially, the post was used to help identify those people who could be exploited during the denazification programs and beginnings of the Cold War. Personnel at the ECIC performed interrogations that were later used to determine if the American intelligence community could utilize the sources as informants. These informants were used to track both former Nazi war criminals as well as develop new intelligence. Agents would gather information on communist activities in all of the sectors of occupation. There was a great emphasis placed on the Soviet Sector and communist activities. As is well known, after the war the relationship between Russia and the Western Allies rapidly deteriorated. Having intelligence agents was imperative to the security of the Western Allies. After the period of denazification the American focus was rapidly changing from the denazification to the 'Cold War.' The Center was used to exploit refugees and displaced persons from the Eastern Bloc countries. These were the days before the Berlin Wall. At the time there was only a cleared field of about seventy-five yards between East and West. Each day the area was tilled, and one could see the footprints of people that had left the Eastern Bloc the night before. Many people were brought to the ECIC and interviewed and housed for a time. We sent classified reports onto Headquarters, EUCOM."

"The ECIC's location was beautiful," recalled Mr. Prejean. "It was a comfortable place to be, located in a village about one or two miles from Oberursel. It was heavily forested, and the buildings we used were old German army barracks. It didn't seem as though it was your usual Army post; it was a much quieter." The on-going daily events were thoroughly regular Army routine with first call beginning each weekday morning at 0615 hours, reveille at 0630, mess call for breakfast at 0645, lunch mess at 1200, Call to the Colors at 1700 hours and the evening mess at 1730.[3] The commanding officer of the ECIC made monthly command inspections of the activities and buildings, reviewing sections such as the "Blew Inn," the barber shop, snack bar, Taunus Mountain Lodge, Blue Room, enlisted mess, barracks, WAC billets, the guard house, the fire station, stockade, theater, message center, mail room, supply and transportation areas.

During 1950 Herr Bayerlein worked for Major Herman L. Halle, Chief of the Projects Branch under the Intelligence Group. Along with the Projects Branch, there were the Interrogation Branch and Control Branch that also reported to the Group. Halle had been promoted from the Operations and Documents Section to the Projects Branch office. With his excellent command of English, Bayerlein was assigned and working in the German PW Exploitation Section. Bayerlein presented his chief with a signed copy of his newly published book of Field Marshal Rommel's memoirs, *"Krieg ohne Hass"* (*"War without Hatred"*).

Although having no official duty involving the former general, Tech Sergeant Prejean was trusted with one of Herr Bayerlein's precious possessions – his money. "From 1952 to 1954 I was stationed in the U.S. Army at the European Command Intelligence Center at Oberursel, Germany. At that time Fritz was working as a Department of the Army civilian employee as an interrogator and an analyst. He was interrogating the informants who had defected from the Eastern Zone of Germany and other points under Soviet control. One of my duties was to issue the monthly paychecks to the civilian employees. I would hand Fritz his check, and he would immediately endorse it and hand it back to me so that I could take it into Frankfurt and cash it for him. That way it saved him some time because he didn't have to go into Frankfurt himself. After the war was over, apparently he was the first general officer prisoner of war to ask for some kind of work to do. So the U.S. Army put him to work in the Oberursel motor pool, changing truck tires. He did a good job and eventually ended up as an interrogator working in the Intelligence Center.

"Fritz once gave us a very interesting briefing on the invasion of Russia and the ensuing campaign – especially their primitive equipment," Mr. Prejean noted. "During the war Guderian and the rest of the command wanted to take Moscow as the capital for an objective and as well as an important rail junction. Fritz explained to us that they were dismayed when the order came from Hitler to cease the advance on Moscow and attack Smolensk and Kiev. As he explained this, Fritz narrowed his eyes and his mouth curled. It clearly upset him to talk of that time. He didn't appear to like the Russians at all."

"Bayerlein was an impressive man," the former sergeant remembered: "he was in top shape, never wasted a moment, had good health and was very astute, alert and snappy. Fritz wore some nice clothing; the double breasted suits were popular back then."

"For the record, the German people at that time were very good to us American military personnel, and they were very helpful. They had been humbled by the war, and in addition they were very appreciative of our presence in the western part of their country. They well understood that if we weren't there, the Soviets would be."

Bayerlein's U.S. Army European Command (EUCOM) Intelligence Center (ECIC) identification card. Bayerlein worked for the U.S. Army Intelligence area from the time he was exonerated by the Denazification Tribunal in October 1947 to 1957. He returned to his hometown of Würzburg and ran an oriental carpet business. (Courtesy of Herrn Willi Dürrnagel)

Left: Bayerlein as an intelligence analyst for the ECIC had the benefit of using a U.S. Army automobile. Here is he enjoying the prestige of the vehicle – a rare privilege of driving and having gasoline – as sister Ellen expressed her excitement over her older brother's good fortune. Nephew Fritz tinkers with the door handles. (Photograph courtesy of Dittmar-Bayerlein Family Collection.) Right: With a newer vehicle provided by the U.S. Army, Bayerlein leaves his city-awarded apartment to drive to Oberursel to his ECIC office. On the tag the "A" was the American Sector, and "B" was for Bavaria. Bayerlein lived in the attic of the apartment building, garnering rent from four tenants. The Morstein family of parents and six children (later growing in size to eight) fondly remember Herr General. Nephew Fritz Dittmar tinkers on his motorcycle. Bayerlein's sister Ellen, her husband and son lived with Bayerlein after their own downtown apartment was destroyed in the firebombing of Würzburg on March 15, 1945. (Photograph courtesy of Dittmar-Bayerlein Family Collection.)

And a Devoted Friend

After the war the trustworthy and devoted *General* Bayerlein worked with the Field Marshal's widow, Frau Lucie Marie Rommel, to publish her husband's detailed manuscripts. Their first book of Rommel's extensive documents was *"Krieg ohne Hass,"* published in 1950 in Germany; and in 1953 the English edition, *The Rommel Papers*, was edited by Sir Basil Liddell-Hart and published by Harcourt Brace. The book became an international bestseller. Liddell-Hart noted on the title page, "with the assistance of *Generalleutnant* Fritz Bayerlein, Lucie and Manfred Rommel." It is obvious from the details in *"Krieg ohne Hass"* that the brunt of the work for the *"Papers"* was carried over and compiled by Bayerlein, Mrs. Rommel and Manfred. Mr. Manfred Rommel recalled with his usual good humor that his role was somewhat less: "I did a lot of typing. You know, after all, Bayerlein was the *General*; and as for me, I was only the former enlisted soldier and clerk!"[4]

Bayerlein stayed as the Rommels' houseguest at their home in Herrlingen. Manfred went to University and studied law. During the 1950s, Bayerlein escorted Mrs. Rommel to various charitable functions designed to establish the organization *"Rommel Sozialwerks,"* and obtain funding to support veterans' families, published of veteran newsletters and magazines and provide maintenance at cemeteries for the soldiers killed during the war. The Rommels and Bayerlein were loyal and devoted life-long friends.

Documenting the Campaigns

The former chief of staff also aided a select group in writing biographies of the Field Marshal. Brigadier General Desmond Young met with Bayerlein and Mrs. Rommel in his research for his book, *Rommel, the Desert Fox* published in 1950.[5] General Young made arrangements for getting a visa for Bayerlein and young Rommel to travel to London. Several others wanted a meeting with the two men also. In 1950, British General Chester

Original caption dated 15 June 1956: "At a band concert given by the 10th Infantry Division Band, Sergeant Jesse Holbert, Headquarters Company, meets General Fritz Bayerlein, former Chief of Staff for Rommel, and Mrs. Rommel, wife of the famous general." (Photograph courtesy of Dittmar-Bayerlein Family Collection.)

Bayerlein, the Field Marshal's wife, Lucie, and their son, Manfred Rommel, worked to edit the Field Marshal's papers, first published as Krieg ohne Hass (War without Hatred) in 1950. (Photograph courtesy of Dittmar-Bayerlein Family Collection.)

Manfred Rommel and Bayerlein pause for a photo session as they work on their second English edition of the Field Marshal's memoirs, The Rommel Papers, – officially edited by Sir Basil Liddell Hart who claimed the lion's share of the credit. Manfred attended University, and Bayerlein had to report back to his job at ECIC in Oberursel as well as answer a plethora of questions from Sir Basil. (Photograph courtesy of Dittmar-Bayerlein Family Collection.)

Bayerlein and Manfred Rommel enjoy a lighter moment from their work. Bayerlein stayed with Lucie and Manfred as their houseguest in Herrlingen. (Photograph courtesy of Dittmar-Bayerlein Family Collection.)

Wilmot arranged a meeting with *General* Bayerlein in London on August 3rd, and again on the 5th, during a visit with Sir Basil Liddell Hart. The three men met again with more discussion on Bayerlein's opinion of Russian T-34 tanks compared to the German Panther. Their primary purpose was to visit with Sir Basil and to attend a meeting with the publisher of the *Rommel Papers*, Harcourt Brace.

Bayerlein worked with many others during the 1950s and 1960s, Dr. Paul Carell-Schmidt was by far one of Bayerlein's favorite authors, as the men forged a lifelong friendship and Carell was invited to many social functions such as the Würzburg *Winterball* and especially as an honored guest at General Bayerlein's birthday celebrations. Another favorite, fellow German author, was Mr. Franz Kurowski, who also worked closely with him. Mr. Kurowski's book, "*Panzer Lehr Division*," was an account taken primarily from General Bayerlein's experiences. It has not been translated into English.

American author John Toland had a bit more difficult time tracking down Bayerlein and getting his cooperation for a book entitled, *The Last 100 Days*.[6] By 1958, Bayerlein's interests were in his new carpet business that was doing quite well and occupying most of his time. Toland's correspondence with one of his helpers in Germany revealed that it took several years before he was able to secure an interview with Bayerlein. However, Toland's associate in Würzburg, Liz Phillip, recalled an experience in gaining information from Bayerlein. In a letter to Toland, dated January 20th, 1958, she wrote: "As you remember, General Bayerlein promised you to give you complete notes and that I was to send them on to you. I tried to contact Bayerlein several times. As it happened, he spent several weeks in London with the Metro Film (I suppose in some advising capacity) and when he came back, he had to get his Christmas business under way and opened a new store. In other words he was too busy to do any work for you. I called him again the other day, and he promised to have the notes by the end of this month. As soon as I get the thing from him, I shall pass it on to you."[7]

In a follow up and frustrated letter to Toland dated March 4th 1958, Liz wrote:

> "I don't know if it will console or irritate you, but I haven't been able to track down the 'slippery carpet salesman,' and to be honest I am tired of trying to contact him. As I told you before, he promised to have the write-up for me by the end of January. I have called him and his dubious assistants several times since then, always with the same result: putting the thing off."

Through another one of Toland's helpful research associates he was able to arrange a meeting with Bayerlein in person, and Bayerlein did, at last, provide a narrative for Toland's book on the combat in the West, in Düsseldorf-Köln, Remagen and the Ruhr pocket capitulation. The two men met on September 14th and 15th of 1963, and hashed through Toland's questions. In his notes, Toland noted his opinion that Bayerlein was a, "strange, nervous man."[8] Bayerlein's health was in early stages of deterioration – effects from the hepatitis and nephritis from the desert war in North Africa. Bayerlein provided a lengthy detailed account of his experiences in the last months of the war.

Bayerlein worked as technical advisor on three films. The most famous was the 1951 Twentieth Century Fox production based on Brigadier Young's book, "*The Desert Fox, The Story of Rommel*" starring actor James Mason in his famous role as the Field Marshal.

Bayerlein left the Army's employment in 1957, taking the time to run his and sister Ellen's two oriental carpet stores in Würzburg. Bayerlein enjoyed the company of many attractive and interesting women. Here they celebrate "Winterball" in 1964, with Frau Friedel Hilgen, Bayerlein's companion, who had a strong wish to be the his wife. A smiling Dr. Paul Carell-Schmidt (r) also enjoys the evening. Dr. Carell-Schmidt wrote many books about the war, including many first-hand accounts recalled from Bayerlein and his former aide, Alexander Hartdegen. Also shown in the photo is Bayerlein's sister, Ellen (3rd from left) next to her husband, Mr. Alberto Rose (2nd from left). (Photograph courtesy of Dittmar-Bayerlein Family Collection.)

Bayerlein's second advisor role was that of Columbia Pictures, "*The Guns of Navarone*," based on the book written by Alistair MacLean. Gregory Peck, David Niven and Anthony Quinn starred in this film. Bayerlein supervised the Greek actors who portrayed German soldiers. This film received seven 1961 Academy Award nominations, which also included Best Picture. "*Navarone*" won the Best Special Effects award for action and adventure movies. The third film Bayerlein was involved in was a German production of "*Rommel 'ruft Kairo*" [*Rommel Calling Cario*] – a rather dismal and ambiguous film of attempted intrigue, but no real action.

The Women in Bayerlein's Life

In their many years together prior to the war, *Fraulein* Hanna Huber devoted herself to Fritz Bayerlein, who was a confessed confirmed bachelor.[9] She made no demands of him, knowing that would end their relationship; so she preferred instead to see him on his own terms. Their relationship began in 1920, when the Bayerlein family moved from the crowded downtown Würzburg apartment to within a block of the Main River in a fourth floor apartment. Hanna was a neighbor's daughter and was a cheerful and hardworking woman. She was immediately attracted to the handsome Fritz. Hanna never considered marrying another man, she adored Fritz Bayerlein and loved him her entire life. Her heart was set for a man she could never have as her husband – so she stayed single. Bayerlein was not faithful to anyone and relished his freedom as a single man to do as he wished. In the post-war years, Hanna would relay her vacation activities to some of her patients, always smiling to herself when she had a rare vacation with Bayerlein. "Hanna had a lot of hope for Fritz," remembered *Frau* Helga Morstein Woods, a long time family friend. Another close neighbor, Frau Christine Singer, recalled that "*Herr General* and *Fraulein* Hanna Huber made such a striking couple – she was very pretty and he was a distinguished looking man. It is a shame they never married."

Hauptmann Alexander Hartdegen, Bayerlein's friend, confidant and aide from Africa to St. Lô, had indulged in a bit of gossip about his commander. He confided to *Major* Bernd Werncke, the Panzer Lehr Division logistics officer that at the age of 19 or 20 Bayerlein had fathered a daughter. The marriage policy of the *Reichswehr* at that time practically prohibited marriages unless the officer or soldier was at least twenty-seven years old, or had served eight years service.[10] To marry, one would have to forfeit his military career unless one's relatives were rich enough to guarantee to the army that the widow and children would be provided for. Mr. Rommel confirmed this policy, stating that his parents were required to have relatives sign for their marriage. With unemployment soaring, the

Parting his lips with a slight smile for the photographer, Bayerlein's eyes sparkle roguishly as though "a thousand devils dance there" – an old German expression.

A 1940 photo of Bayerlein with his sister Ellen (left), and Frau Hart was owner of Wibbelsbacher Höhe a favorite cafe. (Photograph courtesy of Dittmar-Bayerlein Family Collection.)

In the mid-1960s, Bayerlein sits with his brother-in-law's "Cousine Marianne". (Photograph courtesy of Dittmar-Bayerlein Family Collection.)

September 1941 photo of Fraulein Hanna Huber – with the same "thousand devils" – as she looks at Bayerlein. Hanna never married, remaining close and faithful to Bayerlein over his lifetime. On an outing with Matthäus and Ellen Dittmar, and their son Fritz, Bayerlein captures Hanna's feelings for him. Here she stands next to Matthäus Dittmar. (Both photographs courtesy of Dittmar-Bayerlein Family Collection.)

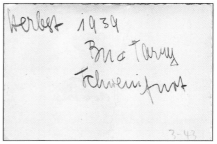

Bayerlein's handwritten note on the back of the photo identifies: "Herbst (Fall) 1939 Bu & Tarmy, Schweinfurt." Evidently the beguiling and beautiful Tarmy was another out-of-town interest for Bayerlein. It is apparent from his photograph collection that he had different women in different towns and villages. (Photograph courtesy of Dittmar-Bayerlein Family Collection.)

Bayerlein listens to his companion, Frau Hilgren, and shows the effects of too much "Sekt", his favorite drink. She had the great hope of becoming his wife. (Photograph courtesy of Dittmar-Bayerlein Family Collection.)

currency devalued and hard political times upon them, Hartdegen said that Bayerlein and the young woman not married and had signed their daughter over for adoption. Hartdegen didn't mention who the woman was, Mr. Werncke recalled.[11] *Frau* Mortstein Woods opined that this woman was not Hanna. "She would have never given up Fritz's baby, no way. She loved him too much." So rumors and mysteries of the man's life continue unsolved.

Usually Bayerlein kept his other relationships out of town, for the most part. As Hanna aged, Bayerlein turned to pursuing much younger women. At least at times, he was sensitive enough not to throw his sexual wanderings under Hanna's nose. In the timeframe of 1938 through 1940, he particularly seemed to be enmeshed in lustful adventures, from the dates of the photographs. In particular, in 1939, one of his fond memories from the town of Schweinfurt was a stunningly beautiful brunette by the first name of "Tarmy" – an unusual nickname. In his bold handwriting Bayerlein scribbled his conquest's first name on the back of her photos, plus the date and town where she lived. Tarmy had a little terrier named "Bu," and he noted its name also, as it was an impressive gesture not to forget her little pet's name. In his private photograph collection, Bayerlein had collected scantily clad females in various stages of dress, or as the case was more appropriately, undress. He also photographed another lovely younger lady laying in the grass in her bathing suite with the straps pulled down. Then she frolicked about in the grassy field with the suite top pulled down to her waist, to the great enjoyment of her photographer. A particular favorite of his was the posing and sunbathing of a woman on Alpine rooftops – *ohne* blouse and brassiere. This must have been an entertainment – or shock – to the passers-by on the streets below.[12] Sticking to the steep tiled roofs also seemed to present a challenge for both photographer and the woman.

Exactly why Bayerlein had these relationships, and why he never wanted to permanently consummate them, so to speak, is unknown. He was notoriously cheap, except when it came to his own entertainment, usually in a red light district, partying with his friends – that was okay with him. Perhaps Bayerlein could not envision the expense of marriage – a larger apartment to pay for, the woman's clothing, and – God forbid – the endless stream of expenses relating to things children needed. His wife would expect to quit her job and raise children; after all he was a *Major*, then promoted to an *Oberstleutnant*. The women perceived him to be a good catch – a career officer – very handsome – and a pleasant, happy man. To Bayerlein, perhaps it was easier, and cheaper, to fool around and then run, leaving disappointed women in his wake. What made the man bolt back to the safety of the garrison can only be surmised. The newest lady friend may have slowed down to look at engagement or wedding rings in jewelry store window, or paused on the street to admire a new baby with its happy mother. At any rate, Bayerlein was astute in translating his girlfriend's inadvertent warning signs that the relationship was becoming serious enough for her to contemplate marriage to him. Marriage he did not want, and whether or nor this was discussed early into the relationship isn't known. Whether he acted irresponsibly or not is the matter of personal judgment and circumstances.

Bayerlein conducted himself as a free and single man and had no commitments of an intimate nature. Postwar, with his high rank of a retired *Generalleutnant* and striking good looks, he was a popular escort. That he was financially secure, with his general's pension, his share of book royalties, his commercial and residential properties in two Würzburg locations, occasional writing for other publications and ultimately his oriental carpet businesses. The women could tick off the man's money and assets in their heads – so *Herr General* was a big hit, as he seemed to loosen his purse strings a bit more in his later years. However, Bayerlein did choose to keep out of marital minefields. One of his friends of 25 years, *Herr* Jürgen Hempel, recalled a particular instance at a popular dance hall in Würzburg. *Herr* Hempel and *Herr General* Bayerlein watched the antics of men and women who were known to be cheating on their spouses. They also to listened the bitter bickering between some of the men and their wives. Turning to his friend, Bayerlein's brow furrowed, and he hissed under his breath, "See all of this now?" he turned and gestured with his back to the crowd, "You can now understand the reason why I've never married!"[13]

In his post-war activities Bayerlein attempted to keep to his pattern of having relationships in different towns, much as he had done before the war. For example, during the 1960s he visited an attractive blonde in the town of Garmisch-Partenkirchen in the Bavarian Alps. He liked to go and watch the ice-skating as the woman had a pretty twelve-year old daughter who skated. His sister Ellen would come along and participate in the cheering section for the little girl. In Austria there was his distant cousin, a woman nicknamed Vrannie that he especially favored as a trusted confidant and friend based upon her letters to him.[14] She was a practical and levelheaded woman.

During the annual *Winterball* party in Würzburg, he escorted yet another attractive woman who clearly was absorbed in the charms of *Herr General*.[15] She was hoping to ensnare the man for the coveted title of *Frau* of *Herrn General*, according to the General's nephew. Evidently the two dated for about five years and she would travel with him on occasion and attend family gatherings. It was no secret the wily woman secretly wished for the wedding band on her finger all the while envisioning holding a rolling pin behind her back to get this man in line once they'd married. But, true to his course, when the old bachelor got wind of the woman's serious intentions to further the relationship into the commitment phase, he'd bolt and run, breaking off the relationship. No matter how sly a woman's approach, her initial intentions, or what she said, Bayerlein seemed to know how long he could be in the woman's good graces and when he should extract himself.

Overall, from accounts of people who knew him, Bayerlein was a warm and affectionate man, a friendly, cheerful companion, and a willing partner. He had a great sense of humor and loved to joke. There was never a dull moment.

Allegations of Statute 175 Involvement

Working for a U.S. Army intelligence service had its pitfalls for Bayerlein. As a German foreign national who was employed in the U.S. Army's intelligence arena, as well as being a former *Generalleutnant* in the Wehrmacht, Bayerlein was a high-profile personality and subjected to routine security review. These checks were conducted to ascertain if a person was a security risk – especially for blackmail. How his name in particular stood out is unknown; however, one such Army intelligence review disclosed an intermittent 1952 through 1954 Frankfurt *Polizei* investigation of Bayerlein for allegedly committing Statue 175 and 175a violations of German Law – the statute prohibiting "Fornication Between Men,"[16] which was a criminal offense at the time.

Bayerlein missed the close camaraderie of the battlefield with his officers and soldiers, and it was obvious that he sought to recapture a time as a pleasant reminder of his front-line action. Bayerlein and his friends' habit of hanging out and drinking at the infamous red light district in Frankfurt became the hot subject of a *Polizei* investigation[17] under the suspicion of indulging in homosexual activities. As an unmarried man in his fifties and with his nocturnal activities – even on his own personal time – Bayerlein was eventually invited by the Frankfurt Police to an interview at their headquarters. Evidently the Frankfurt Police staked out certain *lokals* which were rumored to be "frequented by homosexuals." His marital status was the first red flag to the U.S. American intelligence staff. Colonel Frances E. Fellows, Commander of the 513th MISG, was notified of the suspicion and given photo static copies of the Frankfurt police interviews.

Immediately, as was Bayerlein's custom, he sought the advice of an attorney friend in Frankfurt, Herr Otto Block. Bayerlein naturally denied the allegation. He was never formally charged with the crime due to lack of evidence and witnesses to support the *Polizei* suspicions. Since there was no further legal basis to charge him, the *Politzi* dropped the investigation. Not only the embarrassment for himself, but the criminal charge against him could have resulted in Bayerlein's losing his top-secret security clearance; and without a clearance he would lose his job with the U.S. Army Intelligence Center.

Penalties for the conviction under the Statute would be fines and imprisonment, usually from eight months to one year. In Germany the Statute 175 and subordinate paragraphs were overturned in 1966; all records of routine investigations were destroyed. According to the Wiesbaden district attorney's office, only those files on men who were charged, convicted and sentenced remain on permanent file in the Frankfurt *Polizei* files.[18]

Sir Basil Liddell Hart and the Hostility Manifest

Sir Basil met with American and British officials in Bonn regarding choices for officers in the new *Bundeswehr* (post-war German Army). Discussions between former high-ranking German officers and these officials were on going as to who would be selected to serve in the new German army. During their writing of *The Rommel Papers*, Sir Basil Liddell Hart broached a touchy subject with Bayerlein, stating that he "was sorry to find that there was such hostility to you in various quarters – a fact that will probably not surprise you."[19] Bayerlein was slightly irked when overlooked, his ego suffering a bruise, and royally peeved when Sir Basil aggravated him by broaching this mysterious "hostility manifest" about him. In a furor Bayerlein wrote back to Sir Basil that his former superiors – *Generals von Manteuffel, von Lüttwitz, Geyr von Schweppenburg and von Gersdorff* – harbored personal animosity against him and had been, according to Bayerlein, "spreading such rumors in the Bonn quarters."[20] Sir Basil, the proper Englishman, was taken aback by Bayerlein's reaction and attempted unsuccessfully to mollify him. Evidently, the rumor mill in Bonn constituting former colleagues and superiors of Bayerlein's, according to Sir Basil's letter, stated, "(a) you have been very offensive to other generals in the POW camp, (b) that you had not stayed with them but had taken up work with the Americans; (c) that this showed a lack of loyalty on your part. Of course," Sir Basil's letter continued, "people often hide the 'real reasons' for their attitude."[21] In a long letter that Bayerlein typed himself; he addressed each issue. He asked who the generals were and what was the offense, he cited that he had been in captivity for two years and not released any earlier than anyone else but was in a hospital for a number of months. Finally, Bayerlein responded, that almost all generals took up work with the Americans for the Historical Division and were very anxious and grateful to do so.[22]

Sir Basil liked to keep the waters smooth in order to help where he could, although at times his price tag was high. He cajoled many German officers into making flattering statements that they were his "pupil" or "disciple"[23] and learned everything they knew about mobile tank warfare from his pre-war publications of his theories. Sir Basil did, however, in fairness to the German officers, support their books by endorsing them, was a proponent for the release of their retirement pensions frozen by the Allies and their better treatment as prisoners of war. After Sir Basil and Bayerlein's cooperation on the "*Papers*" their relationship drew to a close in 1956. Sir Basil asked Bayerlein a plethora of questions and requested military analyses in his letters.[24] It was obvious that Bayerlein grew tired of the requests – generally ignoring them or providing a cursory explanation – as he had neither time nor interest to devote to further shore up Sir Basil's reputation as a military genius.

Even though some general officers were listed on a postwar Nazi sympathizer "German Generals Watch List"[25] – such as *General* Hasso von Manteuffel – some found positions in the *Bundeswehr* and prominent elected positions in the German government. There is no doubt that between Bayerlein's high-profile position in Army intelligence and a potential selection for a Bundeswehr position there were a lot of old enemies that would take great satisfaction to see him ostracized and dismissed. Their memories were long and their influence significant.

General von Manteuffel in particular never seemed to forgive Bayerlein for his mistakes and his stalling around the fringes of Bastogne instead of attacking a hopeless cause with devotion and vigor. Von Manteuffel ordered the change to the defensive later during the campaign, but that was his prerogative and beside the point – he was the commander. In a post war interview, von Manteuffel states that the failure at Bastogne was "mainly caused by *General* Fritz Hermann Bayerlein." His first mistake was taking a road that turned into a mud track and second was listening to a clueless civilian regarding enemy strength. Von Manteuffel stated in a post war interrogation, that on December 23rd and 24th he had taken over command and "personally led the Panzer Lehr Division round south of Bastogne, through Remagne and St. Hubert to Rochefort."[26] According to von Manteuffel, Bayerlein's third mistake was at St. Hubert. He caught Bayerlein "loitering around Sibret ... and was a defeatist at the time of the Ardennes Offensive." Von Manteuffel also, "pointed out that he had assumed command of Panzer Lehr Division, when Bayerlein was discharged."[27] So von Manteuffel had his axe to grind with Bayerlein, and subsequently he had a poor opinion of him as a commander. "To Manteuffel, Bayerlein was only a play-actor general," was a conclusion based upon Bayerlein's lethargic command of Panzer Lehr Division during the Ardennes Offensive.[28] Bayerlein had a unique reason for his less than poor performance. In post war interviews regarding his stall around Mageret on the 19th of December, the two hour delay during the night, and his return to get the American aid station to treat a splinter wound, Bayerlein confessed to Sir Basil Liddell Hart[29] and General S.L.A. Marshall[30] that "an American nurse was there and she was very beautiful."[31] Flirting had whetted his appetite for a sexual liaison with a young American nurse. This was sufficient justification for a good reason to stop as any, to Bayerlein's way of thinking. He knew attempting to take Bastogne was a fruitless endeavor anyway. The Americans, Bayerlein knew, would just take it back. He was a realist, but he had to be cautious as defeatism was a court martial offense. Von Manteuffel had an NCO shot for disobedience and failure to follow orders.[32] As one of his Panzer Lehr officers said, "Bayerlein was a highly intelligent man, and he was very clever. Never underestimate him!"[33] It seemed as though Bayerlein was a faster learner than his superiors in this instance. *General* Bayerlein wasn't prepared to pay the cost to waste his men's lives for what he felt were pointless objectives, Hitler order or no Hitler order.

Herr Bayerlein worked for the 513th Military Intelligence Group (MIG)[34] until 1957, wherein, with reasons only known to him, Bayerlein walked away from his job with the U.S. Army and returned to his hometown of Würzburg. He had started an oriental carpet business, the "*Haus der Teppiche*" and was anxious to devote his energies to its success.

The *Verband Deutsches Afrika-Korps Würzburg*

On June 20th, 1954 Bayerlein founded the *Verband Deutsches Afrika-Korps Kreiskameradschaft* of Würzburg. Monthly meetings brought *Afrikaners* and their wives from the local area to visit each other, forge new friendships based upon their shared experiences. Each year the group participates in the memorial service in Herrlingen at the grave of their leader, Field Marshal Rommel. The veterans also remember his chief of staff and honor his memory. The year of 2004 marked the 50th anniversary of Bayerlein's establishing the *Verband*. Through its dynamic and active leaders and veterans, the *Verband* has forged friendship ties throughout the world. They have welcomed and honored the *Biographin* of *General* Bayerlein at the wreath laying in the *Hauptfriedhof* and the 50th Jubilee celebration.

It was unfortunate, but for some unknown reason in his later years, Bayerlein's attendance dropped off, then he came no more. Perhaps his health and his old energy had flagged, his illnesses from Africa caught up with him.[35] So it was time to hand the association to the younger men to carry it into the next decades, and then into the next century. The people of the *Verband* never forgot their founder, and honor him even to this day.

Herr General's Legacy

The story of Fritz Bayerlein's life unfolds, and it lays bare his strengths, his failings, the truth, the legend, the relationships and ultimately the on-going dilemma of the complexity of the man and bringing him to life. The work continues on revealing this man and accurately portraying him in the light of years of social changes. One of his friends summed up Bayerlein as being "two separate men, with separate faces, perhaps this was necessary for his survival during these difficult times."

General Bayerlein never sought notoriety for himself; instead he helped many others and has generously shared his wealth of experiences. At times he grew tired of the discussions about the war and wished to put it behind him and look forward to his last few years in more pleasant activities.

The night before he died, Bayerlein said to one of his friends, "Every old dog has to die." A few minutes past noon on January 30th, 1970 shortly after his 71st birthday, Fritz Bayerlein yielded to the ailments of his African illness that he'd struggled with and suffered from since 1943.

Fritz Bayerlein, his sister Ellen and her son Fritz, lived during a time of political horror and barbarism under the Third Reich. After the war, the rebuilding began in Europe as they looked forward to a future under freedom and democracy. The story of Fritz Bayerlein reveals what one man, one family, experienced. There are as many stories as they are people who made this journey. With love and faith, all is possible.

Bayerlein and his sister, Ellen, in the Bavarian Alps. (Photograph courtesy of Dittmar-Bayerlein Family Collection.)

Uncle Fritz, nephew Fritz Dittmar, Ellen and her new husband, Alberto Rose, stand together for a family memory. (Photograph courtesy of Dittmar-Bayerlein Family Collection.)

One of the last few family photographs. (Photograph courtesy of Dittmar-Bayerlein Family Collection.)

The Field Marshal Rommel legend – as outstandingly portrayed by actor James Mason. The movie was adopted from the biography of Rommel, the Desert Fox, written by Desmond Young. (Photograph courtesy of Dittmar-Bayerlein Family Collection.)

The premier of Rommel, the Desert Fox in Frankfurt Germany. Bayerlein was interviewed by a reporter, and endorsed the film.

Even in his older age – Bayerlein could turn the ladies' heads. Bayerlein, sister Ellen (center) and the ever-hopeful Frau Hilgen (left) enjoy a sunny afternoon. (Photograph courtesy of Dittmar-Bayerlein Family Collection.)

The film's endorsements include: Lucie Rommel, Crüwell, Bayerlein and Dr. Strölin. (Photograph courtesy of Dittmar-Bayerlein Family Collection.)

Bayerlein relaxes at his attic apartment in Würzburg over his second-story carpet shop. (Photograph courtesy of Dittmar-Bayerlein Family Collection.)

Bayerlein served as advisor on several films on Rommel. One in German was "Rommel anrufe Kairo" (Rommel calling Cairo). Another, from Columbia Pictures, was filmed in 1961. The original caption reads: "General Fritz Bayerlein, former Chief Aide to Field Marshal Rommel in the North African campaign of World War II, serves as one of the technical advisers for Carl Foreman's "The Guns of Navarone" on location in Rhodes, supervising the Greek troops appearing in the film as German soldiers. (Photograph courtesy of Dittmar-Bayerlein Family Collection.)

A studio portrait of Bayerlein with the hairstyle fad of the year. This style did not last long with Bayerlein. (Photograph courtesy of Dittmar-Bayerlein Family Collection.)

A more casual and relaxed Bayerlein makes a new friend. He liked animals and treated them kindly. (Photograph courtesy of Dittmar-Bayerlein Family Collection.)

Captivated with the conversation, the Brown Swiss milk cow listens to the man. One wonders what a former Wehrmacht General could possibly say to entertain a cow. (Photograph courtesy of Dittmar-Bayerlein Family Collection.)

Alexander Hartdegen, former aide to Bayerlein, relocated to Brazil in the post-war years. Here he returns in 1973 to Würzburg Germany to pay his respects to his old friend and former commander. The two men forged a lifelong friendship beginning in the African campaign in March 1942. Hartdegen's daughters recalled that their father spoke little about the war, but always referred to Herr General with affection and respect. (Photograph courtesy Hartdegen Family Collection, Brazil.)

Chapter 9 Endnotes

1. Landkreis Obertaunus, Office of Military Government, Land Hesse, Bad Homburg, Germany, letter dated 21 May 1947. NARA, College Park, Maryland.

2. This law states that General Staff officers and general officers are limited in employment to ordinary labor (German Law for Liberation From National Socialism and Militarism, Appendix to the Law, Article 59, Paragraph L). Since the generals were to be discharged into civilian status, they were no longer prisoners of war but employed as indigenous personnel. The Office of Military Government for Germany (US Zone) order was that the demands of the Historical Division would overrule the requirements of the denazification program, and an exception to the general employment policy was made. Per OMG(US) letter dated August 1947, NARA; EUCOM, Occupational History Branch, General Records, NARA RG 338/290/58/33/4 Box 3671.

3. NARA, RG 338/290/73/2/3 Entry 37042, Box 15, General Orders, HQ, 513th Military Intelligence Service Group (MISG), later renamed the 513th Military Intelligence Group (MIG).

4. Mr. Manfred Rommel in visit with author.

5. Desmond Young, "Rommel, the Desert Fox," Harper and Brothers, New York, 1950. 72. Author's Note: In his book, Desmond erroneously states that Bayerlein "fought, from the age of sixteen, as a private soldier." Actually, Bayerlein was registered and drafted as an eighteen year-old – for men with a birth year of 1899 – from the *Gymnasium*, a school that has actually 13 grades and prepares one for University. He was enlisted into the 9th, or "*Neuner*", Bavarian Infantry Regiment, garrisoned in Würzburg, on June 5th, 1917.

6. Library of Congress, Washington, D.C.; John Toland Papers, "*The Last 100 Days*." Box 108, Toland, General Correspondence.

7. Ibid.

8. Ibid., Interviews of German Officers, Box 14, 16.

9. From meeting between Franz Kurowski and Bayerlein (Bayerlein notes).

10. Harold J. Gordon, Jr., "*The Reichswehr and the German Republic 1919 – 1926*," Kannikat Prese Port Washington, N.Y., 213.

11. Author P.A. Spayd's interview with Mr. Bernd Werncke, April 2001.

12. Author's note: Bayerlein had stated for author Paul Carell that "One photograph is worth twenty pages of terrain description." In this case, not having the identity of the women – just the multitude of photographs – author P.A. Spayd made the decision in these instances to use the 'terrain description' in lieu of photos.

13. Conversation with Mr. Jürgen Hempel, October 2003.

14. Family correspondence saved by Bayerlein's sister, Frau Ellen Dittmar-Rose. Family papers made available to the author by courtesy of Herr Fritz Dittmar-Bayerlein, the General's nephew and adoptive son.

15. Conversations with Mr. Fritz Dittmar-Bayerlein, and family friend, Frau Christine Singer. There were numerous family photographs Bayerlein took of his women friends at parties and vacations.

16. Per the German Penal Code, Statute 175 and 175a. (*Strafgesetzbuch, § 175 Unzucht zwischen Männer, § 175a, Schwere Unzucht zwischen Männer*) The German Penal Code of 1871, § 173 – 184b are: "Felonies and Misdemeanors Against Morality and Decency."

17. Der Oberbuergermeister- Polizeipraesident – Kr./7.K Tgb. Nr. Ohne Frankfurt/Main; Gegen Bayerlein: 40 Js 682/54; Frankfurt Main. Kriminalpolizeiliche: Bei Herrn Fritz Bayerlein als Verlageangestellter taetig. Als neue Sache wegen Verdachte nach §§ 175 und 175a StGB. gegen General a.D. Fritz Bayerlein, geboren am 14.1.1899 in Würzburg (*gleichgeschlechtliche* [*trans.* 'of the same sex; homosexual')

18. Hessisches Hauptstaatsarchiv, Wiesbaden Germany. Archivist confirmed Bayerlein's files as destroyed in 1966.

19. Liddell Hart Centre for Military Archives, King's College, London, Reference: LH 9/24/50, letter dated July 4th 1952 to Bayerlein from Sir Basil.

20. Liddell Hart Centre. Letters between Bayerlein and Sir Basil dated July 4th, 11th, 1952. Reference: LH 9/24/50. Reprinted by permission from The Trustees of the Liddell-Hart Centre for Military Archives and quoted by P.A. Spayd, "Bayerlein", 261-264.

21. Liddell Hart Centre, Reference: LH 9/23/50, Letter dated July 4th 1952 to General Bayerlein from Sir Basil.

22. Liddell Hart Centre, Reference: 9/23/50, Letter dated July 11th from Bayerlein to Sir Basil. Author's Note: Reprinted in "Bayerlein" by P.A. Spayd. 262-263.

23. Liddell Hart Centre, Reference: 9/24/204-205; Photographs of many German generals and field marshals – all contain the words, either, "your disciple," or "your pupil." Some more prominent personality photos contained in this series are: Guderian, von Manteuffel, von Schweppenburg, Manstein, Kesselring, von Rundstedt, Blumentritt and Westphal. Sir Basil asked for a photograph of Bayerlein, but evidently he never sent one. Bayerlein was reluctant to be one of the trophies in Sir Basil's collection.

24. Liddell Hart Centre, Reference: 9/24/50. Sir Basil kept copies of his letters and the originals of letters sent to him. This is the most comprehensive and remarkable archive of correspondence found on General Bayerlein.

25. NARA, Watch List of German Generals in the British and U.S. Zones of Germany and in the U.K., File XE 049474, February 46 – Feb 49; Box 37

26. Liddell Hart Centre, Reference: LH 9/24/121, Notes on Interrogation of von Rundstedt, von Manteuffel, Blumentritt and Kruse – Launching of Ardennes Offensive, dated October 1945.

27. Joss Heintz, "*In the Perimeter of Bastogne*," 196.

28. Ibid.

29. Liddell Hart Centre, Reference: LH 9/31/35. Page 13.

30. University of Texas at El Paso Library, Special Collections Department, S.L.A. Marshall papers, MS 186, Box 107, Folder 1711. Marshall's handwritten notes, in a post war interview with General Bayerlein, six undated pages.

31. Ibid.

32. Manteuffel was placed on trial in the late 1950s for ordering an enlisted man court martialed'I started this war with the most wonderful army in Europe: today I've got a muckheap. I have no leaders any more, my generals are incompetent, the officers are no commanders, the troops are wretched.' and shot for failure to follow orders.

33. Interview with a former Panzer Lehr officer by author P.A. Spayd.

34. A confusing array of reorganization and name changes: In April 1947, the Military Intelligence Service Center (MISC #4, Oberursel, Germany) changed names to the 7707th US Army Europe Intelligence Center (ECIC, or USAEUR Intelligence Center). Again a name changed occurred in January 1953: the ECIC was changed to the 513the Military Intelligence Service Group (MISG). In October 1953, the 513th Military Intelligence Service Group (MISG) changed names to the 513th Military Intelligence Group (MIG) NARA RG 338/290/73/2/1/Entry 37042, Box 2, General Orders. Throughout the names changes, the organization was still located at Camp King, Oberursel Germany.

35. *Generalleutnant a.D.* Fritz Hermann Michael Bayerlein died at the *Julisspital* Hospital in his hometown of Würzburg, Germany on January 30th, 1970, just past his 71st birthday on January 14th. His life was considerably shortened due to illnesses he contracted during the North African campaign.

Epilogue

W hen I researched the life of *General* Bayerlein, then wrote and edited his biography, I had no idea that the material I amassed would cover four books. He was a man that history had overlooked – there were the superficial references to *Herrn General,* a quote here and there that gave an indication of his frustration with the war, or his humor and insight. Delving beyond these hints revealed a fascinating character importantly involved on 3 different fronts in World War II and led me to investigate further.

My research is concluded in due course all these boxes will be donated and established as a collection with the Library of Congress, Washington, D.C. It is always the authors' intention to preserve documents for study by future generations.

Please contact: P.A. Spayd, in care of Schiffer Publishing, Ltd., 4880 Lower Valley Road, Atglen, PA 19310, USA.

Bibliography

Books

Bach, Julian, Jr., *America's Germany, An Account of the Occupation*, New York: Random House, 1946.

Barnett, Correlli, *Hitler's Generals*, New York: Grove Weidenfeld, 1989.

Bosch, William J., *Judgment on Nuremberg, American Attitudes Toward the Major German War-Crime Trials*, Chapel Hill: The University of North Carolina Press, 1970.

Browder, George C., *Hitler's Enforcers, The Gestapo and the SS Security Service in the Nazi Revolution*, New York: Oxford University Press, 1996.

Clay, Lucius D. General, United States Army, Retired, *Germany and the Fight for Freedom,* Cambridge, Massachusetts: Harvard University Press, 1950.

— *Decision in Germany*, Garden City, New York: Doubleday & Company, 1950.

Cowdery, Ray and Josephine, *Papers Please! Identity Documents, Permits and Authorizations of the Third Reich*, Lakeville, MN, USM, Inc., 1996.

— *German Print Advertising 1933-1945*, Rapid City, SD, 2004.

Davidson, Eugene, *The Trial of the Germans, An account of the twenty-two defendants before the International Military Tribunal at Nuremberg*. New York: The Macmillan Company, 1966.

Davis, Franklin M. Jr., *Come as a Conqueror, The United States Army's Occupation of Germany 1945-1949*. New York: The Macmillan Company, 1967.

D'Este, Carlo, *Patton, A Genius for War*, New York: Harper Perennial, 1995.

Eisenberg, Carolyn, *Drawing the Line, the American Decision to Divide Gemrany 1944-1949*, New York: Cambridge University Press, 1996.

FitzGibbon, Constantine, *Denazification*, London: Michael Joseph, Ltd., 1969.

Frei, Norbert, translated by Joel Golb, *Adenaur's Germany and the Nazi Past, The Policy of Amnesty and Integration*, New York: Columbia University Press, 2002.

Gansber, Judith M., *Stalag: U.S.A, the Remarkable Story of German POWs in America*, New York: Thomas Y. Crowell Company, 1977.

Gimbel, John, *The American Occupation of Germany, Politics and the Military, 1945-1949*, Standford, California: Stanford Press, 1968.

Gordon, Jr., Harold J., *The Reichswehr and the German Republic 1919-1926*, Kannikat Prese Port Washington, N.Y.

Redaktion: Grübel, Sybille; Schindler, Renate; Spielmann Natascha; Baum Hans Peter; Rosenstock Dirk; Wagner Ulrich, *Aspekte der Verwaltungs, Wirtschafts und Kulturgeschichte Würzburgs im 19. und 20. Jahrhundred,* Veröffentlichungen des Stadtarchive Würzburg, Verlag Ferdinand Schöningh, Würzburg 2002

Kesselring, Albrecht, *The Memoirs of Field Marshal Kesselring*, Presidio Press, CA., 1989. Translation by William Kimber, Ltd., 1953, originally published in German under the title of *Soldat bis zum letzten Tag,* by Athenaum, 1953.

Kramer, Arnold, *Nazi Prisoners of War in America*, Stein and Day, New York, 1983.

Kurowski, Franz, *Knights Cross Holders of the Afrikakorps*, Schiffer Military History: Atglen, PA., 1996.

MacDonald, Charles B., *A Time for Trumpets: The Untold Story of the Battle of the Bulge,* New York, William Morrow and Company, Inc.

Macksey, Kenneth, *Guderian, Creator of the Blitzkrieg*, Stein and Day, N.Y. 1975.

McClatchie, Stanley, *Look to Germany – Heart of Europe*, Rapid City, SD, USM, Inc., 2001.

MacLean, French L., *The Cruel Hunters: SS Sonderkommando Dirlewanger: Hitler's Most Notorious Anti-Partisan Unit,* Atglen, Pennsylvania, Schiffer Military History, 1998.

MacLean, French L., *Quiet Flows the Rhine, German General Officer Casualties in World War II*, Winnipeg, Manitoba, Canada: J.J. Fedorowicz Publishing, 1996.

von Oppen, Beate Ruhm, *Documents on Germany Under Occupation, 1945-1954*, New York, Oxford University Press, 1955.

Orbán, Sándor, Vida, István, *Serédi Jusztinián, hercegprímás, feljegyzései : 1941-1944/[sajtó alá rendezte, az el˝oszót a bevezet˝o tanulmányt és a jegyzeteket írta, Orbán Sándor és Vida István,* Budapest: Zrínyi Kiadó, 1990.

Peterson, Edward N., *The American Occupation of Germany: Retreat to Victory*, Detroit: University of Wisconsin-River Falls, 1977.

Rigg, Bryan Mark, *Hitler's Jewish Soldiers,: The Untold Story of Nazi Racial Laws and the Men of Jewish Descent in the German Military,* Lawrence Kansas, University Press of Kansas, 2002.

Smith, Bradley F., *Reaching Judgment at Nuremberg*, New York: Basic Books, Inc., Publishers, 1977.

Smith, Jean Edward, (editor), *The Papers of General Lucius D. Clay, Germany 1945-1949*, Bloomington: Indiana University Press. A publication of the Institute of German Studies at Indiana University, 1974.

Spayd, P.A., *Bayerlein: from Afrikakorps to Panzer Lehr, the Life of Rommel's Chief of Staff, Generalleutnant Fritz Bayerlein*, Atglen, Pennsylvania: Schiffer Publishing, Ltd., 2003.

Rockenmaier, Dieter W., *Denuncianten*, Würzburg, Germany.

Supreme Headquarters Allied Expeditionary Force, *Handbook for Unit Commanders (Germany),* 15 September 1944.

Toland, John, *The Last 100 Days*, Random House: New York, 1965.

— *Battle, The Story of the Bulge*, Random House, New York, 1959.

United States Senate, Subcommittee to Investigate the Administration of the Internal Security Act and Other Internal Security Laws of the Committee on the Judiciary, *Morgenthau Diary (Germany) Volume I*, U.S. Government Printing Office, Washington, D.C. 1967,

Warlimont, Walter, *Inside Hitler's Headquarters 1939-45*, Novato CA: Presidio Press, Published in Germany under the title: *Im Hauptquartier der deutschen Wehrmacht 1939-1945*.

Redaktion: Dr. Josef Brecht,*425 Jahre Wirsberg-Gymnasium Würzburg,* Würzburg, Germany, Festschrift zum Gründungsjubilaeum, 1986.

Ziemke, Earl F., *The U.S. Army in the Occupation of Germany, 1944-1946*, Washington, D.C.: Center of Military History, United States Army, 1975.

Zink, Harold, Former Chief Historian, U.S. High Commissioner for Germany. *The United States in Germany, 1944-1955*. Princeton, New Jersey: D. Van Nostrand Company, Inc. 1957.

— *American Military Government in Germany*, New York: The Macmillian Company, 1947.

Periodicals:

The Military Review, April 1990, "*Portrait of a German General Officer*," by Lieutenant Colonel Verner R. Carlson, U.S. Army Retired. 69-81.